The Life of Saint Audrey

Il a comence la vie seinte audree
moyne de ely
N bon hume e
en ton porpris
Deueit en sa m...
user son tens
Pur sage deueit son senei
E elui ke poruoit soueur
Dont il est fait e qui le cria
Et quel part il reuertira
Cil qui bien font sunt bonure
E de dieu e del siecle ame
Poruant alonme ses tresors
Puis ke lame se part del cors
A nul ua por deu departi
Et en sa uie departi deserui
Ke ses biens ueinquet ses malices
S on orguil ses mauueises uices
Bien est ki deseit en uie
La den grace z sa compaignie
Ce fu la uirge sainte audree
Al a royne bonure
Ky deguerpi uigne z hauteise
Por auoir ou deu la richesce
Dul apromis a ses feus
Ky sunt ou lui z il ou eus
Li cler li moine li trinite
Ky ont ceste uie despite
Les saintes uirges glorioses
Ky ses firent a deu espuses
Reguem z uiuent z uiueront
Ou deu ki tut cria le mund
Pour sainte audree la roine
Cui bien ne faut ne decline

Hay comence ce liure a faire
J a mestier dut z trauure
De quel linage ele fu nee
Et coin deu foiz fu mariee
Aniz ke par i don mariage
As estuer mouster de son linage
Solom lestore as maiens
En icel tens ke martiens
Pour de roine la seignurie
Lenpire ert tute la baillie
One genz englesi suir nomez
En bretaine sunt ariuez
Cinquante sis z bien cent anz
S z coine saint z das est disanz
Aniz ke saint austin neust
J furent les engles ceo dist
T reis maineres de compaignons
Godlondeis engleis z saxons
Furent ici qui de germaine
E sterent uenuz en bretaine
De la lignee as godlondeis
Furent en gendrez li kenteis
L autre partie des estreis
Furent engendrez des engles
L autre partie des seixons
Ke seixons estreis apeluns
C est auingle a non cele partie
Dont engleis euert la seignurie
De cele genz fu engendree
L a glorieuse sainte audree
Ke mut fu de grant saintee
Et de real dignete
R eduuald fu en icel tens reis
Ce dist lestorie del kenteis

The Life of Saint Audrey

A Text by Marie de France

Translated and edited by
JUNE HALL MCCASH and
JUDITH CLARK BARBAN

Foreword by EMANUEL J. MICKEL

McFarland & Company, Inc., Publishers
Jefferson, North Carolina, and London

Frontispiece: First page of the *Vie seinte Audree*, folio 100v BL Additional manuscript 70513 (by permission of the British Library)

LIBRARY OF CONGRESS CATALOGUING-IN-PUBLICATION DATA

Marie, de France, 12th cent.
  [Vie seinte Audree. English]
  The life of Saint Audrey / a text by Marie de France ; translated
and edited by June Hall McCash and Judith Clark Barban ;
foreword by Emanuel J. Mickel.
    p.   cm.
  Includes bibliographical references and index.

  ISBN-13: 978-0-7864-2653-9
  ISBN-10: 0-7864-2653-5
  (softcover : 50# alkaline paper) ∞

  I. McCash, June Hall.   II. Barban, Judith Clark.   III. Title.
PQ1494.V54E5   2006
841'.1—dc22   2006025400

British Library cataloguing data are available

On the Cover: Saint Audrey stained glass window (*photograph courtesy Mark Ynys-Mon*)

Manufactured in the United States of America

McFarland & Company, Inc., Publishers
  Box 611, Jefferson, North Carolina 28640
    www.mcfarlandpub.com

To our alma mater,
Agnes Scott College,
and to all the extraordinary people there
who were our teachers and mentors.
Deo gratias.

Acknowledgments

As in all such endeavors many people have been helpful along the way. First and foremost, we are deeply indebted to friends and colleagues Rupert Pickens, professor of French at the University of Kentucky, and William W. Kibler, professor emeritus of French at the University of Texas, Austin, for their sensitive readings and comments on the edited text and translation at various stages of the work. Professor Pickens also generously offered to let us include his analysis and rubrics of the source text in this edition (Appendix 2). The suggestions of both scholars have been invaluable in bringing this book to fruition. They are, without question, responsible for many of the strengths it may contain, but are accountable in no way for any weaknesses that may remain. We are also extremely grateful to Emanuel J. Mickel, Jr., professor of French at Indiana University, Bloomington, for agreeing so enthusiastically to write the foreword to this volume.

We offer our thanks as well to Mark Ynys-Mon, webmaster of the Cambridge Churches web site, for permission to use the cover art, a stained-glass window from Saint Peters Church in Bothwell, Cambridgeshire. We also wish to express our appreciation to the British Library for permission to include the frontispiece, the first page of the *Vie seinte Audree* text, folio 100v in the BL Additional manuscript 70513. We are particularly grateful to Michael St John-McAlister, curator in the Department of Manuscripts at the British Library, for his willingness to personally measure the manuscript in order to verify the dimensions of the folio and lined area of f. 100v, when we had three sets of measurements that did not agree. We thank Virginia Blanton, assistant professor of English at the University of Missouri, Kansas City, for her comments on a very early version of the translation and her suggestions for illustrations.

We would particularly like to recognize the work of our research assistant at Middle Tennessee State University, Michael Fletcher, for his careful review of the manuscript text, a task he volunteered to undertake without remuneration as an expression of his passion for learning about the Middle Ages, as well as that of Seth Alder from Publications and Graphics at Middle Tennessee State University for preparing the map and genealogical chart. We also offer our gratitude to Frances Clark Calder, professor emerita of French at Agnes Scott College, for hosting one of our work sessions.

Finally, we want to express our thanks to our husbands, Richard D. Gleaves, Jr., and Eugene M. Barban, for their support, love, and patience throughout this project, which took us not only to London and Ely, but also to work sessions in Kalamazoo, Michigan; Murfreesboro, Tennessee; Black Mountain, North Carolina; Decatur, Georgia; and Jekyll Island, Georgia. It has been an *aventure* from beginning to end.

Table of Contents

THE ANGLO-SAXON
KINGDOMS
IN THE SEVENTH CENTURY

Scale of Miles
0   20   40   60   80

CELTS

Coldingham
Bamburgh

Hexham

NORTH

NORTHUMBRIA

Whitby

SEA

Ripon
York

IRISH SEA

Lincoln

MERCIA

Medehamstede

Dereham

EAST
ANGLIA

Burgh Castle

Ely
Soham

Blythburgh
Dunwich

CELTS

Bury
St.Edmunds

Grantchester

Felixstowe

Exning

Worcester

WESSEX

ESSEX

London

Canterbury

KENT

SUSSEX

JUTES

ENGLISH CHANNEL

FRANCE

Foreword
by Emanuel J. Mickel

It is a pleasure to welcome the new edition of the *Vie seinte Audree* by Professors June Hall McCash and Judith Clark Barban. This current edition of the Old French text, the first in over half a century and only the second to appear in print, offers a new and perceptive look at an important and interesting Anglo-Saxon saint's life. Because the earlier volume of Östen Södergård is less accessible than one would like and does not include a translation into any modern language, this edition, with the first published English translation, is a valuable contribution to medieval studies. Readers will be especially pleased by the editors' excellent notes to the text. There they elaborate on questions of language, comment on elements related to Marie de France's other works, elucidate historical and topographical references pertaining to Anglo-Saxon history, and provide biblical passages and references pertinent to the *Vie seinte Audree*. Also very helpful to the reader are the Index of Proper Names, a map, and a genealogical chart, all illumining the work. The Index of Proper Names is especially helpful in expounding on references to obscure Anglo-Saxon personages. The notes and this index go a long way toward providing the historical and geographical underpinning the reader needs to maintain comfortable understanding of the saint and her *milieu*.

The introduction provides the reader with a clear description of the manuscript and a helpful discussion of the relationship between Marie's *Vie seinte Audree* and the extant Latin version of the saint's life, as it is preserved in the *Liber Eliensis*, composed in the 1170s at Ely, and in the later compilation of the *Acta sanctorum*. But scholars and enlightened readers will be particularly intrigued by the editors' discussion of the question of authorship. In 2002, June Hall McCash published an article in *Speculum* in which she made an eloquent and convincing case for the authorship of four texts (*Lais, Fables, Espurgatoire saint Patriz,* and *Vie seinte Audree*) by a woman who calls herself Marie in each case and once, in the *Fables*, adds "si sui de France." This author, known for

1

years as Marie de France, has been associated with three texts but only tentatively suggested as the same Marie who composed the *Vie seinte Audree*. In their introduction the editors attack the problem of authorship with vigor, setting forth suggestions concerning possible historical figures who might have been our Marie and making more precise references to dating of the works that allow them all to be written by the same author. The editors point out linguistic habits and stylistic similarities between the *Vie seinte Audree* and Marie's other works that are persuasive. Thus scholars can no longer ignore the *Vie seinte Audree* when they discuss all the works of Marie de France.

When Östen Södergård published his edition of the *Vie seinte Audree* in 1955, there was little scholarly interest in the saint's life as a genre either in Latin or Old French. A strong bias of nineteenth and early twentieth century scholarship against didactic and religious literature in particular meant that few publishers would risk editions of this most popular genre of medieval literature. Hence scholars who were interested had to work with manuscripts in European libraries to write about the saint's life—a costly and time-consuming endeavor. In the past thirty years, with the growth of interest in women and women's writings in the Middle Ages both in Europe and North America, the study of religious literature in Latin and Old French, especially the saint's life, has thrived. The interest has centered not just on Old French; there is an abundance of scholarly activity among scholars of medieval English and German. Hence this work is especially welcome, offering as it does not only an accurate edition with an excellent scholarly apparatus, but a clear and readable English translation to help those whose Old French is less than perfect and to give pleasure to the reader who is merely intrigued by this medieval saint and the window this work provides on life in a time so remote from our own.

Emanuel J. Mickel is professor of medieval French literature at Indiana University and is the author of Marie de France *(New York: Twayne, 1974), regarded as one of the most comprehensive studies of the works of Marie. He is a member of the editorial board of* Le Cygne: Journal of the International Marie de France Society.

Introduction

The Manuscript

The Old French *Vie seinte Audree* is preserved on folios 100v–134v of a single manuscript, British Library Additional 70513, a collection of thirteen metrical saints' lives in 265 folios. The codex that contains the *Audree* combines two medieval manuscripts (consisting of a total of thirty-two quires) copied in similar, though clearly distinguishable, hands and with a similar two-column format. However, the presentations differ. Part 1 is vellum and is decorated in simple colored initials and red pen flourishes. Part 2 is parchment and has at the beginning of all but one of the texts large four-line initials (some illuminated), alternating blue initials with red flourishes and red initials with blue flourishes.[1]

The first manuscript (quire i), which has been dated as early fourteenth century, includes eight blank folios, followed by *La Vie de seynte Elizabeth* (1r–4r), *De seynt Panuce* (4r–5v), and *La Vie de seint Paule le Hermite* (6r–8r). The second manuscript (quires ii–xxxii), dated as late thirteenth century, starts on folio 9r and begins with *La Vie del martir* [Thomas of Canterbury] (9r–50v).[2] The first part of the text is lost, and it opens *in medias res* with the last two lines of a five-line stanza. Other texts in this manuscript are *Le Romanz de sainte Marie Magdalene* (50v–55v), *Le Romanz de saint Edward rei* (55v–85v), *La Vie saint Eadmund le Confessur* [archbishop of Canterbury] (85v–100r), *La Vie seinte Audree* (100v–134v), *La Vie seinte Osith* (134v–147r), *La Vie seinte Fey* (147r–156v), *La Vie seinte Modwenne* (156v–222r), *La Vie seint Richard* [bishop of Chichester] (222r–244v), and *La Vie seinte Katerine* [of Alexandria] (244v–265v). All but two of the lives contained in the manuscript are composed in octosyllabic couplets.[3]

The folios of the *Vie seinte Audree*, the eighth hagiographical text in the collection and the fifth in the second manuscript, contain two columns, typically with thirty-four lines per column. The folios of the work measure 250 × 180 mm with a ruled area for text of 196 mm × 135 mm.[4] At the incipit is a decorated initial, the second of only six in the entire manuscript to contain a miniature portrait, in this case 30 × 30 mm, of the saint (see frontispiece). She is

3

standing at a lectern, a book before her, holding the model of a church in her right hand. Her left hand is raised to point to it, as though she is teaching. The miniature places the saint inside the frame formed by the initial letter, and it is one of only three depicted with defining objects.[5]

The codex is particularly interesting since it contains all the only Old French saints' lives known to have been written *by* women: the life of Catherine of Alexandria by Clemence of Barking; the life of Edward the Confessor by the anonymous nun of Barking; and the life of Saint Audrey by Marie. More than half of the saints' lives contained in the collection, seven out of thirteen, are *about* women. It is therefore not surprising that the manuscript was in all likelihood prepared *for* women. As we learn from an inscription on folio 1r: "Cest livere est a covent de campisse"—that is, the codex once belonged to Campsey Ash priory, an Augustinian nunnery in Suffolk founded in 1195 by Theobald de Valoines for his two sisters. There it was intended for reading during mealtimes, as we know from another inscription on folio 265v stating that "ce livre deviseie a la priorie de kanpseie de lire a mengier." The manuscript later found its way to the library of William Arthur, Sixth Duke of Portland in Welbeck, presumably after Campsey Ash priory was dissolved in 1536. It was the only French manuscript (numbered IC1) in his collection.[6] Although bound today in a nineteenth-century brown leather binding stamped with a gold letter "P" at the center of each cover, the two parts of the codex, as mentioned above, date from the late thirteenth and early fourteenth century. It may have been commissioned by Isabel of Warenne, Countess of Arundel, for whom the life of Saint Edmund, Archbishop of Canterbury, was translated from the Latin.[7]

Although the manuscript containing the *Vie seinte Audree* was copied at the end of the thirteenth century, the *Vie seinte Audree* itself displays characteristics of a text written in the late twelfth or, at the latest, the early thirteenth century. (See language section below.) It has been published only once, in a volume edited by Östen Södergård, which appeared more than fifty years ago and is long since out of print.[8]

The entire text of the *Vie seinte Audree* was copied by a single Anglo-Norman scribe, who writes with a beautifully clear hand, though he or she makes a number of errors, omitting words, skipping lines or copying them twice, reversing lines, and occasionally introducing an extraneous word picked up from another line.[9] The scribe was apparently ignorant of the case system that still prevailed in Marie's day and must have found some of the author's forms hopelessly archaic. He or she makes efforts to "correct" or update the language of the text, thereby introducing extraneous syllables or eliminating the case forms no longer used, thus creating a significant number of hypometric or hypermetric lines in the text.

Authorship

The question of authorship is one of the most intriguing issues that con-
front scholars dealing with the *Vie seinte Audree* today. It is not an anonymous
text, as are so many medieval works.[10] On the contrary, it is conspicuously and
self-consciously signed by its author, Marie, in a fifteen-line epilogue that is
remarkably like that of the *Ysopet* or *Fables* of Marie de France, where she declares
that one is "fol ki sui ublie" and where she identifies herself more fully than in
any other text: "Me numerai pur remembrance: / Marie ai nun, si sui de
France."[11] Similarly, in the *Vie seinte Audree*, the author reiterates the notion
that one is "fol ki se oblie" (line 4623) and once again signs her name to impress
it upon the memory of her reader: "Ici escris mon non Marie, / Pur ce ke soie
remembree" (lines 4624–25). Although the name Marie was not uncommon in
the twelfth century, women authors were exceedingly rare, and the probability
that we would find two different female writers of the same name in the same
time period signing their names in such similar and memorable ways is exceedingly unlikely. Nor are those the only similarities between the two epilogues. In
both she reiterates that she has translated the work into French: "En romanz
di" (*Audree*, line 4612) and "en romanz ... dit" (*Fables*, epilogue, lines 1–2). In
the *Vie seinte Audree* she asks the saint to give heed to her work and to save her
soul ("Par sa pité ke a moy entende / Et ce servise a m'ame rende" [*Audree*, lines
4619–20]), in words that clearly recall the same request she made to God in the
Fables: "Kë a tel ovre puisse entendre / quë a lui pusse m'alme rendre" (*Fables*,
epilogue, 21–22).[12]

Memory, both of herself and of the matters she writes about, is a critical
issue in the works of Marie de France.[13] It is equally important and treated in
precisely the same way in the *Vie seinte Audree* as it is throughout the other
works of Marie de France: not as a celebration of received and shared memory,
so common in most saints' lives, but rather as something that must be impressed
upon the reader's mind, like the imprint of a seal in hot wax. Marie frequently
uses expressions like *mettre en memoire* and *faire la memoire* as she constructs her
text for a new audience. Any woman who wished so strongly to have her name
remembered would, it seems, have taken pains to differentiate herself from
another writer of the same name. It would be particularly curious, if the author
of the *Vie seinte Audree* was not the same woman who wrote the *Fables*, that the
wording of the second epilogue is clearly patterned after the first. Yet the author
of the *Vie seinte Audree* seemed ready to believe that her name, Marie, without
any other identification, was sufficient for the work to be remembered as hers.
Was there more than one author named Marie at the end of the twelfth and
beginning of the thirteenth centuries? It seems unlikely, since we can identify
the name of only one other female author writing in French at this same time—
Clemence of Barking, who composed the life of St. Catherine in this same manuscript as the *Vie seinte Audree*. Another text, a life of Edward the Confessor

also contained in the manuscript, was "translaté" by an unnamed nun also from Barking and possibly Clemence herself.[14] But other than these, no other female writer composing in French at the time is known.

The epilogues of the *Audree* and the *Fables* and even the treatment of memory in the *Audree*, which is so similar to the treatment of memory in the works already widely accepted as those of Marie de France, are, of course, not the only reasons for attributing the *Vie seinte Audree* to this same Marie who claims in the *Fables* to be "de France." Additional evidence has been amassed and outlined by one of the editors of this edition in an article published in the July 2002 issue of *Speculum*.[15] Although we will not reiterate all the arguments here, we will point out within the notes of this edition examples of the linguistic similarities, intertextual echoes, and stylistic devices noted in that study. As early as 1955, the text's first editor, Östen Södergård, although he did not attribute the work to Marie de France, had identified the author's French as being from an earlier time than the manuscript and conforming "aux habitudes du continent."[16] While the practices of the scribe, on the other hand, are more typically late thirteenth-century Anglo-Norman, as noted above, it is evident that he or she is copying a text that was originally written much earlier by someone who was indeed "de France."

Although Södergård identified the author of the *Vie seinte Audree* as a nun, in none of her texts, including the *Audree*, does Marie identify herself as a nun. Critics have repeatedly sought to enclose her in a convent in an effort to identify her with such women as the Abbess of Shaftsbury, a Cluniac abbess associated with Reading, and Marie de Boulogne, the latter of whom spent only part of her life in a convent. However, the woman who seems to be gaining ground as the leading candidate for the identity of Marie de France, Marie de Meulan, daughter of Galeran de Meulan (who was himself a poet) and wife of Hugh Talbot, was, from all available evidence, never a nun.[17] Marie de France never identified herself, as did Clemence and the anonymous nun of Barking, as a *religieuse*, nor did she associate herself with a particular abbey.[18] She never used the humility topos so universally adopted by religious figures in their writings. She never apologized for her gender, as did the nun of Barking, who had asked her readers to pardon her "presumptiun" as a woman in translating the life of Edward the Confessor. Instead, the Marie who wrote the *Vie seinte Audree* boldly claims her work, as she did all of her works, without apology and with a determination to have her name remembered. Certainly none of the illuminations contained in manuscripts of the *Fables* (the only images we have of her) depicts Marie as a nun. She is always shown in secular dress, with her hair curling from beneath her headdress. Most of these images date from the thirteenth century, when the historical Marie might well have been remembered by some still living. The religious content of two of her texts, or even the fact that the *Vie seinte Audree* is a saint's life, does not perforce make her a nun. Guernes de Pont-Saint-Maxence, a contemporary of Marie de France, remarked in his life of Thomas

Becket, also contained in the Campsey collection, that hagiographical texts had been composed by "Cler u lai, muïne u dame."[19] What *dame* did he have in mind? Perhaps the woman whom Denis Piramus referred to as "Dame Marie," generally accepted to be Marie de France. She moved easily among the secular nobility, and it was to a "nobles reis" and a certain "cunte Willalme" that she dedicated her first two works. While many medieval women who spent most of their lives in the secular world entered the convent in the later years of their lives, and it is certainly possible that Marie de France did so, nothing in her texts requires us to make that assumption.

The *Vie seinte Audree* was composed, in all likelihood, in Marie's waning years and may have been the last work she wrote and the farthest removed in time from the *Lais*. As a literary text, it is not without its weaknesses. At times, particularly as Marie slogs faithfully through the genealogies of her source text, she seems to bog down stylistically. However, at other times, her interest seems piqued by the more immediate and compelling events of Audrey's story and her determination to remain a virgin, despite her two marriages. Marie is a storyteller above all, and in the narrative moments of the text—and they are many—the direct, more animated style of the author of the *Fables* and *Lais* shines through.

Why would Marie de France—who early in her career, in the prologue to her *Lais,* had eschewed the task of translating Latin texts into *romanz*—decide as she matured to undertake such a project? Perhaps because she had come to understand her role in the context of the use of God-given gifts and talents as Wace had laid it out in his *Vie de St. Nicolas* when he wrote:

> Qui mels set mels deit enseigner
> Et qui plus poet plus deit aider.
> Qui plus est fort plus deit porter
> Et qui plus ad plus deit doner.
> Chescon deit mustrer son saver
> Et sa bonté et son poer
> Et Deu servir, son creatur,
> Et as barons sainz pur s'amur.[20]

[Whoever knows what is best must teach the best and whoever is capable of more must help more. Whoever is stronger must bear more, and whoever has more to give must give more. Each one must demonstrate his knowledge, his gifts, and his ability, and serve God, his creator, and, in his honor, the noble saints.]

Marie had already acknowledged her obligation to use her God-given talents in the opening lines of the prologue to her *Lais:* "Ki Deus ad duné escïence / E de parler bon' eloquence / Ne s'en deit taisir ne celer, / Ainz se deit vulunters mustrer."[21] By the 1190s, when she apparently wrote her last two texts, which deal with religious subjects, she seems to focus more on the latter part of Wace's admonition to serve God and the "noble saints." As she notes in her prologue to the *Vie seinte Audree,* she had come to the conclusion that "An bon hovre e en bon porpens / Devroit chascun user son tens" (lines 1–2), putting emphasis on the word *bon* by using it twice in the opening line of her work.

Few scholars today doubt that Marie de France did indeed turn to the task of translating Latin texts into French, and the *Espurgatoire seint Patriz* is widely accepted as her work. Given the strong similarities of style, the echoed phrases, and the approach to the task of translation, there can be little question that the same woman who wrote the *Espurgatoire Seint Patriz* also composed the *Vie seinte Audree*. Their temporal proximity and even the geographical proximity of the locations where the source texts were produced—Saltrey and Ely (less than twenty-five miles apart)—also suggest that the same Marie translated them both. In fact, the connections between these two texts, coupled with similarity in the epilogues of the *Fables* and the *Vie seinte Audree*, along with the similar incipits of the fables and Audrey's miracles, strengthens the evidence that the author whose commonly accepted name—Marie de France—is derived from the epilogue of the *Fables* was the author of all these texts.[22]

Sources

The Latin text of the life on which Marie bases her translation is preserved in similar forms in both the *Liber Eliensis*, compiled in the 1170s at Ely, and the *Acta Sanctorum*, for which it was edited by Daniel Papebroch (1628–1714). Although neither version corresponds *in toto* to the work of Marie, the actual *vita* (contained in both) constitutes, as Rupert Pickens has noted, approximately three-fifths of her text, ending at line 2646.[23] He argues convincingly that Marie's sources actually consisted of three different works: the life of Saint Etheldreda, an account entitled *De secunda translatione*, and a collection of her miracles, the *Miracula Sancte Etheldrede*. These texts were compiled in a manuscript in the collection of Sir Robert Bruce Cotton (1571–1631), a transcription of which served as Papebroch's base; the transcription was once at Douai Abbey in France, but only portions of it still survive "in the Dean and Chapter library at Ely (formerly Phillips 8174)." The manuscript, or one closely related to it, is housed "in the British Library (Cotton, Domitian A xv), to which [E.O.] Blake assigns the siglum *B*"; Pickens refers to Marie's source as *Douai-B* and dates it 1164–1189.[24] He argues that the *Liber Eliensis* and the *Douai-B* depended not on one another, but on common materials found in the library at Ely, where both were written. The two texts have a virtually identical form of the life of Saint Audrey, or Etheldreda as she is called in Latin. It is interesting to note that Marie herself claims that, while she translated into French the *life* of Saint Audrey that she found in written form ("en latin," line 4614), the miracles were based on oral sources ("les miracles ay oÿ," line 4615). It is tempting to hypothesize that Marie's collection may have served as an earlier vernacular version of the *Miracula*; however, her inclusion in the *Vie seinte Audree* of lines like "Si com en livre l'ay oÿ" (line 484) introduces considerable uncertainty as to whether any portion of her text was actually based on oral tradition, and it is plausible, even probable, that she relied, as Pickens suggests, on written sources throughout.

Language

As noted above, linguistic evidence indicates that the *Vie seinte Audree* was composed toward the end of the twelfth or the beginning of the thirteenth century. By the time the text was copied into the Campsey manuscript a century or so later, many linguistic changes had taken place. For example, the case system had broken down in Anglo-Norman and the case endings that the author appears to have used had little meaning to the scribe. Oftentimes it appears that the scribe has consciously "modernized" words, providing forms more easily recognizable to his or her readers a century later. For example, the older form *honesté* has been altered to the later *honesteté*, thus rendering lines where it occurs hypermetric by the addition of the extra syllable. Where the original text evidently wavered between the earlier *enferté* and the later *enfermeté*, the scribe has uniformly changed them to *enfermeté*, once again creating hypermetric lines. Similarly, the scribe has frequently added a feminine *e* to the word *tel*, making all but one of the lines that contain the newer form of the word hypermetric. On the other hand, in the case of words like *sorurs*, the scribe has ignored the case distinctions and frequently altered the word to *sours*, this time leaving the line one syllable short. Such changes on the part of the scribe help in large measure to account for the highly corrupted language of the text and the unusually large number of metrical irregularities in the otherwise octosyllabic verses.

The language of Marie's other works has been studied by a number of earlier editors, from Warnke and Jenkins to Brucker and Pontfarcy, all of whom have concluded that she wrote in a form of continental French, though they have debated precisely what dialect of continental French she may have used. While there are elements of Francien and Norman, there are also a few Picard characteristics in the various texts. Those same traits are evident in the *Vie seinte Audree*, leading the text's first editor as well as the editors of the present edition to conclude that the author is indeed originally continental and that she lived in England in the late twelfth and early thirteenth centuries. Among the authorial characteristics of the *Vie seinte Audree*, also identified for the most part in the other works by Marie, are the following:

- As is typical of continental works, *en* and *an* are not rimed.
- Elision with *ke* or *que* is optional.
- Vowel sequences requiring diaeresis, preserved in Marie's rhymes (e.g., *veü, eüst, peüst*), had already evolved to diphthongs in England. Although her language did not allow two vowels originally in Latin

hiatus or separated by a consonant to become a diphthong, given the linguistic evolution in England toward syneresis, the scribe apparently read them as one-syllable words, which accounts for a number of metrical irregularities.[25]

- The text wavers between com/come, encor/encore, or/ore, with the final vowel optional, depending on whether or not it was needed for meter. The scribe, who is not at all scrupulous about meter, often includes the *e* when it was clearly not required in the original text.
- We find the use of *e* for *i* in pretonic position, e.g., *devin* for *divin*. Although this may be a scribal characteristic, it is important to note that it also occurs in Marie de France's other works. See, for example, the lai *Eliduc*, line 1180.

The scribe has clearly made his or her impact in a variety of ways, evident in all of the following cases:

- The use of *o* and *u* is inconsistent, wavering between the Anglo-Norman *u* and the continental *o*. While this wavering is, no doubt, due at least in part to scribal changes, such a characteristic might be expected even from the writer herself, who, though she may have been from France, had, by the time the text was composed, lived for a considerable time in England.
- Instead of *a*, one often finds *e* (e.g., *dieble, lermes*).
- The Anglo-Norman orthography *aun* for *an* is frequently used (e.g., *aunte, saunté, aunciens*).
- The use of *ei* for *oi*, typical of Anglo-Norman, is quite common in the manuscript's orthography (e.g., *voleit, aveit, requereit, esteit*).
- The letter *k* is commonly used for *qu* or *c* (e.g., *ke, kar, onkes*).
- The letter *w* occurs frequently, usually in proper names, which may have appeared in the original text in this form. However, occasionally *iw* replaces *iv* (e.g., *siwy*).
- The text also contains a number of examples of the reduction of *ie* to *e* (*matere, arere, maineres*) that may be attributed to scribal changes.

Summary of the Text

The *Vie seinte Audree*, a hagiographical text of 4,625 lines, is based on the life of Saint Etheldreda, known as Audree (or Audrey) in French and Æthelthryth in Anglo-Saxon.[26] She was a seventh-century queen of Northumbria, daughter of King Anna, and lived from about 630 to 679. Though twice married, she remained a virgin throughout her life.

Marie's text begins with a brief prologue, in which the author states the necessity of occupying one's time in a good task and purpose. She reminds readers of the need to keep in mind their creation by God and their need to merit his grace in order to be saved or *gariz*, a term she also uses for physical healing. Her source text includes in great detail Audrey's genealogy (see Fig. 1), which Marie provides in a somewhat perfunctory manner. However, when the text reaches the actual life of Saint Audrey, there is a significant shift in tone and style, toward the narrative qualities scholars find in the other works of Marie de France. She tells us of Audrey's two spiritual marriages, first to Tonbert, who

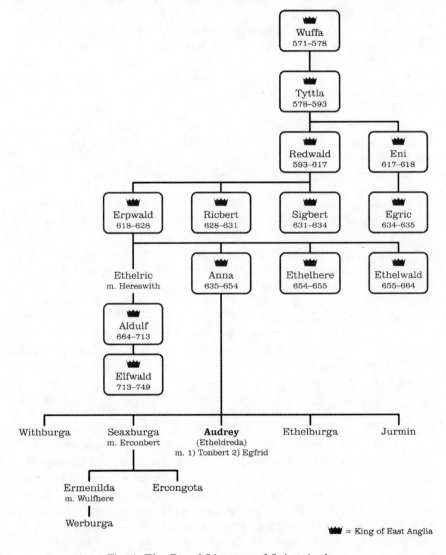

Fig. 1. The Royal Lineage of Saint Audrey

gave her the island of Ely as a portion of her dower, and then, after his death, to Egfrid, King of Northumbria. Like Tonbert, Egfrid at first respected her desire to remain a virgin and lead a religious life, but later he began to insist on his marital rights, and she was forced to flee to avoid violating her vow of virginity. God aided her with a series of miracles in her escape, and she went on to found a double monastery at Ely, where she served as abbess until her death from a tumor in her neck. She was buried in a simple wooden coffin. Her sister Seaxburga succeeded her as abbess. The new abbess arranged for the body of Audrey to be translated to a white marble sarcophagus, made of material found by the monks of the abbey outside the city wall of Grantchester (modern Cambridge), which all believed to have been provided by God. When the body was translated into this special sarcophagus and moved into the church, it was found to be uncorrupted, thus confirming her virginity to those present. This first translation appears at approximately the midpoint of Marie's text.

Invading Danes in the year 870 devastated the abbey and killed the monks and nuns. They tried to break into Audrey's tomb to steal whatever treasure might be therein but were struck blind and killed in the process. Later monks who sought to restore the abbey during the reign of Eadred did not pay proper respect to Saint Audrey's memory and were chased from the abbey. A later king, Edgar, during his reign a century after the Danish invasion, had the convent restored, and once again Audrey's body was translated into the new church, along with those of her sisters.

The text turns finally to Audrey's miracles, which are recounted at length in the latter part of the text. There the reader learns of her powers to cure the sick, the blind, the mute, and the paralyzed, to punish wrongdoers, to eliminate devils that possess the body, and even to help reconcile those with enmity between them. The text concludes with a fifteen-line epilogue in which Marie restates the purpose of her task and identifies herself as author. Having signed her work, "Pur ce ke soie remembree" (line 4625), she concludes with this final verse, a line that curiously stands on its own, without a rhyming line, as though to call attention to itself.

Artistic Assessment

As Jocelyn Wogan-Brown has pointed out, when Audrey's sisters and nieces succeed her as abbesses of the monastery, "the virgin foundress simultaneously disrupts biological lines of filiation [because of her virginity] and creates spiritual genealogies."[27] The text is one that continues to explore, like the *Lais*, the issues of women, their empowerment and disempowerment. Clearly within the spiritual realm, woman has power over whatever obstacles life might present; within marriage, however, she is powerless. Like Guildelüec in the *Lais*, Audrey chooses the realm of the spirit. The *Audree* is a fitting capstone piece to Marie's career and one that underscores the fundamental spirituality of her work.

It is important in the final analysis to look at the *Vie seinte Audree* in the context of Marie's other writings. Although clearly we cannot say for certain when it was written or even be absolutely certain of the order of her works, the *Audree* was in all likelihood composed toward the end of her life in the 1190s. By that time, as noted above, she had abandoned her youthful determination not to do what others had already done—translate a text from Latin into French—which she declined to do in the prologue to the *Lais*. Indeed, this was probably her second, or possibly her third, translation from Latin.[28]

Although the *Vie seinte Audree* shares characteristics with both the *Lais* and the *Fables*, it is temporally and stylistically closer to the *Espurgatoire*, as we might expect. Both texts focus on religious issues and appear to have been written for lay audiences; both are translations from Latin texts that have been identified; both are works about religious quests, one by a male, one by a female, in which salvation and escape are achieved through faith; and the protagonists of both texts must choose between the lay life and the religious life. The male, the *Espurgatoire*'s Owein, decides to remain in the world, while the female Audree takes refuge in the convent; these choices are consistent with what medieval scholarship has shown to be masculine space (open) and feminine space (enclosed). The two texts show many similarities in language and style. Both begin and end with a simple prayer to God. The vocabulary of the two texts is amazingly similar, and even the rhyme words are not infrequently the same.[29] Both remain remarkably faithful to the Latin original in the broadest sense, but Marie also adds, omits, or rearranges information as she chooses in both, and her originality shines through in various ways.

The *Vie seinte Audree* is by no means Marie's best work, but it is one that sheds additional light on her concerns for the problems of women, for the importance of serving God, and for educating "la simple gent" or the laity. While she attempts to include the genealogical materials of the source text (though without a great deal of apparent enthusiasm for this portion of the task), it is clearly the narrative parts of the text that capture her interest, for Marie was, above all, a consummate storyteller. Thus the text is uneven, with some quite lengthy passages worthy of her earlier efforts, while others seem uninspired. Such results are perhaps not surprising when we recall that Marie's art has been at its peak in brief narratives, like the lai and the fable. The *Vie seinte Audree*, on the other hand, is the longest of Marie's works. There are few narrative breaks, with the exception of those between the miracles. There she uses many of the same narrative incipits that may be found in the *Fables*. However, cures from blindness, muteness, paralysis, and dropsy, such as those we encounter in the miracles of the *Vie seinte Audree*, are by their very nature less lively than the antics of the animals and people who populate the *Fables*. One comes away from the work with the feeling that, while Marie may have been passionate about the *life* of St. Audrey, she had rather less enthusiasm for the rest of the text. Nonetheless, it is an important text, not only because it confirms her skills as a dynamic narrator of events, but also because it expands the canon of the works of Marie de France.

Editorial Policy and Translation

The editor of any Old French text is confronted with a number of dilemmas and decisions. Because the BL Add. 70513 is the only surviving copy of the *Vie seinte Audree*, there has been no opportunity to compare its usages to other variants. For this reason, the text's first editor, Östen Södergård, adopted an extremely conservative editorial policy, electing to maintain the 730 defective lines he noted in the text, even though he suggested that "il est souvent facile de voir pourquoi un vers a sept syllabes seulement" and that "le copiste s'est trompé à maintes reprises sur l'emploi de l'élision dans des mots comme par ex[emple] *que*." In cases of hypometric lines, he noted that "un certain nombre de vers de sept syllabes s'expliquent par la synérèse que le copiste employait à tort dans des mots comme: *sue*. Si on le lit avec diérèse: *seüe*, le vers est juste."[30] Even so, he elected to preserve these textual corruptions rather than make any such corrections.

The merits of Marie's text, however, are often obscured by such defects, and we have chosen to establish a text as close to that of the author as is reasonably possible. Although the scribe wrote a beautifully clear hand, he or she seems to have been, by and large, indifferent to the author's meter. The scribe's attempt to shift from the late twelfth-century continental usage of the author to the late thirteenth-century Anglo-Norman usage of the scriptorium has resulted in many metrically defective lines. (See comments on "Language" above.) We have sought to correct the lines where the metrical defect is obvious and easily corrected. Wherever the manuscript is not clearly in error, we have usually chosen to reproduce it as it stands. We have resolved scribal abbreviations, added punctuation and diacritical marks (*tréma, accent aigu, cédille*) as needed, and occasionally made small adjustments required by the sense of the text; all such adjustments are explained in the notes. (An asterisk indicates the presence of a note for that line; notes are listed by line number.) The diacritical marks indicate the diaeresis, help to clarify the meaning (e.g., *traire, traïre*), or point out instances where elision is not permitted by the meter. Only in cases of monosyllabic words like *ke* and *le*, which we have regularly elided before a vowel when required by meter, have we not included the tréma. In the uses of the *tréma*, we have followed the guidelines set forth by Foulet and Speer.[31]

In instances where a metrical defect is caused by an incorrect case usage (e.g., *sours* for *sorurs*) we have corrected the text, thereby usually resolving the metrical difficulty. We have intervened in other instances where the metrical defect is obvious and easily corrected. For example, as Södergård pointed out, the scribe made frequent errors of judgment in his treatment of the optional elision with the word *que*: "Notre copiste a écrit—ce qui arrive souvent aux copistes anglo-normands—*qu'il* là où le vers exige *quë il*."[32] The scribe also wrote *que il* in places that called for *qu'il*. The addition by the scribe of the feminine *e* in the word *tel* has, in ten of the eleven instances where it is used, left the line one syllable too long, making it clear that Marie's original text did not have an *e* on the feminine form. We have made these simple corrections in an effort to reconstruct insofar as possible the original text and meter of the author. In some cases, however, it is impossible to tell what may have occurred in transcription, and we have left these lines metrically defective as they are in the original manuscript. Notable examples of irregularities occur in lines that contain proper nouns, especially place names. Evidently the scribe used a version of the name that was slightly different from the one used by Marie, and thus many of these lines remain hypermetric or hypometric in the text. We have made no effort to change them, unless another spelling that works metrically is attested elsewhere in the text.

We have capitalized references to God for clarity in the text, since without such capitalization some passages may be unclear and also because we are dealing with a religious text. Rejected readings are noted in Appendix 1. The scribe very commonly writes *u* for *n* or vice versa. These we have merely corrected as needed, without noting the hundreds of instances in the rejected readings. We have also routinely resolved *x* to *us* in words such as *viex*.

The reader may notice that the Södergård edition has only 4,620 lines, while ours has 4,625. Södergård skipped one line of the manuscript text in his volume and noted only one possible omitted line by the scribe, when in fact there were at least four and possibly more. As noted above, the manuscript ends on a line without a rhyme, suggesting either an omission on the part of the scribe or, possibly, a deliberate attempt on the part of Marie to call attention to her last line "Por ce ke soie remembree" by leaving it without the second part of the couplet. Such a technique is highly unusual, but the text seems to be complete without another line to match the one ending with *remembree*, and the choice of her closing word is significant in light of her emphasis throughout all her texts on the importance of memory. Although we have included in our line count the various lacunae (with the exception of the final line which may have been deliberate), it is impossible to tell precisely how many other lines may have been omitted. Certainly there are passages where logic suggests lacunae in the text, and we have noted these instances with a note. All things considered, we cannot be absolutely certain how long Marie's original text may have been, but we know that it was *at least* 4,625 lines. Where lines have clearly been omitted by the scribe, we use a full-line ellipsis to indicate the omission.

Other types of irregularities occur occasionally when the scribe's eye has strayed to another line and an extraneous word may appear in the text. For example, line 12 of the manuscript text contains the word "departi," which evidently has been picked up from the preceding line, as it makes no sense whatever in this one. for this reason we have altered, the line "Et en la vie departi deservi" to read "Et en la vie deservi."[33] Not only has the scribe omitted lines, in one instance he or she has copied a line twice. The second copy is not included in the line count and has been omitted from the text. No ellipsis is used to indicate the omission. These instances have been pointed out in the notes and in the rejected readings. When words or phrases seem to have been omitted by the scribe, we occasionally propose possible word(s), placing them within brackets to indicate clearly that they are our additions to the manuscript text.

Our translation seeks to communicate the essential meaning of the Old French text and to elucidate and interpret the original wherever necessary. Although we have remained as close to the Old French text as possible, at times English usage demands changes where line-by-line translation would be stilted and unnatural. Occasionally inversions of information contained in one line will be transposed to another in an effort to provide a naturally flowing English text, which we hope can stand alone. We have also sought to use the punctuation and syntax of English in our translation, for clarity and logic, without distorting the meaning of the original language. As in the Old French text, asterisks indicate commentary in the notes. Whereas the notes on the Old French text comment on linguistic, stylistic, and textual matters, notes on the translation deal with issues such as poetic technique, biblical or patristic allusions, historical or cultural matters, or matters peculiar to the translation. Notes on both the Old French and the English include comments on intertextuality.

Whenever possible, we have attempted to maintain the verb tenses of the original; however, we have always chosen to use verb tenses common to the syntax of English usage. For example, we often used the past tense in lieu of the historical present, which sounds artificial and inappropriate in English although even today it is commonly used in French. We have occasionally added words which do not change the basic meaning, but which help us to present clearly the meaning, both explicit and implicit, of the Old French text. Above all, we have sought to provide a translation into English that will give the reader the flavor of Marie's work, insofar as it can be rendered in another language so far removed from her own time.

Notes to Introduction

1. The life of Saint Foy begins at the bottom of 147r almost as though it were a continuation of the previous text. There is no large initial or image to designate its incipit. For a more detailed description of the manuscript, see Delbert W. Russell, "The Campsey Collection of Old French Saints' Lives: A Re-examination of its Structure and Provenance," *Scriptorium* 57 (2003): 51–83.

2. This title is written in a modern hand.

3. The life of Thomas Becket is written in five-line monorhymed stanzas, and the life of St. Modwenna is written in quatrains.

4. We are grateful to Michael St John-McAlister, curator in the Department of Manuscripts at the British Library, for verifying these measurements, which were taken on folio 100v and may vary slightly on different folios. The text's first editor, Östen Södergård, gives the manuscript dimensions as 254 × 192 mm. He gives no indication as to where he took his measurement. He also suggests erroneously that the manuscript (not noting the two parts) is entirely on vellum.

5. Richard of Chichester holds his crosier, and Saint Catherine holds her wheel.

6. See Louis Karl, "Notice sur l'unique manuscrit français de la bibliothèque du duc de Portland à Welbeck," *Revue des langues romanes* 54 (1911): 210–29.

7. Jocelyn Wogan-Browne, *Saints' Lives and Women's Literary Culture c.1150–1300: Virginity and its Authorizations* (Oxford, England: Oxford University Press, 2001), p. 7. See also notes 10 and 11 on this same page. Others who have mentioned this possible patron include Simon Gaunt ("Saints, Sex, and Community: Hagiography," in his *Gender and Genre in Medieval French Literature* [Cambridge, 1995], pp. 180–233) and Delbert Russell, "The Campsey Collection," 64–66. An alternate possibility has been proposed by Virginia Blanton, who has suggested that the book could have been a gift from Maud de Ufford, Countess of Ulster, when she entered the convent of Campsey in 1347 ("St. Æthelthryth's Cult: Literary, Historical, and Pictorial Constructions of Gendered Sanctity," Ph.D. dissertation, State University of New York, Binghamton, 1998, pp. 272–307).

8. Östen Södergård, ed. *La Vie seinte Audree, poème anglo-norman du XIIIe siècle* (Uppsala: Årsskrift, 1955).

9. It is possible that the scribe was a nun at Campsey, though that is by no means certain.

10. We are using the term "anonymous" in its literal meaning, derived from Latin: One whose name is not known and not given. We are aware of Howard Bloch's recent book, entitled *The Anonymous Marie de France*, in which he gives anonymity an entirely different meaning—essentially one about whom we know very little (see pp. 8–9). However, it is important that Marie self-consciously signed all her works. She certainly had no intent to remain anonymous.

11. Marie de France, *Les Fables*, ed. Charles Brucker, 2d ed. (Paris, 1998), epilogue, line 8, 3–4. Other line references are to this edition and will be cited within the text.

12. For additional similarities see June Hall McCash, "*La Vie seinte Audree*: A Fourth Text by Marie de France?" *Speculum* 77 (2002): 744–77.

13. See Logan Whalen, *Marie de France and the Poetics of Memory*. (Washington, D.C.: Catholic University Press, forthcoming); see also McCash, 752–53.

14. For an argument in favor of Clemence's authorship, see William MacBain, "The Literary Apprenticeship of Clemence of Barking," *AUMLA: Journal of the Australasian Universities' Language and Literature Association* 9 (1958): 3–22.

15. See McCash, 744–777. Other scholars who have suggested that Marie de France might be the author of the *Vie seinte Audree* include Emanuel Mickel (*Marie de France* [New York: Twayne Publishers, Inc., 1974], pp. 143–44, and Michael J. Curley, who, as translator of the *Espurgatoire* would have been well familiar with her style (*Saint Patrick's Purgatory: A Poem by Marie de France* [Binghamton, NY: Medieval and Renaissance Texts and Studies, 1993], p. 7. Other line references are to this edition and will be cited within the text.). Richard Baum has also suggested that the *Vie seinte Audree* deserves consideration in any discussion of Marie de France's authorship, though he argues that we are dealing with more than one author in the various works. See his *Recherches sur les oeuvres attribuées à Marie de France* (Heidelberg, Carl Winter, 1968).

16. Södergård, p. 39. Bloch mistakenly states that Södergård attributed the text to Marie de France (*Anonymous Marie*, p. 3).

17. Marie de Meulan was first proposed in 1932 by U.T. Holmes ("New Thoughts on Marie de France," *Studies in Philology*, 29 [1932]: 1–10; "Further on Marie de France," *Symposium* 3 [1949]: 335, 338–9). Others have agreed and presented additional evidence: See, for example, R. D. Whichard, "A Note on the Identity of Marie de France," in *Romance Studies Presented to*

William Morton Dey, ed. by U. T. Holmes, A. G. Engstrom, and S. E. Leavitt (Chapel Hill: University of North Carolina Studies in Romance Languages and Literatures, 1950), pp. 177–81; P. N. Flum, "Additional Thoughts on Marie de France," *Romance Notes* 3 (1961): 52–56; P.N. Flum, "Marie de France and the Talbot Family Connections," *Romance Notes* 7 (1965): 83–86. See also P.R. Grillo, "Was Marie de France the Daughter of Waleran II, Count of Meulan?" *Medium Aevum* 62 (1988): 269–74. The most compelling recent arguments have been set forth by Yolande de Pontfarcy, "Si Marie de France était Marie de Meulan," *Cahiers de Civilisation Médiévale* 38 (1995): 353–61; see also her edition of the *Espurgatoire seint Patriz* (Louvain: Peeters, 1995), pp. 50–53.

18. Both Dominica Legge (*Anglo-Norman in the Cloisters* [Edinburgh: Edinburgh University Publications, 1950], p. 75) and Jocelyn Wogan-Browne (p. 90) have sought to connect the author of the *Vie seinte Audree* with the convent of Chatteris, but the evidence presented thus far is unconvincing. Although it is true that she mentions Chatteris in the text of the *Audree*, it is also mentioned in her Latin source. Thus, there is no compelling reason to assume that she was a nun there. Chatteris is, however, located about halfway between Saltrey (modern-day Sawtrey) and Ely.

19. *La vie de saint Thomas le martyr*, ed. Em[manuel] Walberg (Lund, 1922), p. 9, stanza 33.

20. Wace, *La Vie de St. Nicolas: Poème religieux du XIIe siècle*, ed. Einar Ronsjö (Lund: Gleerup, 1942), lines 23–30. It is widely believed that Marie was familiar with Wace's works. See, for example, Lucien Foulet's article, which suggests the possibility of her indebtedness to Wace for her English place names ("English Words in the *Lais* of Marie de France," *Modern Language Notes* 20 [1905]: 108–10).

21. Marie de France, *Lais*, ed. Alfred Ewert (Oxford: Blackwell, 1944; Reissued London: Bristol Classical Press, 1983), lines 1–4. Other line references are to this edition and will be cited within the text.

22. McCash has argued elsewhere that there can be little question that the Marie who wrote the *Espurgatoire* is the same as the author of the *Vie seinte Audree*. (June Hall McCash, "*L'Espurgatoire seint Patriz* and *La Vie seinte Audree*: A Stylistic Comparison," International Medieval Congress, Leeds, England, Summer, 2003). The author of the *Espurgatoire* has, of course, long been accepted by most as Marie de France. But there is even more compelling evidence to link Marie de France, author of the *Fables* from which we derive her name, to the *Audree* than to the *Espurgatoire*. The similarity of the epilogues of the *Fables* and the *Audree* and the similar incipits to the *Fables* and to Audree's miracles is persuasive. The weakest evidence is that which links the three of these texts to the *Lais*, though the presence of both the *Lais* and a text of the *Fables* in a single manuscript, the Harley 978, as well as the similar treatment of memory in the various texts, adds considerable support to the argument. Thus, while we are inclined to believe that the same woman was the author of all four texts, one might argue that we are still dealing with two Maries, the Marie of the *Lais* and that of the other three works in question, the woman who identified herself as Marie de France.

23. Rupert Pickens, "Marie de France Translatrix: *La Vie de seinte Audree*," unpublished paper delivered at the International Medieval Congress in Leeds, England, summer 2003, 8, 14 (cited with permission). Södergård identifies the source text as that preserved in the *Acta Sanctorum*. Following the lead of Christine Garrison, Jocelyn Wogan-Browne, and Virginia Blanton-Whetsell, McCash also identified it as the *Liber Eliensis*. Marie clearly follows the life that is contained in essentially identical forms in both the *Liber Eliensis* and the *Douai B*, although one of her self-appointed tasks seems to be to abbreviate it as much as possible. However, after the life itself, beginning with line 2653, she follows the order of chapters found in *Douai-B* and not the *Liber Eliensis*, as she also does in the miracles (beginning with line 2789), thirty-seven of which are scattered throughout the *Liber Eliensis* while an additional eighteen are found only in *Douai-B*.

24. Pickens, p. 6.

25. See Jenkins, p. 38.

26. Jocelyn Wogan-Browne describes the text as "a blending of hagiography and historiography" (*Saints' Lives and Women's Literary Culture*, p. 210.

27. Wogan-Browne, p. 210.

28. Many scholars accept as one of her sources for the *Fables* the Latin *Romulus Nilantii*. Sahar Amer has also suggested that Arabic sources close to Marie's text, notably *Kalilah wa Dimnah*, may also have influenced her work. See *Ésope au féminin: Marie de France et la politique de l'interculturalité* (Amsterdam: Rodopi, 1999).

29. Examples of similarities in Marie's word preference include such words as *deservir* (used 6 times in the *Audree*, 9 times in the *Espurgatoire* and the phrase *Al Deu servir*, or a slight variant, used 13 times in the *Audree*, 8 times in the *Espurgatoire* (though not at all in Clemence of Barking's life of Saint Catherine, where one might expect similar language). Marie also shows a propensity to use the same rhyme words in both texts (e.g., *en oreisons et en afflictions*). McCash has explored the similarities in greater detail in "The *Espurgatoire seint Patriz* and the *Vie seinte Audree*: A Stylistic Comparison."

30. Södergård, p. 38.

31. See Alfred Foulet and Mary Blakely Speer, *On Editing Old French Texts* (Lawrence, Ka.: Regents Press of Kansas, 1979). Many editions use the tréma over *io* (e.g., *religïon*). However, since *io* is always bisyllabic in Old French, we have followed the recommendation of Foulet and Speer and omitted it. See also Peter F. Dembowski, who seems to endorse these ideas in "What Is Critical in Critical Editions?" in *"De sens rassis": Essays in Honor of Rupert T. Pickens* (Amsterdam: Rodopi, 2005), pp. 169–81.

32. Södergård, p. 38.

33. Södergård had also made this correction.

Select Bibliography

Manuscripts

British Library, Cotton Domitian A xv (B).
British Library, Additional 70513.

Old French Editions and Latin Sources

Liber Eliensis. Ed. E. O. Blake. London: Royal Historical Society, 1962.
Marie de France. *Lais*. Ed. Alfred Ewert. Oxford: Blackwell, 1944; reissued London: Bristol
    Classical Press, 1995.
_____. *Les Fables*. Ed. Charles Brucker. Louvain and Paris: Peeters, 1998.
_____. *L'Espurgatoire Seint Patriz*. Ed. Yolande de Pontfarcy. Louvain and Paris: Peeters, 1995.
_____. *Saint Patrick's Purgatory: A Poem by Marie de France*. Ed. and trans. Michael J. Curley.
    Binghamton, NY: Medieval and Renaissance Texts and Studies, 1993.
Södergård, Östen. Ed. *La Vie seinte Audree, poème anglo-norman du XIIIe siècle*. Uppsala: Årsskrift,
    1955.
Vie de saint Thomas le martyr. Ed. Emmanuel Walberg. Lund: Gleerup, 1922.
Vita Sanctae Etheldredae. In *Acta sanctorum*, June, 4, cols. 489–576. Ed. Daniel Papebroch.
    Antwerp: Société des Bollandistes, 1628–1714.
Wace. *La Vie de St Nicolas: Poème religieux du XIIe siècle*. Ed Einar Ronsjö. Lund: Gleerup, 1942.

Translations

Liber Eliensis: A History of the Isle of Ely From the Seventh Century to the Twelfth. Trans. Janet Fair-
    weather. Woodbridge, England: Boydell, 2005.
Sellar, A.M. *Bede's Ecclesiastical History of the English People: A Revised Translation*. London: G.
    Bell and Sons, 1917.
The Fables of Marie de France: An English Translation. Trans. Mary Lou Martin. Birmingham,
    AL. Summa Publications, 1984.
The Lais of Marie de France. Trans. Glyn S. Burgess and Keith Busby. London: Penguin, 1986.

Secondary Sources

Albertson, Clinton, S. J. *Anglo-Saxon Saints and Heroes*. New York: Fordham University Press,
    1967.
Amer, Sahar. *Ésope au féminin: Marie de France et la politique de l'interculturalité*. Amsterdam:
    Rodopi, 1999.

Baum, Richard. *Recherches sur les oeuvres attribuées à Marie de France.* Heidelberg: Carl Winter, Universitätsverlag, 1968.

Blanton, Virginia. "King Anna's Daughters: Genealogical Narrative and Cult Formation in the *Liber Eliensis.*" *Historical Reflections/Réflexions Historiques* 30 (2004): 127–49.

Blanton-Whetsell, Virginia. "*Imagines Etheldredae*: Mapping Hagiographic Representation of Abbatial Power and Religious Patronage." *Studies in Iconography* 23 (2002): 55–107.

Bloch, R. Howard. *The Anonymous Marie de France.* Chicago: University of Chicago Press, 2003.

Brooke, Christopher. *The Saxon and Norman Kings.* New York: Macmillan, 1963.

Burns, Jane. *Medieval Fabrications: Dress, Textiles, Cloth Work, and Other Cultural Imaginings.* New York: Palgrave Macmillan, 2004.

Chadwick, Henry. *Augustine.* Oxford: Oxford University Press, 1986. Reissued 1996.

Clanchy, M.T. *From Memory to Written Record,* 2nd ed. Oxford: Blackwell, 1993.

Dembowski, Peter F. "What is Critical in Critical Editions?" In "*De sens rassis*": *Essays in Honor of Rupert T. Pickens.* Eds. Keith Busby, Bernard Guidot, and Logan Whalen. Amsterdam: Rodopi, 2005.

Elliott, Dyan. *Spiritual Marriage: Sexual Abstinence in Medieval Wedlock.* Princeton, NJ: Princeton University Press, 1993.

Farmer, David Hugh. *The Oxford Dictionary of Saints,* 5th ed. Oxford: Oxford University Press, 2003. Reissued 2004.

Flum, P. N. "Additional Thoughts on Marie de France." *Romance Notes* 3 (1961): 52–56.

_____. "Marie de France and the Talbot Family Connections." *Romance Notes* 7 (1965): 83–86.

Foulet, Albert, and Mary Blakely Speer. *On Editing Old French Texts.* Lawrence: Regents Press of Kansas, 1979.

Foulet, Lucien. "English Words in the *Lais* of Marie de France." *Modern Language Notes* 20 (1905): 108–10.

Godfrey, John. *The Church in Anglo-Saxon England.* Cambridge: Cambridge University Press, 1962.

Grillo, P. R. "Was Marie de France the Daughter of Waleran II, Count of Meulan?" *Medium Aevum* 62 (1988): 269–74.

Holmes, Urban T. "New Thoughts on Marie de France." *Studies in Philology* 29 (1932): 1–10.

_____. "Further on Marie de France," *Symposium* 3 (1949): 335–39.

Jones, Trefor. *The English Saints: East Anglia.* Norwich: Canterbury Press, 1999.

Karl, Louis. "Notice sur l'unique manuscrit français de la bibliothèque du duc de Portland à Welbeck." *Revue des langues romanes* 54 (1911): 210–29.

Legge, Dominica. *Anglo-Norman in the Cloisters: The Influence of the Orders upon Anglo-Norman Literature.* Edinburgh: Edinburgh University Publications, 1950.

_____. *Anglo-Norman Literature and Its Background.* Oxford: Oxford University Press, 1963.

MacBain, William. "The Literary Apprenticeship of Clemence of Barking." *AUMLA: Journal of the Australasian Universities' Language and Literature Association* 9 (1958): 3–22.

McCash, June Hall. "*La vie seinte Audree*: A Fourth Text by Marie de France?" *Speculum* 77 (2002): 744–777.

_____. "*L'Espurgatoire seint Patriz* and *La Vie seinte Audree*: A Stylistic Comparison." Unpublished paper delivered at the International Medieval Congress, University of Leeds. Summer 2003.

Mickel, Emanuel J., Jr. *Marie de France.* Twayne's World Authors Series 306. New York: Twayne, 1974.

Nankivell, John. *Saint Wilfrid.* London: Society for Promoting Christian Knowledge, 2002.

New Harvard Dictionary of Music. Ed. Don Michael Randel. Cambridge, Mass.: The Belknap Press of Harvard University Press, 1986.

Pickens, Rupert. "Marie de France Translatrix: *La Vie Seinte Audree.*" Unpublished paper delivered at the International Medieval Congress, University of Leeds, July-August 2003.

_____. "Marie de France Translatrix: *L'Espurgatoire Seint Patriz.*" *Le Cygne* 1 (New Series) 2002: 7–24.

Piponnier, Françoise, and Perrine Mane. *Dress in the Middle Ages.* Trans. Caroline Beamish. New Haven and London: Yale University Press, 1997. Second printing, 2000.

Pontfarcy, Yolande de. "Si Marie de France était Marie de Meulan." *Cahiers de Civilisation Médié-vale* 38 (1995): 353–61.

Reaney, P. H. *The Place-Names of Cambridgeshire and the Isle of Ely.* Cambridge: Cambridge University Press, 1943.

Robertson, Duncan. *The Medieval Saints' Lives: Spiritual Renewal and Old French Literature.* Edward C. Armstrong Monographs on Medieval Literature 8. Lexington, KY: French Forum, 1995.

Russell, Delbert. "The Campsey Collection of Old French Saints' Lives: A Reexamination of its Structure and Provenance." *Scriptorium* 57 (2003): 51–83.

Sellar, A. M. *Bede's Ecclesiastical History of the English People: A Revised Translation.* London: G. Bell and Sons, 1917.

Sneesby, Norman. *Etheldreda: Princess, Queen, Abbess and Saint.* Ely: Fern House, 1999.

Stock, Brian. *Augustine the Reader: Meditation, Self-Knowledge, and the Ethics of Interpretation.* Cambridge, Mass.: The Belknap Press of Harvard University Press, 1996.

Whalen, Logan E. *Marie de France and the Poetics of Memory.* Washington, D.C.: Catholic University of America Press, forthcoming.

Whichard, R. D. "A Note on the Identity of Marie de France." In *Romance Studies Presented to William Morton Dey.* Eds. U. T. Homes, A. G. Engstrom, and S. E. Leavitt. Chapel Hill: University of North Carolina Studies in Romance Languages, 1950, 177–81.

Wogan-Browne, Jocelyn. "Wreaths of Time: The Female Translator in Anglo-Norman Hagiography." In *The Medieval Translator 4.* Eds. Roger Ellis and Ruth Evans. Binghamton, NY: Medieval & Renaissance Texts & Studies, 1994.

_____. "'Cler u lai, muïne u dame': Women and Anglo-Normal Hagiography, in the Twelfth and Thirteenth Centuries." In *Women and Literature in Britain 1150–1500.* Ed. Carol Meale. Cambridge: Cambridge University Press, 1993, 66–75.

_____. "Rerouting the Dower: The Anglo-Norman Life of St. Audrey by Marie (of Chatteris?)" In *Power of the Weak.* Eds. Sally-Beth MacLean and Jennifer Carpenter. Champaign-Urbana: University of Illinois Press, 1995.

_____. *Saints' Lives and Women's Literary Culture c.1150–1300: Virginity and Its Authorizations.* Oxford: Oxford University Press, 2001.

Yorke, Barbara. *Kings and Kingdoms of Early Anglo-Saxon England.* London: Routledge, 1990.

Other Resources

An Anglo-Norman Dictionary. Ed. Louise W. Stone, William Rothwell, et al. London: Modern Humanities Research Association, 1977–92.

Catholic Bible: Personal Study Edition. Gen. ed. Jean Marie Heisberger. Oxford: Oxford University Press, 1995.

Einhorn, E. *Old French: A Concise Handbook.* Cambridge: Cambridge University Press, 1974.

Godefroy, F. *Dictionnaire de l'ancien français et de tous ses dialectes du IXe au XVe siècle.* 10 vols. Paris, 1880–1902.

_____. *Lexique de l'ancien français.* Paris: Welter, 1901.

Gossen, Charles Théodore. *Grammaire de l'ancien picard.* Paris: Klincksieck, 1970.

Greimas, Algirdas Julien. *Dictionnaire de l'ancien français: Le Moyen Age.* Paris: Larousse, 1995.

Hindley, Alan, Frederick W. Langley, and Brian J. Levy. *Old French-English Dictionary.* Cambridge, England: Cambridge University Press, 2000. Reprinted 2004.

Holy Bible. New International Version. Grand Rapids, MI: Zondervan, 1978.

Kibler, William W. *An Introduction to Old French.* New York: Modern Language Association of America, 1984.

Pope, Mildred K. *From Latin to Modern French with Especial Consideration of Anglo-Norman.* Manchester: Manchester University Press, 1934. Reprint 1952.

Tobler, Adolf, and E. Lommatzsch. *Französisches Etymologisches Wörterbuch.* Bonn, Basel, Leipzig, 1928.

Vising, Johann. *Anglo-Norman Language and Literature.* London: Oxford University Press, 1923.

THE LIFE
OF SAINT AUDREY

Ici comence la vie seinte Audree, noneyne de Ely

fol 100v col 1

An bon hovre e en bon porpens
Devroit chascun user son tens.
Pur sage devroit hon tenir
Celui ke porroit sovenir*
Dont il est fait, qui le cria,   5
Et quel part il revertira.
Cil qui bien font sunt honuré
E de Dieu e del siecle amé:
Poy vaut a home ses tresors
Puis ke l'ame se part del cors   10
S'il ne l'ha por Deu departi
Et en sa vie deservi
Ke ses biens venquent ses malices,
Son orguil, ses mauveises vices:
Gariz est ki desert en vie   15
La Deu grace et sa compaignie.

Ce fist la virge sainte Audree
La roÿne bon[e]üree
Ky deguerpi regne et hautesce
Por avoir ou Deu la richesce   20
Que il a promis a ses feus
Ky sunt ou lui et il ou eus:
Li clerc, li moine, li hermite
Ky ont ceste vie despite,
Les saintes virges glorïuses   25
Ky se firent a Deu espouses
Regnent et vivent et vivront
Ou Deu ki tut cria le mund.

Pour sainte Audree la roïne,
[Li] cui bien ne faut ne decline,   30
Hay comencé ce livre a faire.

fol 100v col 2

Ici m'estuet dire et retraire
De quel linage ele fu nee
Et com deus foiz fu marïee.
Ainz ke paroil dou mariage   35
M'estuet moustrer de son linage.

Solom l'estoire as ancïens

Here begins the Life of Saint Audrey,
nun of Ely*

For a good work and for a good purpose
should each person use his time.
It would be wise
for everyone to remember
5   what he is made of, who made him,
and whither he shall return.*
People who do good are honored
and loved by God and also by the world.
Since the soul will [one day] leave the body,
10 earthly possessions are worth very little
if one has not shared them for the sake of God
nor in this life been a worthy person
whose good works outweigh his misdeeds,
pride, and evil vices.
15 Saved is the one who during his lifetime
has merited the grace and fellowship of God.

The virgin Saint Audrey lived that way,
the blessed queen
who gave up her kingdom and high position
20 in order to have in God the riches
He has promised to His faithful ones
who are in Him and He in them.
Clerks, monks, hermits,
who have disdained this earthly life,
25 and glorious saintly virgins
whose marriage is to God,
now live and will [forever] live and reign
with God the Creator of the world.

I have undertaken to write this book,
30 in honor of Saint Audrey the queen
whose goodness has never faded nor diminished.
I will start by retracing
her lineage, then I will tell
how she was married twice.
35 But before I speak of marriage,
I must show her lineage.

According to the history recorded by the ancients,

En icel tens ke Marcïens
Hout de Rome la seignurie,
L'empire et tute la baillie,   40
Une genz, Engleis sunt nomez,
En Bretaine sunt arivez
Cinqante sis et bien cent anz,
Si com saint Bedes est disanz,
Ainz ke saint Aüstin venist,   45
I furent les Engleis, ceo dist.
Treis maineres de compaignons
Godlondeis, Engleis, et Seixons
Furent icil qui de Germaine
Esteient venuz en Bretaine.   50
De la lignee as Godlondeis
Furent engendres li Kenteis;
L'autre partie des Estreis
Furent engendrez des Engleis;
L'autre partie des Seixons,   55
Ke Seixons Estreis apeluns.
Est Aungle a non cele partie
Dont Engleis eurent seignurie:
De cele genz fu engendree
La glorïeuse sainte Audree   60
Ke mut fu de grant sainteté
Et [fu] de real digneté.
Redwald fu en icel tens reis,
Ce dist l'estoire des Kenteis.
Titulus out son pere a non,   65   fol 101r col 1
Ulf son aol, si le trovom;
De cest Ulf furent apellé
Ulfinges li reis et nomé.
Aprés icel rei Redwald
Regnat un sen fiz Erkenwald   70
Ke par le bon rei Edwine
Se torna a la ley divine.
Cist Edwin[e]s estoit [li] reis,
Sire et mestres de[s] Norhombreis;
Par son seint amonestement   75
Converti cist liu et sa gent.
Occis fu, poi de tens dura.
Sigilberz, son frere, regna:*
Bons cristïens fu sanz dotance.
Cist jeta le païs d'errance   80

in the time when Marcian
was the leader
40 of the powerful Roman Empire
a people called Angles*
arrived in Britain.
Saint Bede says
the Angles had been there
45 a good one hundred fifty-six years
before Saint Augustine came [to England].
There were three types of people
who came into Britain
from Germanic lands:
50 Jutes, Angles, and Saxons.
From the line of the Jutes
the inhabitants of Kent were engendered.
Another group of East Angles
were engendered directly from the Angles.
55 Yet another group came from the Saxons,
a group we call the East Anglian Saxons.
Their area had East Anglia as its name,
and the Angles held it in their lordship.
From these people a woman
60 of great holiness and royal dignity
was born:
glorious Saint Audrey.
According to the history of the people of Kent,
Redwald was king at that time.
65 His father was named Tyttla,
and we are told that Wuffa was his grandfather.
From this Wuffa, the kings of that dynasty
were called by the name "Wuffings."
After King Redwald
70 one of his sons, Eorpwald, ruled.
Through the efforts of good King Edwin
he was converted to the Holy Law [Christianity].
Edwin was king,
lord, and master of the Northumbrians.
75 Through his saintly admonition
the whole area and all its people were converted.
But he was killed and reigned only a short time.
His brother Sigbert later reigned.
He was a undoubtedly a good Christian man,
80 for he brought the land back out of its erroneous faith*

Par saint Felix, un sen ami:
Eveskes fu, mut le creï,
En France ert a lui acointez
Dementres qu'il fu eissilliez.
Kant de son essil vint ariere   85
Felix manda par sa preiere:
Vint a lui, eveske le fist
De Dounemoc, ou il le mist;
Par precher et par sainteté
Converti il cele cité.   90

En icel tens que ge vus di
Sigilberz son regne gerpi:
En Bedrichesworde l'ai oï*
Que a moinage se rendi.
A Egeriz, le suen parent,   95
Dou reiaume la cure rent
Ki en cel tens une partie
Del reiaume avoit en ballie.
Mut soffri cist bataillie et guerre*   fol 101r col 2
D'un rei Penda qui en la terre   100
Vint ocians de Merchenelande:
Sa poüsté vout qu'ele espande.
Quant Egeriz ne pout contendre
Ne la terre vers eus defendre,
Sigilberz volrent faire issir   105
De son moinagë et partir
Pur eus aider et conforteir
Et lur corages afermeir.
De s'abeïe le geterunt
Et a force ou eus le menerunt   110
En la bataillie ou cil esteient
Ki encontr'aus se combateient.
Membra lui par religion
De sa sainte profession:
Autre armeüre ne voloit   115
Fors une verge k'il tenoit.
Occis fu en cele bataillie
Et Egeris li reis sanz faillie.
Totes lur hoz et leur mainees
Hont occises et detrenchees.   120
Trente set anz furent passés
Et sis cenz puis que Deus fu nees

with the help of his friend Saint Felix.
Felix was a bishop, and I am quite sure
Sigbert made his acquaintance in France
while he was there in exile.
85   When he returned from exile,
he sent for Felix, who, upon his request,
came to him; then Sigbert made him Bishop
of Dunwich and seated him there.
Through his preaching and holiness
90   Felix converted that city.

During this particular time
Sigbert gave up his throne.
I heard that he went to Bury Saint Edmunds
and became a monk.
95   He left the kingdom to Egric,
one of his relatives,
since he already held part
of it in his power.
Egric endured a series of wars
100   with a certain King Penda
who came marauding to that area from Mercia,
seeking to expand his power.
When Egric could no longer contend
nor defend his lands against the Mercians,
105   the East Angles decided to make Sigbert leave
his monastic life and come back
to help strengthen their army
and bolster their courage.
So they took him by force from his abbey
110   and made him go with them
into battle against the men
they were fighting.
Mindful of his faith
and his holy profession,
115   he refused any weapon other
than the staff which he held in his hand.
He was killed in this battle,
and so was Egric the king.
All their troops and the entire army
120   were killed and cut to pieces.
Six hundred and thirty-seven years had passed
since the birth of God [Christ]

Quant ceste aventure avint si
Que jeo vos ay cunté ici.

Le fiz ainnez, un noble vassal   125
De noble linage et de real,
Regna aprés l'occision:
Anne le rei l'apelloit hom.
Cest rois fu pere sainte Audree
La roïne bonn[e]üree.   130
Kant le regne out bien en justise,
Si honura mut une eglise
Que en Cnaresburc estoit   fol 101v col 1
Ou Phurseüs manoit
Ke, par la grace et par l'aïe   135
Sigilberz, out cele abbeïe.

Annë ert reis de la cuntree
Sainte vie et bonn[e]üree
Mena et tint mut sagement.
Femme prist al lou de sa gent: 140
De ceste dame trovom nous
Ke digne fu de tiel espous
Et de linage et d'honesté
Et de bone moralité.
Tant furent de Deu espiré   145
Ke tost s'estoient aturné
A Deu servir lur creatur
Et a povres doner de[l] lur.
Tres noble engendr[e]üre et digne
Heurent ensemble et mult benigne: 150
Deuz fiz, quatre fillies haveient.
Norir les firent cum meuz pooient.
Li uns fu Aldulfs apellez,
Jurmins fu li autres nomez;
Des fillies [ert] Sexburg l'ainznee,   155
Tres noble dame et alosee;
La secunde out non Edelberge
En qui toz [biens] meint et herberge;
La tierce avoit a non Audree,
Saintiesme virge et honuree;   160
La quarte suer Withburc out non,
Mut fu de grant religion.
Sachez ke [celes] quatre soers

when this event took place
just as I have related it to you here.

125   The eldest son, a noble vassal
of a high and royal lineage,
ruled after the slaughter.
His name was King Anna,
the father of Saint Audrey
130   the blessed queen.
When he had duly established his rule,
he then richly endowed a church
in Burgh Castle
where Fursey,
135   through the kindness and support
of Sigbert, held the abbey.

Anna was king of the land.
He led a holy and blessed life
and ruled wisely.
140   At the behest of his people he took a wife*
who, we learn,
was quite worthy of such a husband
because of her lineage and honorable name,
and also because of her high morality.
145   The couple were so inspired by God
that they soon turned
to serving God their creator,
and gave of their wealth to the poor.
Together they produced
150   very noble, well-bred, and kind children:
They had two sons and four daughters
who were brought up in the best possible manner.
One son was called Aldulf;
the other was named Jurmin.
155   The oldest of the daughters was Seaxburga,
a very noble and praiseworthy lady.
The second one had the name Ethelburga,
a woman full of every virtue.
The third daughter was named Audrey,
160   a most holy and honored virgin.
The fourth sister was very devoutly religious;
her name was Withburga.
Know that these four sisters

Deservirent bien en lur jurs
Ke ou les cointes virges pristrent   165
L'oille ke en lur lampes mistrent,
Ke ja meis ne seient estaintes   fol 101v col. 2
Dont les nonsages font les pleintes.
En Aldulfs, fiz al rei l'ainzné,
Dist saint Bedes, ot grant bonté.*   170
En Jurmins out grant sainteté,
Devotion et honesté.
De ceste dame dist ici
Dont si bon linagë issi
Ke Hereswidë out a non,*   175
Fillie Herici un baron:
Cist fu nefs le rei Edwine
A ki Norhomborlond acline.
Sexburg, la fillie Anne l'ainnee
A Herchenbert fu marïee,   180
Rois de Kent, si come nos dist
Saint Bede ke le livre fist.
Aldulfs fu rois puis le decés,*
Et Edelwold regna aprés.
La merë Aldulf, Hereswid,   185
Fu suer, ceo conte li escrit,
Sainte Hilde une bone dame,
Abbesse mult de noble fame,*
Et furent fillies Herici,
Ceo havé vos devant oï.   190
Alvriz out lur aol a non,
Fiz [de] Edwine le baron.
Hereswide, dont jeo vous di,
Out heü un autre mari
Dont ele out une fillie bele,   195
Sedrete out non, virge et pucele.
Sexburg, par le conseil sa mere,
Al quint an del regne son pere
A Erchenberc fu marïee
Ky l'a en Kent ou li menee.   200
Eldeberge virginité   fol 102r col 1
Promist a Deu et chasteté:
Rendi sei en religion.
En icel tens dont nos parlom
Out en Bretaine meinte eglise   205
Fundé et faite a Deu servise

were quite praiseworthy in their lifetime.
165 Like the wise virgins, they brought
oil to put in their lamps
so that the lamps would never go out—
for which [oversight] the foolish ones lamented.*
Aldulf, the king's eldest son,
170 was extremely good, according to Saint Bede.
Jurmin was saintly,
devoted to God, and noble of character.
The lady [King Anna's wife]
came from a good family.
175 Bede says that her name was Hereswith,*
the daughter of a certain baron Hereric.
He was the nephew of King Edwin
to whom Northumbria was subject.
Seaxburga, Anna's oldest daughter,
180 was married to Erconbert,
a king of Kent, as Saint Bede
who wrote the book tells us.
Aldulf was king after Anna's death,*
and Elfwald reigned after him.
185 The writing tells us that Aldulf's mother, Hereswith,
was the sister
of Saint Hilda, a good woman
and an abbess of great and noble repute.
These two were the daughters of Hereric.
190 But you have heard all this before.
Their grandfather was named Edfrid,
son of the noble Edwin.
Hereswith, whom I have mentioned,
had had another husband
195 by whom she had a beautiful daughter
named Sethryd, a young virgin.
Seaxburga, following the advice of her mother,
in the fifth year of her father's reign
was married to Erconbert
200 who took her to live with him in Kent.
Ethelburga promised her virginity
and chastity to God
and gave herself over to religion.
During this particular time
205 there were a number of churches
founded in Britain and built for the service of God,*

Ou plusors lur fillies metoient,
A Deu esposer les fesoient,
Si comë il ooent les lois
E les costomes de François.   210
Fillies et neces et parentes
Fesoient noneines où grant rentes:
A Calke, a Briges, et alliors
Furent rendues des meilliors.
A Briges fu mise Sedree   215
Ky de l'autre seignur fu nee,
Et Eldeberge ensemble ou li
Ky fu del naturel mari.
Wythburg, ki la puisne[e] fu,
Espire[e] estoit de vertu.   220
Fiz des rois la voleient prendre
Mes el ne voleit mie entendre:
Richesce et parentee despit;
En solitaire liu se mist,
Pur avoir la Deu compagnie   225
Vout avoir solitaire vie.
Aprés la mort son pere Anna
A Dereheam se herberga.

La beneïte virge Audree
En une vile renomee,   230
Exninge [l']apelë hom,
Si come en livre le trovom,
Fu nee, ceo dist en la vie
Ke saint Bedes testimonie.   fol 102r col 2
En s'enfance mut bonement   235
Se contint et mut sagement,
Et tot jurs creut en amendant
En dit, en fait, et en semblant;
De tote gent estoit amee
Et mut preisee et mut dotee.   240
A nul home vivant ne fist
Moleste ne que li nosist.
Del comencement de s'enfance
Mist ele entente et voilliance
D'estre sobre et en charité   245
Mainer et en virginité.
La compagnie de son pere
Tint sainte Audreë et sa mere

in which many [parents] placed their daughters
and had them married to God,
thus they followed the laws
210 and customs of the French.
Daughters and nieces and female relatives
became nuns, bringing with them large endowments.
The best ones went
to Chelles, Brie, and other similar places.*
215 In Brie they put Sethryd,
who was born of Hereswith's first husband,
and together with her they put Ethelburga
who was born of the natural [second] husband.
Withburga, the youngest daughter,
220 was inspired by virtue.
They tried to make her wed the son of a king,
but she would have none of it.
She held no regard for wealth and lineage,
and went away to an isolated place,
for she wanted to lead a solitary life
in order to have the companionship of God.
After the death of her father, Anna,
she lived in Dereham.

The blessed virgin Audrey
230 was born in a famous city
known as Exning,
as we find mentioned in the book
which tells her life story
to which Saint Bede bears witness.
235 During her childhood she behaved
very well and properly,
and as she grew she constantly improved
in speech, behavior, and appearance.
She was greatly loved, admired,
240 and revered by everyone.
She never quarreled
or did harm to any human being.
From the beginning of her childhood
she set her mind and will
245 on being sober and on living in charity
and remaining a virgin.
Saint Audrey went in the company
of her father and mother

D'aler aorer a sainte eglise
[Et] entendi al Deu servise, 250
[Ne] del giu ne de l'envoisure
De ses compaignes n'aveit cure.
Mut se merveillient si parent
De son noble contenement:
Entr[ë] eus le dïent sovent 255
Ke la Deu grace en li resplent.
Sainte Audree metoit grant cure
Ke sa vie fust chaste et pure.
Ceo siecle despist et haÿ,
Orgueil ne vice n'out en ly. 260
D'un sage home fu bien li diz
En la sainte virge acompliz,
Ke dist ke veilliesce d'aage
Est nonsuillé vïe al sage.

Come ceste virge ert issue 265
D'enfance [ele] fu parcr[e]üe,
De sa bieuté et sa valur
Parloient mut li plusur,
Et loinz et pres [en] fu portee   fol 102v col 1
La novele et la renomee. 270
Roi et prince la demandeient
Pur sa beauté la coveitoient
Et pur la grant valur de ly
Ke chacuns en avoit oÿ,
Mes ele suspiroit souvent 275
Pur la chambre u ele s'atent
C'est le paleis [de] Jesu Crist,
A ki virginité promist.
En oreisons toz jurs manoit,
Sa char dantoit et destreignoit. 280

Issi avint ke si parent
Par le devin porveiement,
Pur ceo ke la virge ert d'aage,
Ly purvirent ou mariage
D'un prince ki la requereit: 285
Tonbert out non, haut home esteit;
Grant entente et grant paine out mise
Pur ly avoir et mut requise.
Tant la requist et tant pria

to pray in church
250 and hear the mass.
She had no interest in games or the merriment
of her company of friends.
Her parents marveled
at her noble comportment.
255 They often remarked to each other
that the grace of God shone in her.
Saint Audrey was very careful
to lead a chaste and pure life.
She disdained and despised this world.
260 There was no pride or any vice in her.
This saintly virgin illustrated
the adage that says
that the unsullied life of a wise person
equals the wisdom of ripe old age.*

265 The virgin had grown out
of childhood and was now mature.
People spoke at length
about her beauty and her worth.
News of her and her reputation
270 had spread both far and near.
Kings and princes asked for her hand;
they desired her because of her beauty
and also because each had heard
of her worthy comportment.
275 But she herself often longed
for the chamber she awaited:
that is, the palace of Jesus Christ
to whom she promised her virginity.
She spent every day in prayer;
280 overcoming and restraining the flesh.

Then it came about
through Divine Providence
that because the virgin was of age,
her parents decided to give her in marriage
285 to a prince who was asking for her hand.
He was an important man named Tonbert
who had made every attempt
and many requests to have her.
He asked her parents and begged for her so much

Que son pere lui otria.   290
Come sainte Audree l'oÿ
Mut se dolut et mut fremi,
Et contredist a son pooir
Pur ceo k'ele voleit manoir
En la vie qu'ele out enprise   295
Et qu'ele avoit a Deu promise.
Par la divine purveiance
Ly changa sa esmaance:
Pur l'auctorité de son pere,
De ses parens et de sa mere,   300
Assenti et fu marïee
Et a icel prince esposee.

Deuz anz entiers, cum m'est avis,   fol 102v col 2
Ainz que son peres fu occis
Fu sainte Audree marïee   305
Et de l'ydle d'Ely douee.
Pur la plenté k'a ou mareis
D'anguillies et de peissons freis
Fu cest'ydle nomé issi:
D'*ales* en engleis dist hom *ely*.   310
Ciz mareis fu donc granz et larges
De viles et de bons mesnages
En cest mareis est Rameseie
Et l'abbeïe de Thorneie,
Plusurs autres ke jeo ne puis   315
Nomer, si cume escrit le truis;
Chateriz est en ydle d'Ely.
Ceste matere lais issi,
Kar revertir voil a l'estoire
Dont en romanz fas la memoire.   320

Sainte Audree dont nos parlon
Fu mut de grant religion
Pur Deu garda virginité
Et toz jurs menoit en chasté:
Ceuz ke la virge conoiseient   325
A grant merveillie le teneient
K'ele gardoit en mariage
Virginité et pucelage,
Mes de ço ne doit nul doter
Ke Deus ne puisse bien tenser   330
Ceuz ke li servent et aorent

290   that her father finally consented.
        When Saint Audrey heard of it,
        she moaned, trembled all over,
        and protested as best she could,
        for she wanted to continue to live
295   the life she had undertaken
        and promised to God.
        However, through Divine Providence
        her feelings changed.
        Thus on the authority of her father,
300   her relatives, and her mother,
        she agreed and was given
        in marriage to that prince.
        I believe it was two full years
        before her father was killed
305   that Saint Audrey was married
        and given the isle of Ely as her dower.*
        The island derived its name
        from the abundance of eels
        and fresh fish in the marshland:
310   for *ales* in English one says *ely.**
        This marshland was expansive
        and contained towns and fine houses.
        Ramsey is located there,
        the abbey of Thorney,
315   as well as several others I am unable
        to name, yet I have found it all written down.
        Chatteris is on the island of Ely.
        But I will not pursue this subject,
        for I wish to return to the main story
320   which I am recording in French.

        Saint Audrey, of whom we are speaking,
        was devoutly religious.
        She kept her virginity for God
        and lived a chaste life daily.
325   Those who knew the virgin
        marveled at her,
        for though she was a married woman, she kept
        her virginity and maidenhood.
        In such matters one should never be perplexed
330   or think that God cannot protect
        those who faithfully serve

Et en son servise demeurent.
Legerement pout trespasser
Ses mals ke il volt conforter.
Ceste espose mit son pöer,   335
Tote s'entente et son voler
Ke ensure pout en sa vie   fol 103r col 1
Nostre dame sainte Marie
Ke Joseph out en mariage
E fu virge tout son aage.   340
Ceste virge bon[e]üree
De jur en jur fu tormente[e]:
Pour danter sa char et destreindre
La covint en martire maindre
Et en amone et en chasté   345
Mena sa vie en son heé.
Son mari et ele entendi
Ke demener lur vie issi
Estoit mut greindre sainteté
K'acompleir autres volunté.   350
En briés tens Tonbert morut
Saintement, si come deut:
Ensemble ou la Deu compaignie
Receut la corone de vie,
Par deserte de chasteté   355
Ly a Deu son regne doné.
Icist out vescu ou s'espuse
Sainte Audree la glorïuse
Treis anz devant son obit,
Issi com saint Bedes nos dit.   360
Un cors, un cuer, et un talent
Heurent cist espiritelment;
N'out entr'eus nule departie
N'estrif mes douce et sainte vie.
Ja soit ice ke saint' Audree   365
Plorast e fuest aukes troublee
Pur la mort Tonbert son amy:
Son corage s'en esjoÿ
Kant delivre estoit del servage
K'ele out del jou [del] mariage   370
[E] de l'enpechement del mond,   fol 103r col 2
Ke la gent avuegle et confund
Kydoit la virge estre delivre,
Toz jurz sanz mariage vivre.

and worship Him,
for He can easily cure
the ills of whomever He wishes to help.

335　Once married, Saint Audrey concentrated all her efforts
and intently set her mind on
emulating through her own life
Our Lady, Saint Mary,
who was married to Joseph

340　but who remained a virgin all her life.
This blessed virgin [Audrey]
was tormented day after day,
for in order to overcome and restrain the flesh
she had to live as a martyr.

345　Thus she devoted her life
　　to charity and chastity.
She and her husband agreed
that to live that way
would be holier

350　than to give in to any other desire.*
After a short time Tonbert died
a holy death, as befitted him.
In the presence of God's company
he received the crown of life.

355　Because of his chastity
God awarded him His heavenly kingdom.
He had lived for three years with his wife,
glorious Saint Audrey,
before he died,

360　as Saint Bede tells us.
The couple was spiritually united:
one in heart, body, and desire.
Between them there was no disagreement
or strife, only a sweet and saintly life.

365　Although Saint Audrey
wept and was somewhat troubled
at the death of Tonbert, her dear friend,
inwardly she rejoiced
to be free from the servitude

370　she had endured under the yoke of marriage
and from the hindrance of this world,
which blinds and confuses people.
The virgin believed she was now free
to live forever without marriage,

D'amone fairë et prïere   375
Estoit la virge costumere:
Des lermes aorneit son cors
Ke de ses ieus issoient hors.
Des lermes fist son oignement,
A Deu crioit merci sovent,   380
Envis seroit onkes trovee
Pucele que fust marïee,
Ke ne fust vencue et surprise
Par icel charnel coveitise.
Par sa seintisme chasteté   385
Et par sa grant virginité
Parvint a noces saluables
Ky durent et sunt parmenables;
Par sa deserte et chasté pure
La garda Deus de sullieüre.   390
Nul ne se doit desesperer
Ke bien ne peüst averer
Tel aventure en nostre tens
Ke Deus donast vertu et sens.

Plusurs demandent en quel page   395
Hom trueve escrist cel mariage
Com[e] saint Bede dist ici
De la virge et de son mari.
Ky en cercha la veire estoire
Pur mestre la vie en memoire,   400
Com put nul sa vie treiter
En mariage sanz suillier,
La mere Jhesu Crist le fist
Ke Deus a sen oës elist:
Ele garda en mariage   405   fol 103v col 1
Virginité et pucelage.
Autres unt heu icele vie,
Sainte eglise le tesmonie.
Mut unt estrivé de tel ovre,
Mes l'estoire nos le descovre,   410
Si com dist en collacïun
Des peres k'en lisant trovum.

Deuz auncïens homes estoient
Jadis ki a Deu requeroient
Ke il lur mostra[s]t lur bonté   415

375   to continue giving alms and saying prayers
       as was her custom.
       Tears flowing down from her eyes
       became the jewels adorning her body,
       and tears became her fragrant ointment,
380   for she often cried to God for mercy.
       It would be difficult to find
       a young married woman
       who has not been compelled and overwhelmed
       by carnal desire.
385   But Saint Audrey, through her holy chastity
       and virginity
       made a worthy marriage
       which lasts eternally.
       Because of her merit and pure chastity
390   God kept her from any stain.
       No one should be disillusioned
       if he cannot confirm
       in our day a story like this one
       in which God bestowed such virtue and good sense.

395   Many people ask in what book
       they can find a description of a marriage
       like the one Saint Bede relates here
       about the virgin and her husband
       (Bede had sought out the true story
400   in order to record her life for posterity),
       for no one can lead a married life
       without sullying themselves.
       Yet the mother of Jesus Christ did so,
       whom God chose for His purpose:
405   she kept her virginity and maidenhood
       throughout her marriage.
       And others have led such a life—
       the Holy Church bears witness to it.
       This subject has been much debated,
410   but the following story reveals it to us
       exactly as it is said in mealtime texts*
       by the Church Fathers when we read them:

       There were two men of yore
       who asked God
415   to reveal to them their religious standard

Ou il furent, en quel degrié.
Une voiz vint ke lur disoit
K'en Egipte un prudom manoit
Eucaliste, ceo dist en sa vie,
Et sa femme avoit non Marie.　　　　　　420
Uncor n'erent mie venuz
A lur force n'a lur vertuz.
Ces deuz hastivement alerent
Loinz en Egipte ou cil autre erent.
Eucalist[e] les vit venir,　　　　　　425
Sa table mist pur eus servir:
Ewe clere fist aporter
Pur lur pez et lur meinz laver.
Ceus li distrent k'il ne pot estre
K'il manjassent einz ke son estre　　　　　　430
[Ne] lur eü[s]t mustré e dist
Et com il o sa femme vit.
Cil lur respondi humblement
« Pastor sui. As bestes entent
Garder. Ceo est ma femme ici.　　　　　　435
Tel vie mein com jeo vos di. »
Ceus le demanderent avant,
Il ne respont ne tant ne quant.*　　　　　　　　　　fol 103v col 2
Ceus li dïent apertement
Ke par le Deu aveiement　　　　　　440
Sunt la venuz pur encercher
Quel vie il meine ou sa mulier.
Quant Eukalistes ceo oÿ,
Poor out, si lur respondi:
« Kant que Deu nos preste ou ses dons　　　　　　445
En treis parties les partons:
As povres est l'une partie,
De l'autre sustenons la vie,
La tierce en hospitalité
Ky nos requiert par charité.　　　　　　450
Puis ke ceste dame esposay
Charnelement ne la tochay:
La nuit dormons totdis seor sas,
El demein revestons nos dras.
Tresqu'a ceo jur, sachez de fy,　　　　　　455
Ne sout nul ceo que jeo vos dy. »
Ceus s'en partirent a ytant
Le rei de ciel glorifiant.

and how well they were measuring up to it.
A voice came and said to them
that in Egypt there lived a good man
called Eucalist, so it says in this story,
420   and his wife was named Mary.
      [The voice said that] they had not yet arrived
at the level of strength or virtue of this couple.
Immediately these two men made the long journey
to Egypt where the couple lived.
425   Eucalist saw them coming
and set his table to serve them.*
He had fresh water brought
to wash their feet and hands.
[But] they told him
430   that they would not eat until
he had told them about his life,
especially what his life was like with his wife.
He answered them humbly:
"I am a shepherd. My job is to keep animals.
435   And this is my wife here.
I tell you that such is the life I lead."
The men asked for more details,
but he did not say a word.
Then they told him quite frankly
440   that under the guidance of God
they had come there to investigate
what kind of life he was living with his wife.
When Eucalist heard this,
he became frightened and answered them:
445   "Whatever God gives us from his bounty
we divide into three parts—
one part for the poor,
with another part we sustain our own lives,
and the third part is used in hospitality,
450   which is required of us out of charity.
Since I married this woman
I have not touched her carnally.
At night we always sleep in sackcloth bags;*
in the morning we put our clothes back on.
455   Be assured that until this day
no one has known what I am telling you."
Then the two men departed,
glorifying the King of Heaven for this.

Pur Tonbert et pur sainte Audree
Ay ceste aventure contee,   460
K'hom ne doit doter ne decreire
Que la lur vie ne soit veire.
En toz ordrers et toz degrez
[Et] en chascune dignitez
Coneut Deus ceus de sa mainie   465
Ky a lui cest a compaignie.
Ne richesce ne povretez
Ne sucrest mie saintetez:
Hom n'est parfiz par obscurté
Ne dampnez s'il est en clarté.   470

Al dozeime an Anne le roy
Fu morz Felix, si com jeo croy,
Ke evesques estoit sacrez   fol 104r col 1
De Donemoc, preuz et senez:
A Saham fu li ber portez   475
Et ensevelez et enterez.
Lingtinges un ber i funda
Une eglise qu'il honura:
Moines [i] mist grant
    compaignie
Et fit iluc riche abbeïe;   480
Werfred out lur abbes a non,
Uns hom de grant religion.
Iluc est l'entree d'Ely,
Si com en livre l'ay oÿ.
Cist Felix fist edefïer   485
A Saham primes un moster
Et a Redeam une eglise
Ou l'em fesoit le Deu servise.
Mes li paien et li Danois
Ky haïrent Deu et ses loys   490
Destriurent celui et roberent
Et les serjanz Deu en osterent.
Mes en tens que Cunit regna
Les os saint Felix remua,
Si les fist porter a Rameseye   495
Ou sa faste est bien renome[e].
Cist saint Felix benignement
Baptiza rei Anna et sa gent

I have related this story
460   for the sake of Tonbert and Saint Audrey
so that no one would doubt or disbelieve
that the story of their life is true.
In all orders, in all ranks,
in every position
465   God knows those who belong to Him,
for each one of them has fellowship with Him.
Neither wealth nor poverty
increases saintliness at all.
A person is not perfected through obscurity
470   nor is he condemned if he is in the light.

I believe it was in the twelfth year of King Anna's reign,
that Felix died.
This worthy and wise man had been consecrated
Bishop of Dunwich.
475   The body of the noble man was brought to Soham
and was buried and returned to the earth.
Lutting, a baron, had founded
a church there, which he endowed.
He installed a significant number of
        monks
480   and established a rich abbey there.
Their abbot was named Werfrid,
a man of great piety.
The entrance to [the island of] Ely is located there,
so I have learned from a book.
485   Felix had built
first a monastery in Soham,
then a church in Reedham
where people worshipped God.
But the pagan Danes
490   who despise God and His laws
robbed it, destroyed it,
and took away the servants of God.
During the reign of King Cnute
the bones of Saint Felix were removed
495   and carried to Ramsey
where his feast day is well known.*
Saint Felix had lovingly
baptized King Anna and his family

Et fist ke tute la contree
Par baptesme ert regendree.　　　　　500

Li rois Annes dont nos parlames
Devant en sa vie mostrames,
Ja soit ice que il fuist reis
D'Engletere sur les Engleis
Ne vout aver humaine gloire　　　　　505
Par poissaince de sa victoire,
Qu[e] el se fist a ses procheins　　　　　fol 104r col 2
Et al poeple doz et humeins,
As prestres, as clers acceptable
Et a poeple mut amiable:　　　　　510
Pensa k'en sa grant digneté
Ne menera orgueil ne fierté.
Grant devocion out li ber
De Deu servir et cotiver
Et d'eglises edefier　　　　　515
Plusors fist aparaillïer
Del regne fu leaus garderes
Et as orphanins fu bon peres;
Les vefves meintint et ayda
Et doucement les governa.　　　　　520
Ceus ki eurent mestier d'aïe
Socorut, ne lur faillit mie,
Et loinz et pres ky a lui vint
Il le conseillia et meintint.
Pour la grant bonté de ceo roy　　　　　525
Et pur s'onesté et sa foy,
Com il fu bon rei et bon pere
Et pur venir a la matere,
Avom de li parlé et dist
Ceo que nos trovom en escrit.　　　　　530
De Kenewal, un roy puissant,
Mostre l'estoire ici avant.
Kinegeles fu pere cestui,
Cil tint le regnë aprés lui.
Icil despit le Deu servise　　　　　535
Et renea son sacrifise.
La ley Deu aÿ et despist
Et tote s'ovre contredist.
A femmë out la suer Penda,
Mes pur un' autre la lessa　　　　　540

and caused the whole region
500   to be born again through baptism.

We have already mentioned King Anna
and shown how,
although he was a king
of England over the Angles,
505   he did not want to have human glory
through the importance of his renown.
So he made himself gentle and humane
to his acquaintances and to the people,
gracious to priests and to clerks,
510   and very amiable to everyone.
He decided that in worthy comportment
he should not be boastful or proud.
The noble man was devoted
to serving and worshipping God
515   and to building churches,
of which he completed many.
He was a loyal steward of the kingdom
and a good father to orphans.
He supported and aided widows
520   and governed them with kindness.
He succored and never failed
anyone in need of help.
He counseled and supported
whoever came to him whether from far or near.
525   In order to get to the main story
we have told at length
what we find in the written record about this king
because of his goodness,
his honor, and his faith,
530   and because he was a good king and a good father.
Now I will tell the story
of Cenwald, a powerful king.
His father was Cynegils,
and Cenwald reigned after him.
535   He refused to worship God
and renounced His sacrifice.*
He hated and scorned the law of God
and opposed His entire work.
Cenwald's wife was the sister of Penda,
540   but he left her for another woman

K'il prist et l'autre deguerpi,   fol 104v col 1
Par quei tut son regne perdi.
Penda pesa de sa soreur
Dont il li fist grant deshonur,
K'il deguerpi pur autre prendre: 545
Mut li f[e]ra, s'il pot, cher vendre.
Grant ost et grant gens assembla
Et soer Kenewald les mena.
Cil n'out aÿe ne socurs,
Si l[i] estuet aler ailliurs.   550
Tout son reaume deguerpi
Et au rei Anne s'enfuï:
Cil bon rei Anne le retint
Treis anz entiers, issi avint
Ke il receut crestïenté   555
Et creance de verité.
Roy Anne ki l'out retenu
Bonuré et saint home fu
De sainteisme et noble lignee
Ki mut ert par Deu eshaucee: 560
A seintes dames fu il pere
Dont nos treitons ceste matere.
En païs ke roy Anne tint
Kenewald crestïen devint:
Felix l'enoint d'oillie et de cresme,   565
Anne fu parrin del baptesme.
Aprés iceo tant l'eÿda
K'en West Sexoine repeira,
Son patremoine raconquist
Et cele gent a sey souzmist.   570
Tost fu la novele seüe
Et par Engleterre espandue:
Mut loerent Anne le roy
De sa bonté et de sa foy,
Ke tel amor out ver celui   575   fol 104v col 2
[Ke] plusurs se joinstrent a lui.
Merchenelande suelement
Haioit rey Anne mortelment,
Cil ke ert sire de la terre.
Envers li comença la guerre.   580
Ly rois Annes hastivement
Contre Penda vint ou sa gent:
Trop trova forz ses enemis,

whom he took as his wife, abandoning the first one,
and for this he lost his entire kingdom.
Penda was distressed over his sister
whom Cenwald had greatly dishonored
545 when he left her to take another wife,
so he would do all he could to make him pay dearly.
He assembled a great army of many troops
and led them against Cenwald.
Since Cenwald had neither reinforcements nor protection,
550 he was obliged to go elsewhere.
He left his entire kingdom
and fled to King Anna.
Good King Anna kept him
for a full three years; and it came about
555 that while he was there
he embraced Christianity and believed the truth.
King Anna, who had retained him,
was a blessed, holy man
of a saintly and noble lineage,
560 a man on whom God had bestowed great honors,
for he was the father of the sainted ladies,
the central figures of this written narrative.
Thus in the land held by King Anna
Cenwald became a Christian.
565 Felix anointed him with oil and chrism,
while Anna was designated his godfather at baptism.
After this, with Anna's great [military] aid,
he returned to Wessex,
reconquered his patrimony,
570 and subjugated the people to his rule.
Soon the news of all these events
spread throughout England,
and people highly praised Anna, the king,
for his goodness and faith.
575 They had such respect for him
that many formed alliances with him.
Only [the king of] Mercia
had a mortal hatred for King Anna.
The leader of Mercia
580 began a war against him.
Although King Anna came quickly
against Penda with his forces,
he found his enemies too strong,

En la bataillie fu occis.
El dis et neveisme an fina   585
Ke terre tint et guverna,
Cincquante et katre et sis cenz anz,
Si come saint Bede est disanz,
Fu [i]ceo fait dont nos parlom
Puis la Deu incarnation.   590
Edelbert, ses freres, regna,
Le regne tint et governa:
Plus jofne fu, mes aprés ly
A roy esluirent icestuy;
Cil fu mut bien del roy Penda   595
En sa subjection regna.
En une vile en la contree
Ke Bliyeborc fu apellee
Fu le cors rey Anne portez,
Enseveliz, et enterrez,   600
Ou mut par grant devotion
Honorent le cors del baron.
L'estoire dist k'enseveliz
Fu iluec[ques] Jurmin son fiz,
Mes puis fu son cors remué   605
Et a Bedrichesworde aporté:
La vile piert ore iceo non
Et Saint Edmund l[a] apellom
Pur le roy glorïus martir   fol 105r col 1
Ke en cel liu deigna gesir.   610
Les Estengleis furent dolent;
La roïne out grant marrement
Puis la mort Anne, son seignur:
Richesce et terrien honur
Despit, et come pelerine   615
Ala en France la roÿne;
A Chailons en unë egleise
Se mist la dame en Deu servise;
En ordre se mist et fu none
Pur la parmanable corone.   620
Saint[e] Hylde, sa suer, [y] vint
Pur li ensivre et l'ordre tint
En cele seintime abbeïe
Mena chescune sainte vie.
Kant fu passé le premer an   625
Un eveske, saint Aÿdan,

and was killed in the battle.
585 He died in the nineteenth year
of his reign.
Six hundred fifty-four years
after the incarnation of God,
according to Saint Bede,
590 this event took place.
Then his brother Ethelhere reigned,
exercising authority over the kingdom.
He was much younger, but after Anna
they elected him king.
595 Ethelhere enjoyed the favor of King Penda
and ruled in subjection to him.
The body of King Anna was carried
into a regional town
called Blythburg,
600 where it was buried and enshrined.
They honor the body of the baron there
with great devotion.
The history states that
his son Jurmin was also buried there,
605 but later his body was removed
and taken to Bederickswode.
The city has lost that name
and we now call it Bury Saint Edmunds
in honor of the glorious martyr king
610 who deigned to make that city his final resting place.
The East Angles were filled with sorrow,
and the queen deeply grieved
after the death of her husband Anna.
She scorned riches and earthly honor,
615 and, as a pilgrim,
went to France.
She placed herself in God's service
in a church at Chelles
where she entered holy orders and became a nun
620 awaiting the eternal crown.
Saint Hilda, her sister,
soon followed her and took orders there.
In this most holy abbey
each one led a holy life.
625 But at the end of her first year there,
a bishop, Saint Aiden,

Vout sainte Hylde par prïere
En son païs torner arere.
Al secund an dont jeo vous dy
Penda li fel que Deu haÿ,   630
Homicide fu de ces roys
Ke amoient Deu et ses loys:
Roy Sigilber et Egeris
Et Anne fu par lui occis,
Oswald et le [bon] roy Edvine,   635
Si com l'estoire nos divine.
Oswald fu des Norhombreis,
Ceo dist l'estoire, et sire et reys.
Seur Oswy ky puis regna
Penda li fel grant gent mena,   640
Trente legions et mut plus
A eus conduire ou trente deuz.
De Elfrid, fiz Oswy, lisom   fol 105r col 2
Ke [ot] une sule legion:
Par la Deu grace et par s'a[ï e]*   645
Ou sa petite compaignie
Pur son pere se combati,
Penda et tot son ost venquey.
Oswy out un autre fiz
K'en ostagë out Kenewiz: 650
Merchenelande out en baillie
Cele dame par seignurie.
Cil fiz [de] Oswy out a non
Egfrid, issi l'apelloit hom:
Cist devoit prendre sainte Audree   655
La reïne bon[e]üree
De cui vie et de cui victoire
En cel livre mis en memoire.
Oderwold fu fiz [de] Owold
Qui deut Oswy aÿder   660
Son oncle et sa honte venger.
Contre les so[e]ns fu o Penda,
Car il creüt et espera
Que le regne son pere eüst
Et nul encontre lui estut.   665
En ceste bataillie fu morz
Penda ou li toz ses esforz,
Ses trente et ses mainïe[e]s
Et ses aés sont ples[sï]ees,

called Saint Hilda back
to her own country.
Then the next year,
630   evil Penda, who hated God,
and who was the murderer of those kings
who loved God and his laws,
(Kings Sigbert and Egric,
Anna, Oswald, and King Edwin
635   were killed by him,
so the history tells us,
and we learn that Oswald
was king of the Northumbrians.)
led a great army
640   against Oswy who reigned at that time,
coming against him with at least thirty legions,
perhaps thirty-two.
We further read that Ethelfrid, son of Oswy,
commanded only a single legion,
645   but by the grace of God and by His help,
with his little company
he fought for his father and
vanquished Penda and his entire army.
Oswy had another son
650   whom Cynewise [wife of Penda] was holding hostage.
This lady possessed Mercia
through her seignorial rights.
The latter son of Oswy was named Egfrid,
that is what he was called.
655   He was the one who would marry
Saint Audrey, the blessed queen,
whose victorious life
I have recorded in this book.
Oswald's son Ethelwald
660   should have helped Oswy
avenge his uncle and his disgrace.
[Yet] he allied himself with Penda against his own people,
for he was hopeful
that he would inherit the kingdom of his father
665   and that no one would stand against him,
but he died in this battle.
Penda and all his forces,
his thirty [legions], his armies
as well as those of his allies were destroyed

Par la grace ke Deu dona   670
A Oswy suer ceus de la.
Dona li ber a faire eglises
Doze viles mut bien asises:
Sa fillie Alfled en l'une mist,
A Deu servir none la fist.   675
En treszimë an roy Oswy
Iceste bataillie venqui   fol 105v col 1
K'il out tenu reaume et terre
De ceus ke li m[e]ürent guerre.
Ceus de Merchenelande occist   680
Et ceus d'autre terre conquist,
Si mist entre eus crestïenté
Et dreite foy et leauté.
En quart an esmurent grant gerre
Vers li les barons de sa terre.   685
Preveement par traïson
Le fiz Penda, Ulfer par non,
Ellurent a estre leur roy:
[A] Oswy mentirent leur foy,
Ulfer amoient et siuvoient   690
Et come leur roy le servoient.
Et cist Ulfer se maria
La fillie Herconbert esposa,
Ermenild ke lui fu donee,
Fillie Sexburg, seur sainte Audree.   695
Icist Ulfer out de s'espouse
Une fillie mut glorïuse,
Werburch out a non la pucele:
Virge vesqui la Deu ancele.
Ulfer regna dis et set anz,   700
Si com saint Bedes e[st] dizanz.
Puis fu occis roy Edelher
Et Edelwolz regna li ber,
Ly tiers freres Anne, le bon rey.
Cist ama Deu en droite fey,   705
Ententif fu al Deu servise,
Et mut honora sainte eglise.
Aprés roy Anne voleit traire
Sen frere a totes honors faire.
En le tens Edelwold fu un ber,   710
Suthelm issi l'oÿ nomer,   fol 105v col 2
De Estreis Seixons rois estoit:

670   by the grace that God gave
      to Oswy against those people.
      Oswy then allocated twelve well-placed cities
      for the purpose of building monastic churches.
      He placed his daughter Elfleda in one of them,
675   making her a nun to serve God.
      It was in the third year of Oswy's reign
      that he won this battle
      by which he took the kingdom and land
      from those who had waged war against him.
680   He put to death the ones from Mercia
      and those conquered from allied lands.
      He established Christianity, good faith,
      and loyalty among the people.
      But four years later the barons of his land
685   fought against him.
      Secretly, by treason, they elected
      a son of Penda named Wulfhere
      to be their king.
      They broke faith with Oswy;
690   instead they loved, followed, and served
      Wulfhere as their king.
      Then Wulfhere took as his wife
      the daughter of Erconbert,
      Ermenilda, who was given to him in marriage.
695   [She was] the daughter of Seaxburga, sister of Saint Audrey.
      Wulfhere had by this wife
      a most glorious daughter
      named Werburga:
      a maiden, servant of God, who lived as a virgin.
700   Wulfhere reigned seventeen years,
      according to Bede.
      After King Ethelhere was killed,*
      the baron Ethelwald,
      third brother of good King Anna, reigned.
705   He loved God with upright faith,
      was attentive to God's service
      and greatly honored the holy Church.
      He wanted to honor his brother King Anna
      and follow his example.
710   In the time of Ethelwald there was a baron
      I have heard called Swithelm,
      a king of Essex

Idles coutivoit et servoit.
Cil soleit sovent repairer
A Edelwold k'il out mut cher, 715
[Et i]cil requeroit sovent
K'y[l] lassast le coutivement
Des idles et sa fause loy
Et si creut en le Veray Roy.
Suthelm creüst ceo k'il li dist: 720
Li et autres baptizer fist
D'un eveskes, Ceddes out non,
Hom fu de grant religion.
Edelwold le leva et tint
Des fonz quant a baptesme vint. 725
Suthelm cinc anz [aprés] vesqui,
Ne regna plus, idunc fini.
Aprés cestui Alduf regna,
Fiz roy Anne ke Deu ama,
Frere la virge sainte Audree 730
Ke ci devant avom nomee.
La fillie Alduf, Edborc, fu none
Et abb[e]esse a Rependone.
Ceste sainte dame fist traire
Un sarcu qu'ele avoit fait faire 735
De plum. Al serf Deu l'envoia,
Cuthblac, ke dedenz reposa
En un bucel qu'el li tramist
Ou l'em son cors ensevelist.

Ci reparole del mari 740
Sainte Audree ki tost fini,
Tonbert qui l'avoit espousee
Et ke d'Ely l'avoit doee.
Aprés sa mort s'en est alee
A son doaire sainte Audree. 745 fol 106r col 1
La se restout, illuc manoit
Pur ceo ke sotir leus estoit.
N'avoit cure de la noblesce
Del secle ne de la richesce.
Silence tint et sainte vie 750
Mena icele Deu amye.
En cele idle ou ele habitout
Plenté d'eaue et d'arbres i out.
En l'entré et tot environ

who worshipped pagan gods.
He often went to see
715 Ethelwald who was very dear to him.
Ethelwald urged him
to abandon the worship
of idols and his false religion
and to believe in the True King.
720 Swithelm accepted what he said.
Then Ethelwald had him and others baptized
by a bishop named Chad,
a man of great piety.
When he came to be baptized
725 Ethelwald received him from the baptismal font.
Swithelm lived five [more] years,
he died, and that was the end of his reign.
After Ethelwald, Aldulf reigned,
the son of King Anna who loved God,
730 and the brother of the virgin Saint Audrey
whom we have mentioned above.
Edburga, the daughter of Aldulf, was a nun
and abbess at Repton.
This saintly lady had a sarcophagus
735 made out of lead and brought to her.
She sent it to the servant of God,
Guthlac, who was laid to rest therein,
with his body wrapped in a linen shroud
that she had provided for him.

740 Now I will return to Tonbert,
Saint Audrey's husband who died early.
He had married her
and endowed her with Ely.
After his death Saint Audrey went away
745 to her dower lands
where she could live
in a place of solitude,
for she had no interest in the nobility
or riches of this world.
750 This woman, friend of God,
led a quiet and holy life there.
On this island where she was living
there was an abundance of water and trees.
At the entrance and all around the island

Nul n'i entra si par nief non.   755
Ceus k'ele vit ke Deu amoient
Et en religion manoient
Ajousta a sey par amor
A servir Deu son creator.
De jeüner et de vellier   760
S'amegri pur ly travaillier;
En Deu servir mist son poër
Pur la celestiene joie aver.
Greignur duceur, greignur franchise
Senti la dame en Deu servise   765
Et de plaire son creatur
Ke d'aver terrïen honur.
Checon jur creut en sainteté,
En devotion et bounté.
Del saint Espirit ert suspris   770
Le desir k'en son quer out mis.
Par les travaus k'ele suffri
Tut [les] charneus desirs venqui.
La victoire de sa bounté
Et de sa grant virginité   775
Fu par tut le regne espandue
Et entre le poeple s[e]üe.
En cel tens, si com ge recort,
Eg[el]frid regna en ceo nort: fol 106r col 2
En ceo roi out mut grant bontez,   780
Evrewich fu sa chief citez.
Cist noble roy out grant amur
Vers sainte Audree par honur
Pur les biens k'il oÿ de ly:
Mut grant richesces li offri   785
Et granz doaieres a doner
Par quei la peüst espouser.
Ceste dame ces dons despit
Et les granz offres k'il li fit.
A son poër le contredist,   790
Pur Deu ou son curage mist:
De sa requeste fu chargee
Et de ses offres ennuyee.
Kant ver li ne poet espleiter,
S'en ala ses parens prier.   795
[Mes] tant l'ont ses parens requise
Ne pot desdire en nule guise.

755   there was no approach except by ship.*
       Saint Audrey surrounded herself
       by people who loved God
       and who were living a religious life
       so that together with them she might serve God her Creator.
760   In working for Him by fasting and keeping vigils
       she grew thin,
       expending all her energy to serve God
       in order to have celestial joy.
       The lady found greater sweetness,
765   greater nobility in divine worship
       and in pleasing her Creator
       than in having earthly honor.
       Her holiness,
       devotion, and goodness increased daily.
770   She was living in accordance with the desire
       nourished in her heart by the Holy Spirit.
       Through the works that she performed
       she vanquished all her carnal desires.
       Word of her pervasive goodness
775   and victorious virginity
       spread throughout the kingdom
       and became known among the people.
       At that time, as I recall,
       Egfrid, a very good man,
780   reigned in the north
       where York was his chief city.
       This noble king developed a strong and honorable love
       toward Saint Audrey
       because of the good things that he had heard of her.*
785   In an effort to marry her
       he offered to give her very great riches
       and a large dower.
       But the lady scorned these gifts
       and the generous offers he made her.
790   She resisted him with all her might
       for the sake of God to whom she had given her heart.
       In fact, she was burdened by his request
       and distressed by his offers.
       When she could not succeed in discouraging him,
795   she went to plead with her family.
       However, her relatives so insisted on the marriage
       that finally there was no way she could refuse.

Tout encontre sa volenté
Lors a la virge gra[a]nté.
En setme an k'Anne fu occis, 800
Son pere, par conseil d'amis,
Prist la virge ceo mariage,
Sanz volenté de son curage.
En cel tens sen uncle regna,
Ed[el]wold ki ly conseillia. 805
Cil out le regne aprés son pere
Et aprés Edelher son frere.
A Egfrid fu [donc] espousee
La beneïte sainte Audree.
Cil fu le fiz le roy Oswy, 810
Si come en livre l'ay oÿ.
[Li] roy Oswy fu fiz Elfriz fol 106v col 1
Et Elfriz fu le fiz Elriz.
Cil tint le regne noblement.
Trente anz fu sire d'une gent 815
Ky Dereÿens sont nomez
Et en cel tens sy apellez
De ceo ke sy eurent a non
Cele gent en lur region.
Pur ceo nus mostre en ceste escrit 820
Saint Gregoire, kant il les vit,
Jefne gent ky a Rome vindrent,*
Pur Engleis devant eus se tindrent:
A Deu dist loënge de ceus
Pur la beauté k'il vit en eus 825
E dist k'en iceles contrees
Dont issi beles genz son neez
Estuet mestre sanz demorance
Espandre [de] Deu la creance.
Ore repeir au rey Oswy, 830
Le roy Oswold qu'avez oÿ,
Cil ky par Penda fu occis:
Une sereur eurent cil roy
Ky ama Deu par dreite foy.
Ebbe out a non, a Coludy 835
Fu noneine et autres ou ly.
Seur les autres estoit mestresse
Et tint l'ordre cum abb[e]esse.*
Fiz et fillies out Oswy,
Le rey dont il nos conte icy. 840

Quite against her will,
then, the virgin agreed to the marriage.
800 Thus in the seventh year after her father, Anna,
had been killed, on the advice of her loved ones
but without the consent of her heart,
the virgin accepted this marriage.
At this time her uncle Ethelwald,
805 who counseled her, was king.
He held the kingdom after her father
and after Ethelhere, his brother.
So the blessed Saint Audrey
was married to Egfrid,
810 son of King Oswy,
as I have read in the book.
Now King Oswy was the son of Ethelfrid,
and Ethelfrid was the son of Ethelric.
Oswy reigned nobly
815 for thirty years over a people
who are still called Deirans today
just as they were at that time,
for that was the name
of the people in that region.
820 Concerning these people Saint Gregory told us in his writings
about the first time he saw them:
some young men who had gone to Rome*
were standing there before the Romans claiming to be Angles.
Gregory praised God for them
825 because of the beauty he saw in them.
He went on to say that in those countries
where these beautiful people were born
a [religious] teacher was needed immediately
to spread belief in God.
830 But getting back to King Oswy
[and] King Oswald, whom you have heard
was killed by Penda,
these kings had a sister
who loved God with upright faith.
835 Her name was Ebba.
She was a nun at Coldingham along with others
over whom she was mistress,
for she held the order as abbess.
Oswy, the king we are talking about now,
840 had both sons and daughters.

Ly einez de ses fiz out non
Elfrid, issi l'apelloit hom;
Egelfriz out non li puisnez,*
Cil fu mut de son pere amez.
Elfrid fu roy de Dyrïens,   845
Egelfriz de Bernicïens.
Elfrid fu de si grant aage   fol 106v col 2
Ne pot tenir son heritage.
Egelfriz fu pruz et vaillianz
Et ert bachelier de trente anz,   850
Courteis et larges a doner
Et mut vaillianz d'armes porter,
Et mut fu bien cist Egelfriz
De l'erceveske, saint Wolfriz.
Ou quart livre de ceste estoire   855
Dont seint Bede feit la memoire
Fu cele virge, seinte Audree,
A cest Eg[el]frid esposee.
Volentiers li constresteut
Si ele osast, si ele peut.   860
O sei a Eg[el]frid menee
Cele virge bon[e]üree
Sanz nule charnel coveitise,
Par quei el perdist sa franchise.
La u les autres coveitoient   865
Seculers deliz et amoient,
La virge s'estoit atornee
A Deu; des angles fu gardee.
Plusurs anz garda chasteté
Ou le roy et virginité: 870
Egfrid le roy et sainte Audreė
Seinte vie et bele ont menee.
Seinte Audree et le roy Egfrid
Lur erceveske saint Wolfrid
Amerent mut et si le cruerent;   875
Meinte bone ovre par li firent,
Et il ama eus durement
Et conseillia mut lëaument.
Pais et joie et plenté de bien
Fu en son tens de tote rien: 880
Par tut venqui ses enemis   fol 107r col 1
Et grant pais tint en son païs.
La glorïuse seinte Audree

The eldest of his sons was named
Ethelfrid, that is what they called him.
The next born was named Egfrid
who was much beloved of his father.
845 Ethelfrid was king of the Deirans,
Egfrid over the Bernicians.
Ethelfrid was so old*
that he could not manage his inheritance.
Egfrid was noble and valiant,
850 and was a young man thirty years old.
He was courtly and generous in giving
and very valiant in bearing arms,
and he had good relations with
the archbishop Saint Wilfrid.
855 In the fourth book of the history
which Bede recorded,   .
the virgin Saint Audrey
was married to Egfrid,
although she would willingly have rejected him
860 if she had dared and if there had been any possibility.
So Egfrid took away with him
    this blessed virgin
devoid of any carnal desire
which might cause her to lose her noble character.
865 While others desired
and enjoyed secular delights,
the virgin had turned toward God
whose angels guarded over her.
For a number of years she kept her virginity
870 while living with the king.
King Egfrid and Saint Audrey
together led a holy and beautiful life.
Both of them loved their archbishop,
Saint Wilfrid, very much.
875 They trusted him.
and did many good works through him;
and he in turn loved them dearly
and counseled them loyally.
There was peace and joy
880 and an abundance of goods of all kinds in his time.
Egfrid vanquished his enemies on all sides
and maintained peace in his country.
Glorious Saint Audrey

Une noble eglise a fundee
En l'honorance saint Andreu,   885
Augustaldeus noment ce liu.
Sainte Audree genz assembla,
Homes et femmes, si les mena
Ensemble ou li a cele eglise
Pur establir la Deu servise.   890
Owine, un home mut sené
Et de mut grant auctorité,
Amena la roïne ou ly.
Moines estoit k'avons oÿ
A cui Deus especialment   895
De ces secriez fist mustrement.
Cestui fist seinte Audree mestre
De cele eglise et de cel estre.
Tel home avint bien [a l']eglise
A moustrer le Deu servise.   900
Honeste fu et convenable
Et a pople mut acceptable.
Tut fu a [le] siecle manant
Son quer estoit en Deu voilliant.
Enaprés la conversion   905
La roïne, dont nos parlom,
S'y converti cist Oswy,*
Moines devint et tut guerpy.
De seint Chede out oï conter
Grant bien, s'ala a lui parler;   910
Come a li s'estoit apremez,
Tut furent ensemble acointez,
Il le receut ou ses amis
En le biens k'il fra mes tut dis.
Par Deu [e] par son mostrement   915   fol 107r col 2
Vist Ewine les angles sovent
A Seint Chedde aler et venir
Pur conforter le son desir.

A la mateire revendrons
K'un roy dont ci parlé avons,   920
De la joie et de grant barnage
K'il out de cel haut mariage
De la roïne sainte Audree.
Quant [ele] ly fu espusee
Par duçur et amur la ceint,   925

founded a noble church
885   in honor of Saint Andrew
in a place they named Augustaldeus.
Saint Audrey had brought along with her a group of people,
both men and women, whom she took
into that church
890   to establish divine worship there.
The queen had brought with her
Ovin, a very wise man*
and one with great authority.
He was an extraordinary monk, as we have heard,
895   to whom God directly
revealed His secrets.
Saint Audrey made this man master
of that church and of its religious life.
Such a man was well suited to the church
900   to teach divine worship,
for he was honorable and affable
and very gracious to the people.
He had been living in a secular state,
even though his heart was desirous of God.
905   Inspired by the way of life of
the queen Saint Audrey,
Ovin had been converted,
become a monk and abandoned all.
He had heard many good things about Saint Chad,
910   so he went to speak with him.
Once they had met,
the two became quite well-acquainted,
and Saint Chad received him among his friends.*
Concerning the good that he will do, I will say more later.
915   By direct revelation from God,
Ovin often saw angels
coming and going to Saint Chad
to minister to him.*

Let us return to the matter
920   concerning a king we have already mentioned
and the joy and great nobility
that he derived from his high marriage
with the queen Saint Audrey.
Once she had married him,
925   he surrounded her with sweetness and love,

Mes son corage pas ne veint.
Le roy forment se merveillioit
Ke son corage ne tornoit;
Tant ert de grant religion
Noit et jur fu en oreison.   930
Come le roy pur son delit
Ert cochiez en son real lit,
Si com Deu plesoit somellioit,
Et la roÿne se levoit.
En oreison et en prïere   935
Ert, ne voleit venir arïere.
Seint Espiriz la governa
Ky en son quer se herberja:
Par sa seinte inspiration
La guarda de corruption.   940
Fort fu encontre totes vices
Et haÿ del mund les delices.
Unkes ne pot estre entamee
En cors ne en quer violee,
Unkes ne vout pur son seignur   945
Par prïere ne par amour
Lessier k'el ne fust en servise
Jhesu Crist ou ele s'ert mise.
Garder vout sa virginitee   fol 107v col 1
K'a Deu out promise et voee,   950
Meuz vout mener issi sa vie
K'aver a home compaignie:
Ele ert ensemble ou son baron
Non par charnel conjunction.
Le roys fu engreis et emflee   955
Kant de ly n'out sa volentee.
Par deuz foiz estriva a lui,
Unkes ne pur ceo la venqui.
Kant il vist ceo k'il ne pooit
Faire de ly ceo k'il voloit,   960
Ou grant ire plus egrement
Wout qu'ele feïst son talent,
Et come plus il l'anguisa,
Plus defensable la trova.
Tot son crüel porposement   965
Venqui la virge et son talent.
[Li] roy Egfrid sed et entent
K'en sa chambre preveement

but he did not conquer her heart.
The king was truly amazed
that he could not direct her heart's affection toward him.
Her religious fervor was so intense
930 that she was in prayer night and day.
Whenever the king lay
in his royal bed awaiting his pleasure,
it pleased God to have him fall asleep.
The queen would then get up
935 to pray and make supplication;
she did not want to get back in bed.*
The Holy Spirit living
in her heart governed her.
By His holy inspiration
940 she was kept from corruption.
She was strong against all vices
and disdained the pleasures of the world.
Never would her body be penetrated
nor her heart violated.
945 Never for her lord Egfrid's
beseeching nor for his love,
did she want to leave the service
of Jesus Christ to which she had committed herself.
She wished to keep the virginity
950 that she had promised to God.
That is the way she preferred to live
rather than to have intimacy with a man.
She was indeed united in marriage with her husband,
but not by carnal relations.
955 Unable to have his way with her,
the king became irritated
and twice he tried to force her,
but he could never subdue her that way.
When he saw that he could not do
960 with her what he wanted,
he became extremely angry
and even more ardently wanted her to do his bidding.
But the more he tormented her,
the more resistant he found her.
965 The virgin and her will vanquished
all his cruel intention.
Finally King Egfrid realized
that he could not overcome her in any way

Ne la veintra en nule guise.
Purpensa soy d'une cointise   970
K'as ordenez s'en ira plaindre,
Par eus la vout faire destraindre,
Mes Deus en sa gloire benigne
Vist bien de l'enemi malingne
K'il vout la virge tresbuchier   975
Et son purpens faire less[i]er;
Mes la virge dont ge vous dy
Venqui bien son premer mary,
Et l'autre aprés dont ge vous cont.
Mut preisa poy les biens del mund.   980

Nul ne doit aveir mescreance
Ke grant vertu et grant poissance
N'eüst la virge en honesté   fol 107v col 2
De guarder sa virginité.
Ceste chose fu espandue   985
Par Engleterre et bien s[e]üe
Par lui predome creoient
Et afermeient et disoient.
Cist roy Egfrid par sa espouse,
Sainte Audree la glorïouse,   990
S'amenda et mut la cremi:
Pur le granz biens k'il vit en li
Ne le voleit mes esforcier*
N'estriver a lui n'atochier;
Ja soit iceo k'il n'eurent mie   995
Ensemble charnel compaignie
Ne fu la virge sainte Audree
Meins dame ne meins honoree.
Le roy fu mari par semblance
Mes non d'ovre ne de fesance: 1000
Non de roÿne en mariage
Sanz volenté et sanz curage
Et sanz charnel delit sentir
Out la virge pur Deu servir.
Le roy estoit mut curïus   1005
D'avoir ceo qu'avient a espous
Et que l'espose li doit faire,
Mes il ne pot la virge atraire
Ne par promesse ne par don,
Par bien proier ne par sermon.   1010

when they were alone in his bedchamber.
970 So he devised a clever trick:
he would go complain to the ordained priests
and get them to constrain her.
But God in his benign glory
knew that the crafty Enemy*
975 was trying to cause the virgin to stumble
and abandon her resolution.
But this virgin was able
to overcome her first husband
as well as the one I am telling you about,
980 for she had little regard for the pleasures of the world.

Let no one doubt
that the virgin truly had
enough virtue and control
to guard her virginity.
985 This fact circulated
and was well known throughout England.
Wise people believed it,
declared it to be true, and spread news of it.
Inspired by his wife,
990 Saint Audrey the glorious,
King Egfrid amended his ways and began to revere her.
He saw such goodness in her
that he did not ever want to force her
or quarrel with her or even lay a hand on her.
995 And so it was that they never had
carnal relations together.
But the virgin Saint Audrey
was not considered less a lady or less honored.
The king was married in appearance,
1000 but not in marital acts.
The virgin had gained the title of queen by a marriage
that was against her will and against her heart
and in which she experienced no carnal pleasure
in order to serve God.
1005 Yet the king was still desirous
of having a husband's due
from his wife.
But he could not persuade the virgin—
neither by promises nor by gifts,
1010 nor by pleading with her, nor by admonishing her.

Par ces amis le roy Egfrid
Plusurs foiz requist seint Wolfrid
Mut li promist riche lüer
Pur la reïne conseillier
Qu'ele lessast son vou ester   1015
De sa virginité garder,
Rendist a lui ce qu'el devoit   fol 108r col 1
Si come espouse a espous doit.
Si come saint Bede nos dit
Par plusurs lius en son escrit,   1020
Kant le roy vit e entendi
Del saint erceveske e de lui
Le conseil et l'enhortement
Ke entr'eus deus estoit sovent,
Par la grace de charité   1025
Vout ensivre lur volenté:
En vein promist le roy Egfrid
Ses granz lüers a saint Wolfrid
Pur la reïne amonester
Fors a Deu servir et amer.   1030
Com [plus] ala en son message,
A plus aferma le corage
De la virge bon[e]üree
Ky a Jhesu Crist s'ert donee.
Ensemble furent dozë anz   1035
Le roy et ele conversanz
Dedenz sa chambre en chasteté,
Et garda sa virginité.
Grant grace out de Deu receüe
Kant ne pooit estre vencue,   1040
Kar issi come ele venqui
Le quer de son primer ami,
Par la force [de] Jhesu Crist
Venqui ele l'autre, ceo dist.
Tel fu de Deu la volunté   1045
K'il ne voleit que violé
Fuest cil temple seintefïé,
Kar a ly s'estoit otroié.
Perpetüel virginité
Out la virge en Deu [de]claré: 1050
En munde ert reïne honurable   fol 108r col 2
Et a Deu fu mut acceptable.
Mut fu curïeus sainz W[o]lfriz

Through the intermediary of his friends, King Egfrid
on several occasions sent word to Saint Wilfrid,
promising him a rich reward
if he would advise the queen
1015   to let go of her vow
to keep her virginity,
and to give him what she ought,
as was her wifely duty.
As Saint Bede tells us
1020   in several places in his writings,
when the king took into consideration
all the advice and exhortation
that both he and the holy archbishop
often gave her
1025   with kindness and love,
he expected her to do their bidding.
But it was in vain that King Egfrid promised
his great reward to Saint Wilfrid
to admonish the queen
1030   anything except to love God and to serve Him.
The more Wilfrid went to see her,
the more he strengthened
the blessed virgin's resolve
that she had been given to Jesus Christ.
1035   They were together twelve years,
the king and she, coexisiting
chastely within his bedchamber;
and she kept her virginity.
She received much grace from God,
1040   allowing her not to be conquered.
For just as she had dominated
the heart of her first husband
by the power of Jesus Christ,
she overcame the next one also, we are told.
1045   It was the will of God
that this sanctified temple
not be violated in any way,
for it had been given to Him:
the virgin had pledged
1050   perpetual virginity to God.
In the world she was an honorable queen,
and to God she was highly acceptable.
Saint Wilfrid truly did not want

Ke la virge pur les deliz
Del siecle ne perdist son tens, 1055
Et k'el ne chanjast son porpens.
Par la seinte grace divine
Ver le roy et ver la roÿne
Se contint l'erceveske bien:
Il ne vousist pur nule rien 1060
Ke le roy eüst ver ly ire
Ne ke la roïne fust pire
Del conseil k'ele avoit eü
Et ke de Deu out receü.
Le message porta souvent 1065
A la virge espiritelment.
Kant il devoit parler del roy,
Si l'amonesta de la foy
Et de joies celestïens
Pur despire les terrïens. 1070
Par cointise, par grant verdie
Fist saint Wolfrid la departie
De la dame et de son espous
K'en la chambre a[l] Roy Glorïus
Pot recevoir de sa deserte 1075
De la peine k'ele a deferte.
En conseil seint Wolfrid s'e[s]t mise,
A Jhesu Crist s'est del tot prise;
La charité de Deu servir
Le fist emplir [tot] son desir: 1080
Par le devin porveement
Vint en aïe a meinte gent,
Car il estudioit sovent
Nuit et jur mut piteusement
Coment il po[oi]t aïder 1085   fol 108v col 1
Ceus k'il aveit a conseillier.
Ceste dame dont nos parlum
Ama sainte religïun:
Ceus et celes k'ele quidoit
Ke Deu servissent honuroit. 1090
Desseur toz les autres ama
Saint Wolfrid ky la conseillia
Et saint Cuthbert pur sa bonté
Et pur sa tres grant honesté.
A saint Cuthbert dona sovent 1095
De son aver mut largement.

the virgin to alter her purpose
1055 or waste her time
   with the pleasures of this world.
With divine grace
the archbishop behaved politely
toward both the king and the queen,
1060 for he certainly did not want
the king to be angry with him
nor the queen's situation to be worsened
because of the counsel
she had received from God through him.
1065 He delivered the message [from God]
to the virgin in a very spiritual manner.
When he had to speak on behalf of the king,
he simply instructed her concerning the faith
and the celestial joys one receives
1070 when one rejects earthly pleasures.
Politely but cleverly
Saint Wilfrid brought about the separation
of the lady from her husband
so that in the chamber of the Glorious King
1075 she might receive the reward
she would merit for her suffering.
She entrusted herself to Saint Wilfrid's counsel
[and] gave herself completely to Jesus Christ.
The love of serving God
1080 fulfilled all her desire.
Through divine guidance
Saint Wilfrid helped many people,
for he contemplated night and day
with great compassion
1085 how he could help
those whom he had to advise.
The lady of this narrative
loved the Holy Faith.
She esteemed men and women
1090 whom she believed served God.
But above all others she loved
Saint Wilfrid who advised her
and Saint Cuthbert for his goodness
and his great integrity.
1095 To Saint Cuthbert she often gave
very generously of her wealth:

D'or et de saie sainte Audree
Fist une estole bien ovree
Et un fanon k'el li tramist;
Pieres precïeuses i mist. 1100
Ces aornemenz sont gardé
A Durthaim par [mut] grant chierté;
En l'onor Deu par remembrance
L'eglise fait une monstrance.
L'amur des deus ert covenable, 1105
Kar ele ert a Deu acceptable:
Virges furent et chastement
Tindrent lur vie et seintement;
Li uns avoit l'autre en memoire
Ke Deus le menast en sa gloire. 1110
En plusurs leus fu de la dame
Dite novele et bone fame:
Mut fu coveitee de gent
A vooir pur amendement;
A tote gent ert amiable 1115
E duce et pie et revoable.
Dreiture ama, dreiture tint,
Dreiturelement se contint.
Nul delit ama ne nul estre   fol 108v col 2
Fors d'aver la joie celestre. 1120
Matin ala a seinte eglise
Et entendi a[l] Deu servise.
La vie de ceste roïne
Fu a meinte gent discipline.
Nature bone l'enfanta,* 1125
Volenté virge la garda;
La grace [de] Deu la garda
Ke en sun quer se herberja.

Ky poet remembrer en corage
Le jeu k'ele out en mariage 1130
Et de charnel temptation
Kant ele fu ou son baron,
Fors de ceste virge honoree
Ke Deus a [a] son oes gardee?
Desirant fu d'estre delivre 1135
Del mariage et en Deu vivre:
Par le seint Espir[i]t coneut
La seinte joie ou aler deut.

Saint Audrey made a finely-worked stole
and maniple out of gold and silk,
adorned it with precious stones
1100   and gave it to him.
These adornments are still kept
with great affection in Durham.
To honor God in memory of Saint Cuthbert
the church made a monstrance for them.
1105   The love between these two [Cuthbert and Audrey] was proper
and acceptable to God
for they were both virgins who led
chaste and holy lives.
One was always mindful of the other,
1110   [praying] that God would bring each of them into His glory.
News about the lady and her great fame
was spoken of in various places.
Many people desired
to see [her] in order to amend their ways.
1115   She was kind to everyone
sweet, pious, and helpful.
She loved righteousness, held fast to righteousness,
and lived a righteous life.
She had no love for pleasure or any way of life;
1120   other than seeking celestial joy.
In the mornings she went to the holy church
and heard mass.
The life of this holy queen
was a model of discipline for many people.
1125   From Nature's womb, she was born good,*
and, by her own will, she remained a virgin,
sustained by the grace of God
that dwelt in her heart.

Who else could fathom
1130   the yoke she bore in marriage
or the temptation of the flesh
when she was with her husband
other than this honorable virgin
whom God had kept for His own purpose?
1135   She wanted to be free
from marriage and desired to live only in God.
The Holy Spirit taught her about
the celestial joy to which she was destined to go.

Relement voit l'em ke cil ke sont*
Et ky conversent en ce mond   1140
Despisent charnel coveitise
En lour corage les atise:
Fort chose est al chargé de vices
D'ateindre del ciel les delices.
Pur ces choses, je ne vos ment,   1145
Ceste dame espiritelment
Voleit del siecle estre delivre
Ke ou Deu pot manoir et vivre
Non relement mes nuit et jur
Requist et pria son seigniur   1150
Congié k'ele peüst partir
De ly pur Jhesu Crist servir.
Le roy ne ly granta nïent,   fol 109r col 1
Me[s] mut en out le quer dolent.
Roy Eg[el]frid bien entendi   1155
Ke s'el se departist de li
Tot n'i eüst il compaignie,
Ja mes n'avroit joie en sa vie.
Ver le roy ert mut corïuse
Ceste roïne glorïuse   1160
De faire le departement,
Mes il l'en escundui sovent.
Tant com plus il l'en esc,onduit,
Plus l'en anguissa et requist
Car ele avoit tot son desir   1165
A l'espous ky ne peust morir.
Ou gemissement et ou plur
Li roqueroit par grant doçur,
Car ele sout bien sanz dotance
K'en li estoit sa delevrance.   1170
Le riche drap k'elë avoit
Ne si amy qu'ele v[e]oit,
La richesce d'or et d'argent
Ne porreit müer son talent,
Nepurüec tant l'angoissa   1175
Que a grant peine le granta:
Mut out le quer joieus et lé
La roïne de cel congié.
Le veil receut de saint Wolfrid
A noneine la benesquit   1180
Et prist ou sey grant compaignie

Rarely does one see people
1140 living in this world
reject the lust of the flesh
and extinguish it in their hearts.
But it is a difficult thing for one laden with vices
to obtain the joys of heaven.
1145 For these reasons, and this is the truth,
this woman deep in her soul
wanted to be set free from this world
so that she could live in the presence of God.
Not occasionally, but night and day
1150 she begged her husband
for permission to leave him
in order to serve Jesus Christ.
The king granted her nothing of the sort,
and her request grieved him.
1155 King Egfrid indeed realized
that if she left him
he would never have her company again,
and never have any joy in his life.
Although the glorious queen
1160 was quite eager
to separate from the king,
he refused it time and again.
But the more he refused it,
the more she tormented and begged him,
1165 for all her desire was set upon
the Husband Who can never die.
Weeping and sighing
she asked him very sweetly,
for she was well aware
1170 that her deliverance could come only from him.
Neither the fine clothes she had,
nor the friends she frequented,
nor the wealth of gold or silver
could change her mind.
1175 Despite all, she so troubled her husband
that finally, with great sorrow, he granted her request.
The queen was overjoyed
because of this permission to leave.
She received the veil from Saint Wilfrid,
1180 and he blessed her as a nun.
She took a large group of people with her

Si s'en ala en l'abeïe
La u seinte Ebbe conversoit
Ou noneines qu'el governoit.
Aunte fu le roy Eg[el]fri,   1185
[Et] suer [fu] Oswald et Oswy:
Abb[e]esse ert en Coludi,   fol 109r col 2
La cité ert nomez issi.
Pur son grant bien, pur sa franchise,
Vindrint plusurs a seinte eglise   1190
Et Owines nomeement
Ki fu mestres de cele gent.
Sivi sa dame seinte Audree
Ke en Coludi est alee;
Cil Owines devinement   1195
Les secriez Deu oÿ sovent:
Sachiez k'il nes oblia mie.
Ainçois ke receut monial vie
En plusurs terres fu contee
La novele de sainte Audree,   1200
Et plusurs de ceus ky l'oïrent
Despirent le mond et guerpirent,
A religion se tornerent
Et lur vies en amenderent.
Sainte Audree vint a l'eglise,   1205
A Deu s'uffri en son servise.
Terrïene joie et honor
Despist pur Deu son creator,
Son chief fist veler et fu none
Pur la parmenable corone: 1210
Pur priveté, veire, aspre, et dure*
Estoit tote sa vest[e]üre.
Donc a primes li resembla*
K'ele ert roïne et donc regna
Del siecle se senti delivre,   1215
En Deu regnoit et voloit vivre.
Ou li porta ses vestemenz
Et ses reals aornemenz,
Le or et argent k'ele avoit
Et ceo k'a lui apartenoit   1220
Pur amender cele maison   fol 109v col 1
Ou receut sa religion.
Ceste roïne fu parfite
En Deu servise ou se delite

when she went into the abbey
where Saint Ebba lived
with the nuns she governed.
1185   Ebba was King Egfrid's aunt,
the sister of Oswald and Oswy.
She was the abbess of Coldingham—
that was the name of the city.
Because of her extreme goodness and noble character
1190   many people came into her church,
Ovin in particular,
who was the spiritual leader of Saint Audrey's people,
followed his lady
when she went to Coldingham.
1195   By divine revelation Ovin
often heard secret things from God.
Rest assured that he never forgot them.
Even before she embraced the monastic life
the story of Saint Audrey
1200   was told in many lands,
and quite a few of those who heard it
rejected the world
and turned to the religious life,
amending their ways because of her.
1205   Saint Audrey came into the Church,
and offered herself to the service of God.
She disdained earthly joy and honor
for the sake of God her creator.
Her head was veiled; she became a nun
1210   in order to gain the eternal crown.
In self-deprivation, all her clothing
was mottled, harsh, and coarse.
Now for the first time it seemed to her
that she was a queen, and so she reigned.
1215   She felt free from the world.
In God she reigned, and in God she lived.
She brought her [rich] garments
and her royal adornments with her—
her gold and silver
1220   and all that belonged to her—
to be used to improve the monastery
where she had entered religious life.
Because of her merit, her blessedness,
and her proven devotion,

Par deserte et bon[e]üree   1225
Et en passion esprovee;
En discipline et en seinté
Cotiva la divinité.
Semblance out en la soue vie
De deuz soreurs Marthe et   1230
    Marie:
Marthe ensuï de travaillier
[Et] Marie de Deu prïer.
La novele de sa bounté
Estoit cressanz en honesté,
Si cresoit sa devotion   1235
Tuz jurs ver Deu en oroison.
Seur les autres fu curïuse
De Deu servir et vertüeuse.
Bien entendi en un seul an
Ke menor peine et meins de han   1240
Out el jeu de religion
Ke suffrir l'estre ou son baron
Par sa sainte religion
Et par sa grant devotion.
Par l'essample d'humilité   1245
Et par sa grant benignité
Deservi illuec la hautesce,
Del ciel la joie et la leesce.
Ele fu tenue a maistresse.
Destregnanz si com abb[e]esse   1250
De bien faire vout enseignier
Iceus ki en avoient mestier.
Verrement estoit sainte Audree
De noble victoire aournee,
Kar ceste virge glorïuse   1255   fol 109v col 2
Avoit esté deuz feiz espouse,
Primes au duc et puis au roy.
Grant merveillie fu de la foy
K'ele garda a Jhesu Crist
A cui virginité promist: 1260
Amdeuz venqui saintë Audree
Iceus ky l'eurent espousee.
Virge remist et virge fu,
A Deu a bien son vou rendu,
Cil ki garda les treis enfanz   1265
Ou for, ou ert li feus ardanz:

1225   the queen was impeccable
        in the service of God, and she delighted in it.
        She worshipped the Deity
        in self-discipline and in holiness.
        Her life resembled
1230   that of the two sisters Martha and
           Mary:
        Martha pursued work,
        Mary chose to pray to God.*
        Saint Audrey was increasingly
        reputed for her goodness,
1235   and her devotion to God
        was intensifying daily through prayer.
        She was more eager than the others
        to serve God, and she was more virtuous.*
        Within a year she came to realize
1240   that she endured less pain and suffering
        under the yoke of religion
        than she did while living with her husband.
        Through her religious faith
        her great devotion,
1245   her example of humility,
        and her great kindness
        she earned high ranking in the monastery
        as well as heavenly joy and contentment.
        She was even considered mistress of the house.
1250   Compelled as if she were the abbess,
        she wanted to teach those who needed to learn
        how to do good works.
        Truly Saint Audrey was crowned
        with noble victory,
1255   for this glorious virgin
        had been married twice:
        first to a duke and then to a king.
        It was a great miracle of faith
        that she remained faithful to Jesus Christ,
1260   to whom she had promised her virginity,
        and overcame both of
        these men who had wed her.
        She was a virgin and remained a virgin,
        thereby fulfilling her vow to God.
1265   He who preserved the three youths
        in the fiery furnace*

Garda la virge chaste et pure
De tote charnel sueillieüre.

Ceste glorïuse roïne
En seint ordrë, en discipline, 1270
Se mist si com des einz mostrames
Et de sa seinteté parlames.
Roy Egfrid del departement
K'il fist de li mut se repent.*
Anguisseus est et si plein d'ire 1275
Ne set ke faire ne que dire:
Tel düel a en son curage
Et nuit et jur pur poi n'enrage.
Le roy par conseil de sa gent
Ke sa dolur veient sovent 1280
La vout geter de sa maison
U ele aveit conversion.
Pleins est espris de deverie
Est alé tresqu'a l'abbeïe
Ou grant compaignie de gent: 1285
La vout geter de ceo covent.
Sainte Ebbe ke ceo covent tint
Sout ke le roy cele part vint.
La glorïuse seinte Audree fol 110r col 1
A conseilliee et enhortee 1290
K'ele voit en liu solitaire
Ou il ne puisse aver repaire.
Sainte Audree hastivement
Par le devin porveement
En l'ile d'Ely est alee 1295
Dont ele fu primes doee.
Cele ki einçois fu roïne
Del regne prist la discipline
En l'eglise ou la compaignie
K'elë ou primes establie. 1300
Ne se fist pas haute abb[e]esse
Ne desur les autres maistresse,
Mes humble, simple, obeïsanz
A totes les autres servanz,
Car ele entendi come sage 1305
Ceo ke dist la devine page:
Cil ki en mond ont plus hautesce
Deivent aver gregniur simplesce:

kept the virgin chaste and free
from any carnal stain.

This glorious queen
1270 submitted herself to the discipline of a holy order,
and her saintliness
has already been described.
King Egfrid deeply regretted
the separation from her that he had made [possible].
1275 He was so tormented and full of anger
that he did not know what to do or say.
He constantly felt such grief inside
that he almost lost his mind.
On the advice of his people
1280 who often saw his suffering,
the king decided to force her out of the convent
where she had taken up residence.
He was so consumed with anger
that he went all the way to the abbey
1285 with a great company of people,
intending to take her by force out of the convent.
When Saint Ebba, the abbess of the convent,
learned that the king was coming that way.
She advised
1290 glorious Saint Audrey
to go off to an isolated place
where he would not have access.
Saint Audrey,
with the help of Divine Providence,
1295 quickly headed for the island of Ely
which was part of her first dower.
She who once was queen
of the realm took on the discipline
of the church with the community
1300 that she had first established.
She did not make herself head abbess
nor mistress above the others,
rather she was humble, simple, obedient,
a servant to all.
1305 For she wisely knew
what the Holy Word said:
those who are exalted in this world
will be brought low;

Ky en ce siecle s'humilie
Enhauciez iert, ne faudra mie.   1310
Ja soit ceo k'ele quida vivre
En repos et estre delivre,
Si out ele temptation
De l'enemi et agoillion:
De l'apostre fu bien li diez   1315
En la sainte virge acompliez
Ky dit ke tuz les meilliurs sunt
Temptez et gregniurs peines ont.
Aprés la dame ala li rois
La ou [ele] ert en cel mareis.   1320
Par droite force la vout prendre,
Mes el ne le voloit attendre.
A Jhesu Crist d'eternité   fol 110r col 2
Comanda sa virginité:
Priveement s'en est alee   1325
De cel liu la bon[e]üree.
Desur un tertre s'en ala
Deuz compaignes ou li mena
Ky mut furent de li privees:
Sewar et Oswen sont nomees.   1330
En engleis est cist mont nomé,
Goldeborch et apellé,
Et en latin ravons oÿ
C'om l'apelle Goldeburch cy.
Cil Dieu ki bien garde sa gent   1335
En mer et en autre torment
Fist ke la mer multiplia
Et icel tertre environa.
Si com cil del païs conterent,
Set jours entiers i demorerent   1340
Sanz viande et sanz gareison
Furent iluec en oreison.
Deu fist la mer lesser son cours,
Merveillie fu de tel secours.
[Li] roy Egfrid mut longement   1345
I fu et n'espleita nïent,
Ne s'osa mestre dedenz l'onde,
Car trop estoit lee et parfonde,
Si esch[a]pa la Deu amie
Del roi la force et la rustie.   1350
Par sa pitié l'ad Deus gardee

but whoever humbles himself in this world
1310   will be exalted, and this without fail.*
Although she thought to live
in peace and to be free,
even so she was goaded
by the Enemy and Tempter.
1315   The words of the apostle were indeed*
fulfilled in the saintly virgin
when he said that only the best people
are tempted and have greater suffering.*
The king went in pursuit of the lady
1320   there in that marshland where she was.*
He wanted to take her by direct force.
But she was not going to wait for him [to arrive],
for she had vowed her virginity
to Jesus Christ for all eternity.
1325   So the blessed lady
slipped out
and climbed up to a hilltop
taking with her two female companions
who were among her closest friends:
1330   Sewara and Sewenna were their names.
In English this mountain
is called "Goldeborch"
(and we have also heard it called
"Goldeburch" in Latin).*
1335   God who takes care of his own
both at sea and in any peril
caused the sea to swell up
and surround that hill.
According to the people of the region
1340   the women remained there a full seven days
without food or any provisions.
They simply prayed.
God caused the sea to leave its normal course—
and such a rescue was a miracle.
1345   King Egfrid waited there for a long time
but he could do nothing.
He did not dare enter the water
for it was too wide and deep.
Thus the friend of God escaped
1350   the power and brutality of the king.
Through His compassion God kept her

Del roy Egfrid et delivree.
Cil secriez lius estoit garni
De la Deu grace et repleni.
Une haute roche i avoit   1355
Ke un de[s] costés aceignoit,
Entaillié ert la pere dure: fol 110v col 1
C'estoit merveillieuse aventure;
Et la mer ke desouz estoit
Ou ele au tertre se tenoit   1360
En pes se tint sanz departir
Si ke hom ne poet avenir.
Ceste novele fu portee
Par tote la terre et contee.
Tuz ceus ke oïerent la fame   1365
Distrent ke Deus garda cele dame.
Le roy avoit dol et destresce
Kant il veoit sur la hautesce
De la roche ou se pout tenir
La dame, einz l'en estoet partir.   1370
Le roy s'en va grain et iré,
A Everewic est repeiré.
De l'erceveske saint Wolfriz
Se pleint, mut fu ver li mariz:
De se[s] conseils n'ert mes privez   1375
Ne de s'amur aseürez;
Long tens aprés l'a esloigné
Et hosté de l'ercevesqué.
Kant roy Egfrid s'aparceüt
Ke son entente rien ne valeut   1380
De sainte Audree porchacier,
Si prist Ermenborc a muellier.
Sainte Audree et celes ki sont
Sur le rochier grant seif ont.
Mut furent les dames grevees   1385
Et de la grant seif tormentees.
Sainte Ebbe, la bone abb[e]esse,
Ke sur les autres ert maistresse
Sainte Audree pria et dist
K'e[lle] nostre seigniur requist   1390
K'un pou d'eawe par sa bonté   fol 110v col 2
Lour envoiast par charité
Ky en desert fist del rochier
Issir l'eawe a son poeple aider.

and rescued her from King Egfrid
by preparing and providing this secret place
through His grace.
1355 There was a high rock
that formed part of the coastline.
The hard stone had been hollowed out.
This was a miraculous occurrence:
the water at the base
1360 of the hill where she stood
stayed there without moving,
so that no one could come near her.
News of this was reported
throughout the region,
1365 and all those who heard about it
said that it was God who protected the lady.
The king was sad and quite distressed
when he saw the lady on top
of the rock where she was able to stand her ground.
1370 But there was nothing he could do except depart.
The king went his way upset and angry
and headed back toward York.
He complained about the Archbishop Wilfrid
and was quite vexed with him.
1375 He would never again be privy to his counsel
nor assured of his love!
Afterwards he removed him from the archbishopric
and sent him away.
When King Egfrid finally perceived
1380 that his effort to pursue Saint Audrey
was worthless,
he took Eormenburga as his wife.
Saint Audrey and those who were with her
on the rock became very thirsty.
1385 The ladies were really quite
bothered by their great thirst.
Saint Audrey called to Saint Ebba,
who was mistress over the other [nuns],
and asked the good abbess
1390 to beseech Our Lord
to send them a little water
out of His kindness and love,
He Who in the desert caused water
to issue from the rock in order to help His people.*

Ceste dame par grant douçur   1395
En a requis son creatur.
La roche dure si ovri*
Et l'eawe douce s'en issi
Dont les dames furent mut lees
Et del beivre resainees.   1400
Uncore i cort cele fontaine,
As malades est douce et seine.
Ensorquetut mut grant vertu
Fist del leu ou ele fu
Car si com ele aloit montant   1405
Sur le rochier et descendant
Perent les pas de sainte Audree
Com cire qui fust eschaufee.
Iluec fist Deus, ç'avons oÿ,
Quatre granz miracles pur ly.   1410
Li un fu ke Deu la garda
Et dë Egfrid la delivra;
Li autre, com la mer i creut
Et come mur en pes s'esteut;
Le tiers si fu de la fonteine   1415
Ke del rocher sourt clere et seine;
Le quart des piés ki enfondrerent
Sur le rochier uncore i perent.
Ceus del païs testimonient
Ces quatre miracles et dient,   1420
Car saint Bede ne pooit mie
Par seul conter iceste vie
Fors tant com il en out enquis
Par la bone gent del païs.

Nul ne doit doter ne mescre[i]re   1425   fol 111r col 1
Ke ceste chose ne soit veire
K'ele fust virge ou deus mariz
Et despist tus charneus deliz:
Ceo fu par Deu et par s'aïe,
Merveillie en avom de l'oïe.   1430
Grant tesmonie a sainte Audree
K'en virginité fu gardee
De l'erceveske saint Wolfrid,
Des clers, des lais, de Kinefrid.
Ensurquetut saint Wolfrid di[s]t   1435
A ki le roy sovent promist

1395   Ebba kindly
       made the request of her Creator.
       The hard rock then opened
       and fresh water issued forth.
       The ladies greatly rejoiced over it
1400   and were refreshed by the drink.
       This fountain still flows,
       sweet and wholesome to the sick.
       Most importantly, Saint Audrey brought great honor
       to this place where she was stranded,
1405   for wherever she mounted
       or descended the rock
       her footprints appeared
       as if sealed in melted wax.
       Now we have heard about the four great miracles
1410   that God performed there through her:
       the first was that God protected her
       and delivered her from Egfrid;
       another was how the water swelled around
       and stood still like a wall;
1415   the third was concerning the fountain
       that came out of the rock clear and clean;
       and the fourth—about the footprints melted
       into the rock, which are still visible today.
       The people of the area attest
1420   to these four miracles and tell all about them
       (For Saint Bede could never
       by himself recount this life
       unless he had inquired about it
       from the good folk of the land).

1425   No one should doubt this fact about her
       or think erroneously
       that she was not a virgin who had two husbands
       and rejected all carnal pleasure,
       for it came to pass through God and His help,
1430   and we are amazed to hear about it.
       There is firm verification
       that Audrey remained a virgin
       from the Archbishop Saint Wilfrid,
       from clerks, from lay people, from [the physician] Kynefrid—
1435   most especially from the testimony of Saint Wilfrid
       to whom the king often promised

Terre et aver et grant loër
Pur la roïne conseillier
K'a li atornast son corage
Si com avent en mariage,   1440
Car i sout bien et entendi
Qu'el le creoit mut et il li.
Digne chose est a remembrer
La seinteté et recorder
De la roïne sainte Audree   1445
Ke a Deu out s'amur donee,
Kar, si com l'escripture dist
Et Bede qui le livre fist,
Plusurs recevrent en sa vie
Santé par li de maladie: 1450
Contreit, aveugle et surd et mu
Par sa preiere orent salu.
La seinte virge, Deu amie,
Out des sages la compaignie
Ky ou lur lampes alumees   1455
Sont as riches noces entrees,
Ne fu la virge pas susprise
Ne de cors ne de cuer maumise
Si com la fillie Jacob fu   fol 111r col 2
Par l'amur le fiz Sicheü: 1460
Ceo fu Dina ke s'en parti,
Sa propre region guerpi
Et ala en autres contrees
Ou dames li furent loees.
Mes la virge pur Jhesu Crist   1465
Terriens honeuremens despist.
Tant fu de l'amur Deu enprise
Qu'ele out corone de justise,
Ja soit k'ele ne fust occise,
Si out ele sur sa char mise   1470
La croiz ou Jhesu Crist sueffri
La mort quant Longis le feri:
En jonne, en veillie, et en plur
Tormentoit son cors nuit et jur.
Pur c'ert ceste virge acollie   1475
En cele seinte compaignie
De celes ke l'estole pristrent:
En sang de l'agniel Deu la mistrent
Et com[e] sages la laverent

land, wealth, and a rich reward
if he would advise the queen
to turn her affection toward him,

1440   as should happen in marriage;
for he firmly believed
that the two [Wilfrid and Audrey] had faith in each other.
It is well worth remembering
her righteousness and recalling

1445   how queen Saint Audrey
had given her love to God.
For, as the book says,
and Bede its author,
many people were healed of diseases

1450   through her during her lifetime:
the lame, the blind, the deaf, and the mute
were cured through her prayers.
The holy virgin, friend of God,
was like the wise virgins

1455   who, with their lamps lighted,
entered into the rich wedding feast.*
Neither her body or nor her heart was violated,
for the virgin was not led astray
as was the daughter of Jacob

1460   for the love of Shechem's son.*
It was Dinah who left,
abandoning her own region,
and went into another territory
where the women were renowned.

1465   But the virgin for the sake of Jesus Christ
rejected earthly honors.
She was so taken with the love of God
that she wore a crown of righteousness.
Although she was not martyred,

1470   she bore on her flesh
the cross where Jesus Christ suffered
death when Longinus struck him.*
In fasting, in vigils, and in tears
she tortured her body night and day,

1475   and for these acts the virgin was accepted
into the holy company
of those who took their garment,
placed it in the blood of the Lamb of God,
and, like the wise ones, washed it,

Devant le trone Deu chanterent. 1480
En ceste dame out si grant bien
C'el tens que Dioclicïen
Eust esté et en tens Neron,
Kant il firent l'occision
Des cristïens de cruel ire, 1485
El ne dota[st] pas le martire;
Denz tormenz com elë avoit
Joieuse et lee se fesoit.
Senz sanc espandre fu martir:
En veillie, en plur, et en desir, 1490
En feim, en soif, et en nuesce.
Pur malades fu en destresce,
[Et] pur les perils de la mer,* fol 111v col 1
Et pur le poplë amender.
Del ciel ama la compaignie 1495
Et haÿ terrïene vie.

Bien est seü de seinte Audree
K'el ne vint onkes par contre[e],
Si com distrent ly ancïen,
K'ele ne monstrat Deu le bien. 1500
[Li] roy Egfrid ne volt lesser
La guerre de li enchacïer.
Ou deuz anceles s'en ala,
Sewen et Seward amena:
Bien sivi le comandement 1505
De Deu et son enseigniement
Ke dit ke cil ki out fait guerre
Deveient fuïr de terre en terre.
Ceste roïne, seinte Audree,
A Hombre vint, si est passee, 1510
A Wytringam [ele] ariva,
Et a Eltham d'ieluec ala:
Hostel requist et hostel out
Ou iceles qu'ele menout.
Une eglise en cel liu fonda 1515
Et deuz granz miracles mostra.
Poy de tens i fu la roïne
Avant vait come pilerine.
En povre habit hors de chemin:
S'en vait ceste dame a tapin 1520
Preveement në en oiance

1480 then sang before the throne of God.*
     In this lady there was so much goodness
     that, had she lived during the time of Diocletian
     or during the time of Nero,
     when they so cruelly
1485 and with such anger killed Christians,
     she would not have feared martyrdom.
     In the torments that she endured
     she was able to feel happy, even joyous.
     Though her blood was not spilled, she was nevertheless a martyr
1490 in vigils, in tears, in want,
     in hunger, in thirst, in nakedness.
     She anguished over the sick,
     over those in danger at sea,
     over all people who needed help.
1495 She loved the company of heaven
     and disdained her earthly life.

     It is well known about Saint Audrey,
     as our forefathers have told us,
     that she never passed through any region
1500 where she did not demonstrate the goodness of God.
     Since King Egfrid did not want to give up
     trying to pursue her,
     she took two servants,
     Sewenna and Sewara, and left.
1505 She indeed followed the principle
     of God who taught
     that those who have engaged in the fight [of faith]
     must flee from one place to another.*
     Queen Saint Audrey
1510 crossed the Humber and then continued on her way.
     She arrived in Winteringham
     and from there went to West Halton,
     where she requested and received lodging for herself
     as well as for those traveling with her.
1515 She founded a church in that place
     and performed two great miracles.
     The queen spent some time there
     before leaving disguised as a pilgrim.
     Dressed in poor clothing, avoiding the main road,
1520 the lady left secretly.
     She would not allow this journey to be discussed

De son eire ne fist parlance.
Tant fu anguiseuse d'errer
K'ele out talent de reposer:
Issi avint par la Deu grace   1525
Que ele vint a une place
Ke mut est covenable et bele   fol 111v col 2
De flurs, d'herbe freche et novele.
La s'est cochie[e] seinte Audree,
Si s'est iluekes reposee,   1530
Mes quant ele s'est enve[il]lie[e],*
De son baston s'est merveillie[e]
Qui estoit sec, ore fu cruz,
Fluriz et fueilliz et branchuz.
Pur ice fait a Deu rendirent   1535
Grace ke le miracle virent.
Ceus del païs tes[ti]monient*
Ceo miracle et pur voir le dient.
Tant creut cist fust et tant leva
Ke ces del païs sormonta.   1540
Edeldrestewë apellom*
Le liu dont nos ici parlom.
En l'onur Deu et sainte Audree
Ja une eglisë ert fondee.

Tost aprés ce qu'ele parti   1545
De l'eglise de Coludi,
Ou ele prist religion,
Fu ars et mostier et maison
Pur le mal ke firent li maistre
Ky deveient garder cele estre.   1550
Un home en cele eglise avoit
Del linage as Escoz estoit;
Adammis out icil a non,
Mut ert de grant religion:
En vigile et en salmodie   1555
Menoit iceo prudom sa vie.
Une nuit fu mut effreez
Adammis et espo[e]ntez
Pur un home ky aparut
Par nuit, ky devant ly s'estut,   1560
Mes cil li dist mut doucement   fol 112r col 1
K'il ne s'espo[e]ntast nïent

either publicly or privately.
After a while she became quite weary of traveling
and needed to rest.

1525 By the grace of God
she came to a place
that was very pleasant and beautiful,
with flowers and fresh grass.
There Saint Audrey lay down
1530 and took her rest.
But when she awakened
she was astonished by her [pilgrim's] staff
which had been made of dead wood but which had now grown
and sprouted branches, foliage, and flowers.*
1535 Then she had them all give thanks to God
that they had witnessed this miracle.
People who live in that region bear witness
to this miracle and declare it to be true.
The staff grew so tall and sturdy
1540 that it surpassed all the trees in the area.
This place
is called Etheldrestowe.*
In honor of God and of Saint Audrey
a church was established there.

1545 Not long after she left
the abbey at Coldingham
where she had entered holy orders,
both the church and the chapter house were burned
because of the evil deeds of the leaders
1550 who were supposed to direct monastic life there.
There was a man in the church
of Scottish descent
named Adammis,
and he was very devout.
1555 This good man spent his life
in vigils and in psalm-singing.
One night Adammis
was terribly frightened
by a man who appeared
1560 and stood before him in the darkness.
But the apparition told him very kindly
that he should not fear at all

Et li dist k'il fesoit grant sens
K'en oürer metoit son tens,
Et qu'il avoit avir[o]nee   1565
Tote l'eglise et puralee:
N'i avoit nul trové, ce dist,
Fors [de] li ky a Deu tendist.
Homes et femmes ouelement
Peccherent en lur fol talent,   1570
Et pur cë ad Deu vengance prise
De ce liu et de ce[s]te eglise.
A seinte Ebbe ky en out cure
Dist Adammis ce[s]te aventure.
Ceste dame en fu mut marie   1575
Kant la novele en out oïe,
Et li dist que malement fist
Kant il erraument ne li dist.
Cil li dist par grant essïence
Ke il dota sa reverence   1580
Et qu'elë en fuest trop troblee
De la novele et mut grevee.
Icele dame chastia
Ceus et celes qu'ele garda,
Mes aprés son decés revindrent   1585
As vices ke eusençois tindrent,
Par quoy Deu vout de la maison
Et d'eus touz la destruction.
Pur l'honorance seinte Audree
Ke en cel liu fu ordenee   1590
Ne voleient lur mals lesser,
Lur cors danter ne chatïer.
Ceo dist que [lessent] apernement*
Des bons et grant espeirement
Iceus qui n'ont devotion   1595   fol 112r col 2
Ne de Deu inspiration.

La glorïuse seinte Audree
Un an puis k'ele fu velee
Out grant travail, ç'avom oÿ.
Repeira en l'ile d'Ely   1600
En sa lige possession
K'ele out de Tonbert, son baron.
Ces deuz anceles ou li furent
Ki tuz les granz travaus conurent.

and said that he did very well
to spend his time in prayer,
1565   for he had been around and about
      the whole monastery
and had found no one
except him [Adammis] who had devoted himself to God.
Men and women equally
1570   were giving in to the sins of their foolish desires,
and that is why God had taken vengeance
On this place and its church.
Adammis related all of this
to Saint Ebba who was in charge of the abbey.
1575   The lady became quite vexed
when she heard about it
and told Adammis that he had acted badly
by not telling her about the situation sooner.
The man very wisely replied
1580   that he feared that the Reverend Mother
might be too upset
and grieved by the news.
Then the lady chastised
the men and women under her responsibility,
1585   but after her death they returned
to the vices they had indulged in before.
For this reason God willed
the destruction of the house and all of those in it.
[Not even] for the honor of Saint Audrey
1590   who had entered orders there
would they leave off their evil-doing;
they refused to control or discipline their bodies.
It is said that those who have no devotion
nor inspiration from God
1595   forsake the lessons learned
from good and great examples.

Glorious saint Audrey,
a year after taking the veil,
encountered great difficulties—we have heard about this.
1600   She returned to the isle of Ely,
her sovereign possession
which she received from her husband Tonbert.
The two servant girls who were with her
also experienced many of her hardships.

Mut fu la dame bien venue　　　　　　1605
Et a grant joie fu receue.
Par la purveiance divine
Vout Jhesu Crist ke la roïne
Fust illuec parmenablement
Et feïst son herbergement.　　　　　　1610
Un seint prestrë, Hunus out non,
Sivi la dame a sa maison.
Cil li mostra des seinz les vies
Et les veraies profecies.
Cist idle ou la dame fu,　　　　　　　1615
Si cum nos avom entendu,
Elge si fu primes nomez,
Et ore Ely est apellez.
Elgë est un non en hebreu,
En glose dist la terre Dieu.　　　　　　1620
Par droit bien est issi nomee;
Kant de primes fu aportee,
En Engleterre la mostrance
De droit baptesme et de creance,
Iceus ky en le ile furent　　　　　　　1625
Crestïenté primes receurent.
En cestë ile sainte Audree
Une riche eglise a fondee.
Pur ce k'ele ert des Estengleis　　　　fol 112v col 1
Del linage as nobles Engleis,　　　　　1630
Par esperit de prophecie
Et par sa seinte noble vie,
Le plusurs ke fillies avoient
Dedens sa garde les metoient
Pur aprendre la loy devine　　　　　　1635
Et de li sen et discipline.
Pur le seint ordre qu'ele tint
Werborc, une pucele, i vint.
Fillie Ermenild sa nice fu,
Deu li dona grace et salu.　　　　　　1640
Mut tint bien sa religion
Et fu de grant devotion.
Sainte Audree Deu mercia
Des compaignes k'il li dona.
En cel tens në avoit asise　　　　　　1645
En cel yle fors une eglise.
Cele destruit le roy Penda;

1605 The lady was warmly welcomed
and received with much joy.
By Divine Providence and
by the will of Jesus Christ, the queen
was to remain there permanently
1610 and make it her home.
A saintly priest, Huna by name,
came to the convent shortly thereafter
and taught her about the saints' lives
and about their teachings of the truth.
1615 Ely, where the lady was living,
as we have understood it,
was first named "Elge"
and is now called "Ely."
Elge is a Hebrew name
1620 which in translation means "the land of God."
It was rightfully named this:
when the teaching
        of true baptism and faith
was first brought into England,
1625 those who lived on this island
were the first to accept Christianity.
Here on the island Saint Audrey
founded a magnificent church.
Because she was an East Angle
1630 in the line of English nobility,
and because of her spiritual nature,
and her admirable holy lifestyle,
many [people]
placed their daughters in her care
1635 to learn from her the divine law,
wisdom, and discipline.
A maiden named Werburga arrived there
to join Saint Audrey's holy order
She was the daughter of Ermenilda, Audrey's niece,
1640 to whom God had given grace and salvation.
She practiced her religion well
and was very devout.
Saint Audrey thanked God
for the companions He had given her.
1645 Until that time only one church
had been established on the island.*
King Penda had destroyed it,

Seinte Audree la redresa:
Maisons, officines i fist
En l'aorner grant peine mist.   1650
Saint Wolfrid ky out tant amé
A la dame le liu gardé
Et lur trova lur estovoir
Et ceo qu'eles deurent avoir.
Saint Bede nos dist k'abb[e]esse   1655
La fist saint Wolfrid et maistresse.
Sainte Audree par sa cointise
A li purchaça grant franchise
Des rois, de[s] ducs, de meint prudome
Par le confermement de Rome.   1660
Cist yle li estoit donee
Et par douaire confermee.
Pur ceo purchaça tel franchise   fol 112v col 2
Qu'el la torna a Deu servise,
Ne voloit mie en nul tens perdre   1665
Ne ke nul se i peust aherdre.
Par previleges purchaça
Ke le[s] franchises conferma.
Par le conseil Aldulfs le roy
Ky mut l'ama par bone foy   1670
S'eglise acreut et amenda:
Son frere estoit, mut li dona.
Saint Wolfrid a Romë ala
Et privilege purchaça
K'estables soient mes a tuz dis   1675
Le[s] donés ke le roy i a mis.
Par le devin purveement
Fu fait icist ordenement:
Qu'el les virges out en baillie
De ces virges la compaignie   1680
Saint Wolfrid, ki virges estoit,
Les meintenoit et governoit.
Semblant fu de la comandise
Ou la mere Jhesu fu mise
Devant la croiz ou il pendi,   1685
Kant saint Johan i vint ou li:
La virge al virge comanda
Ki bien la servi et garda.
Sachiez de voir, pas ne receurent
Greigniur lüer ceus ki einz furent   1690

but Saint Audrey rebuilt it.
She also built a chapter house and outbuildings there,
1650 and went to great lengths to have them all nicely embellished.
Saint Wilfrid, whom she loved so much,
took charge of the place for the lady,
providing them whatever they needed,
attending to their exigencies.
1655 Saint Bede tells us that Saint Wilfrid
made her abbess of the monastery.
Through her shrewdness Saint Audrey
obtained for him important tax exemptions,
approved by Rome,
1660 from kings, dukes, and many noblemen.
Since the island had been given to her
and confirmed as her dower,
she was able to procure this type of exemption,
and she turned it over to the service of God.
1665 She never wanted to lose it
or have anyone to take it away from her.
Through privileges she was able
to confirm the exemptions.
Following the counsel of King Aldulf,
1670 who loved her devotedly,
her church grew and was enriched,
for he was her brother and gave her much.*
Saint Wilfrid went to Rome
And obtained a privilege
1675 that granted to the monastics whom the king put there
security henceforth and forever.
Through Divine Providence
this rule was made:
that Saint Audrey would keep the virgins under her tutelage,
1680 and that Saint Wilfrid, who was also celibate,
would maintain and govern
her company of virgins.
It resembled the command Jesus gave
when His mother was brought
1685 before the cross where He was hanging.
Saint John had come there with her.
Jesus commended the Virgin to the celibate John
who served her and took good care of her.*
Be assured that those who came early
1690 did not receive any greater reward

K'eurent ceus ki aprés venoient;
Al servise Deu se tenoient
La seinte congregation
Dont nos devant parlé avom.
Une reule, un ordenement,   1695
Un corage, un cotivement
Estoit entre eus de bien garder   fol 113r col 1
Cele maison et ordener.
En cronikes avom trové
Ke sis cens ans erent passé   1700
Et setante trois quant l'eglise
Par seinte Audree fu asise
Puis la venue Jhesu Crist,
Issi com seint Bede nos dist.
En brief tens fu la maison faite   1705
Et sainte compaignie atraite
D'hommes et de femmes, ce dist
Seint Bede ki le livre fist.
En l'Escole Englesche ai trovee
K'a Coludi avoit fundee   1710
Un moster et une maison
Pur meintenir religion
Et en plusurs autres contrees
Out autres eglises fundees.

Saint Wolfrid n'out mie oblïee   1715
La compaignie seinte Audree.
Kant il oï qu'ele ert venue
Et en Ely [ert] arestue,
A lui vint pur li conforter,
Enseigner et endoctriner   1720
La droite voie par sermon
De seinte conversation.
Aprés ice li fist maistresse
Saint Wolfrid et haute abb[e]esse,
Et ele bien et seintement   1725
Governa l'ordre et le covent.
Tut son corage, tut son desir
Mist seinte Audree en Deu servir.
En june et en veillie menoit
Et granz asmones departoit.   1730
Bedes nos dist que mut ama   fol 113r col 2
Les seinz et lur festes garda.

than those who came later,*
for all those of this holy congregation
of whom we have just spoken
remained obedient to the service of God.
1695   The house functioned well, for
one rule, one order,
one heart, one worship
existed among them.
In historical chronicles we have found
1700   that six hundred seventy-three years had passed
since the coming of Jesus Christ
when Saint Audrey
established her church,
as Saint Bede tells us.
1705   The house was completed in a short time,
and a holy company of men and women
were drawn to it, so says
Saint Bede, author of the book.
In the English School I have found [recorded]*
1710   that in Coldingham
a church and a monastery were founded
to uphold the faith,
as were a number of churches
in several other locations.*

1715   Saint Wilfrid certainly did not forget
his friendship with Saint Audrey.
As soon as he heard that she had come
to stay in Ely,
he went to strengthen her
1720   and to teach her
the correct way [to live as a nun],
exhorting her concerning holy monastic life.
Shortly after this Saint Wilfrid made her mistress
and high abbess,
1725   and she governed the convent
efficiently and in a saintly manner.
Saint Audrey served God
whole-heartedly and led a life
of fasting, keeping vigils,
1730   and giving out much in the way of alms.
Bede tells us that she especially loved
the saints and regularly observed their feast days.

Puis que la virge out receüe
Religion, s'est si tenue
K'en langes ala nuit et jur   1735
En servise nostre seigniur.
Par trois foiz en l'an se baignia
Aprés celes qu'ele garda:
Kant chacune out ou bain servie,
Aprés baignoit par compaignie.   1740
A la Pasche, ceo dist ici,
A la Penthecoste autresi,
A la Tiphanie veirement
Se baignerent communaument.
Ke de quer est net et mundé,   1745
Le cors peust estre tut lavé.
Ceste dame assidüelment
Mist son seint amonestement
En cele congregation
Ke ou lui ert en sa maison.   1750
A une foiz le jur manga
Fors a festes ke l'em garda.
Ele haÿ come tempeste
Sorfait de manger, mes a feste
Mangoit pur les autres haiter   1755
Et lur abstinence alegier.
Aprés matines tresque'au jur
Entendoit a son creatur
Si d'enferté ne fuest grevee
Ou d'autre cure desturbee.   1760
Lors estoit en afflictions,
En prïeres, en oreisons.
A celui dist sa volunté
Ky gardoit sa virginité.
Ici nos dist del fiz Penda,   1765   fol 113v col 1
Ulfer, ke donckes devia
Merchenelande out governee
Et a cristïeneté tornee.
Cist fu le primer de[s] paiens
K'ileukes devint crestïens.   1770
Tuz les y[d]les aneenti,
Egleises fist et Deu servi.
A Medeshamstede fist
Une eglise en non Jhesu Crist.
Cist liu est ore Borc nomez,   1775

Ever since the virgin's commitment
to the faith, she dressed herself
1735 in a coarse chemise night and day
as she served our Lord.
Three times a year she bathed last
after the women in her care.
After each one had served her turn in the bath,
1740 then each would bathe in a common bath.
It is said that
they bathed as a community
at Easter, at Pentecost,
and also at Epiphany.*
1745 When the heart is pure and clean
then the body can be thoroughly washed.
The lady regularly
gave saintly admonition
to the congregation
1750 with her in the convent.
She ate only once a day
except on the feast days that they kept.
She absolutely despised
overeating, but on feast days
1755 she ate in order to please the others
and to lighten their abstinence.
After matins until the break of day*
she concentrated her attention on her Creator
so she would not be troubled by infirmity
1760 or disturbed by any other concern.
During this time she engaged in acts of humility,
prayers and petitions,
expressing her desires
to Him who had preserved her virginity.
1765 Now the book tells about Penda's son
Wulhere, who died about that time.
He had governed Mercia
and had turned it to Christianity.
He was the first of the pagans
1770 to become a Christian in Mercia.
He destroyed all their idols,
built churches, and served God.
In Medeshamstede, which is now called Peterborough,
he built a monastic church
1775 in the name of Jesus Christ.

De granz richesces est fefez.
Sexuls out primes l'abbeïe,
Un hom de mut honeste vie.
De Merchenelande fu, puis
Eveske si cum escrist truis.   1780
Ci nos dist de la femme Ulfer,
Ermenild, qu'il out a mueillier,
Fillie Sexborc, suer sainte Audree.
Cele out une fillie enfantee
Del roy Ulfer, Werborc out non,   1785
Mut fu de grant religion.
Werborc aprés la mort son pere
Par conseil de sa bone mere
Li siecle despist et haÿ,
Si fu envoié en Ely   1790
En la compaignie s'anteine
Ki la vela et fist noneine.
Tant ama Dieu, tant l'a servi
K'il fist meint miracle pur li.
Edelred puis Ulfer regna   1795
Et le reäume governa.
Un secund roy, Peada, i out*
Ky en cel north, ce dist, regnout:
En icel an dist li escrit   fol 113v col 2
K'il fu par sa femme traïst.   1800
Aprés ice fu le tiers rois
Merewalz sur les Est Angleis.
[Cist] trois rois furent frere Ulfer
Ke le regne out a justiser.
Roy Merewalz out quatre enfanz   1805
D'Emenborc ke fu mut vaillianz.
Fillie Ermenild fu la roïne,
Dame de mut bone doctrine.
Ses enfanz dont ai ci parlé
Furent de mut grant seinteté.   1810
Un fiz i out et treis puceles
Ke mut furent sages et beles.
Merwins avoit li fiz a non.
[Or] des puceles nos dirom:
Milburch avoit a non l'einee,   1815
L'autre Mildrez et puis Mildree.

[I]ci dist pur la renomee

It is endowed with great riches.
Seaxwulf, a man who lived a very honorable life,
was the first abbot.
Then he became bishop
1780 of Mercia, so I find in the writings.*
Next we learn that the wife of Wulfhere,
Ermenilda, whom he had married,
was the daughter of Seaxburga, sister of Saint Audrey.
She in turn gave birth to a daughter
1785 by King Wulfhere. Her name was Werburga,
and she was very devoutly religious.
After the death of her father, Werburga,
persuaded by her good mother,
rejected the world
1790 and was sent to Ely
into the community of her aunt [Audrey]
who veiled her and trained her as a nun.
She loved and served God so well
that He performed many miracles through her.
1795 After Wulfhere, Ethelred became king
and governed [Mercia].
There was a second king, Peada,
who, they say, reigned in the north.
Concerning him the book says
1800 that he was betrayed by his wife.
Then there was the third king,
Merewald, who ruled the East Angles.*
These three kings were brothers of Wulfhere,
who had governed the kingdom.
1805 King Merewald had four children
by Emenburga, his queen of high nobility
and a lady of much good instruction,
who was the daughter of Ermenilda.
All of her children, whom I have mentioned
1810 were very devoutly religious.
There was one son and three girls
who were quite beautiful and well-behaved.
The son was named Merwin,
and here are the names of the girls:
1815 the eldest was named Milburga,
the next Mildred, and then Mildgyth.

The next part of the book tells about

Ke bone fu de seinte Audree.
Plusurs venoient en Ely,
Si s'acompaignoient a ly.   1820
Nobles barons de haut linage,
Riches dames de grant parage*
Et autres de plus jofne aage
Se rendirent de bon corage.
Ja soit k'ele lur demostrast   1825
Les griez de l'ordre et acointast,
Ne se voloient departir
Ne sa compaignie guerpir.
Entres les autres si avint
Ke uns moine profés devint.   1830
Son chapelein avoit esté,
Prestre de grant humilité.
L'abb[e]esse forment l'ama   fol 114r col 1
Pur les granz biens k'en li trova,
Car il fu amonestement   1835
De bien faire a icele gent.
Sexborc, si com out entendu
Par l'angle et par la Deu vertu,
Coveita la subjection
Et le jou de religion.   1840
Ceste dame les descovri
A ses privez k'ele out ou li
Et lur dist: « Ge m'en voil aler
Pur mes amis revisiter,
Ma soreur, la roïne Audree,   1845
Et le païs u ge fu nee.
Ensemble ou li voil estre mise
De sa religion aprise.
En garde Deu vos met ici
[Et] Ermenild, ma fillie, pri   1850
K'ele vos consout et meinteigne,
Si f[e]ra ele que qu'avienge. »
Ne faist gires de porloingnance,
En Ely vint sanz demorance.
L'abb[e]esse Audree, sa suer,   1855
Encontre li vint de bon quer.
En s'abbeïe l'a menee,
De joie plure sainte Audree:
L'une de l'autre est confortee,
En Deu est lur joie dubble[e].   1860

Saint Audrey's excellent reputation.
Many people came to Ely
1820   to join her community:
noble barons of high lineage
and fine ladies from great families;*
even young people
went there quite willingly.
1825   Although she pointed out to them
and made them aware of the severity of the order,
they still did not want
to leave her community.
It so happened that one man
1830   from among them became an avowed monk.
A priest of great humility,
he had been Saint Audrey's chaplain*
whom the abbess dearly loved
because of the goodness she saw in him,
1835   and because he was an example
of well-doing to her people.
Seaxburga, directed
by angels and by the power of God,
desired submission
1840   to the yoke of religion.
She confided this desire
to her close friends there with her*
and said to them: "I want to go away
to see my friends again,
1845   my sister Queen Audrey,
and the land where I was born.
I want to join her community
and receive her religious instruction.
I leave you here in God's care,
1850   and I have asked my daughter Ermenilda
to console and sustain you,
and thus she will do, come what may."
She did not delay
but went to Ely immediately.
1855   The abbess, her sister Audrey,
graciously came out to meet her
and took her into the abbey
where Saint Audrey wept with joy.
They comforted one other,
1860   and in God their joy was doubled.

Pur Deu se mist en povreté
Et guerpi sa grant richeté.
Sa soreur requist la roïne
Le veil pur estre en discipline.
Tut issi com[e] seint Pol fist   1865
Ki as piez Gamaliel se mist:
A grant honur fu receüe   fol 114r col 2
Ceste dame et la retenue.
Mut fu curïuse en servise
Jhesu Crist ou ele s'ert mise.   1870

En cel tens furent mut seüz
Signes et miracles veüs
De la roïne, seinte Audree,
Et de cele seinte assemblee:
En cors ou erent li dïeble   1875
Delivra la virge mirable,
Et de plusurs enfermetez,
Delivra Deus les enfermez
Et cil ki loinz furent d'Ely
Par li nomer furent gary.   1880
De totes gens estoit amee
Ceste roïne et honoree.
Par la devine demoustrance
A ses noneines dist en oiance
K'une pestilence vendroit   1885
Ke suer la maison decendroit.
Pur ce lur a devant moustré
Ke lur quers seient affermé
Et ke lur poors soient mendre
En cele pestilence atendre.   1890
[En] Elge ou icele abbeïe*
Fu ordenee et establie,
Sainte Audree ki dame fu
Par seinteté et par vertu
Tint le covent en honesté   1895
Et garda bien tot son heé.
Pur une grant dissencion
Ke nos ici vos mostr[er]om
Que fu entre le rei Egfrid
Et l'ercevesque seint Wolfrid,   1900
Ki le roy de son sé geta   fol 114v col 1
Ou seinte Audree sejorna

For the sake of God Seaxburga embraced poverty,
abandoning her great wealth.
She asked her sister Queen Audrey
for the veil to enter the order.
1865 All this was just as Saint Paul did
when he sat at the feet of Gamaliel.*
The lady was received into the order
with great honor and was retained there.
She became quite avid in the Lord's service
1870 to which she now dedicated her life.

During her time [as abbess] there were many
signs and miracles witnessed
by the queen Saint Audrey
and by her holy assembly.
1875 Bodies that were demon-possessed
were set free by the marvelous virgin.
And God delivered the sick
from many diseases.
Even those far away from Ely
1880 were healed merely by saying her name.
This queen was much loved
and honored by all people.
Through divine revelation
she told her nuns in the presence of all
1885 that a plague would
descend upon their house,
and that she had warned them in advance
so that their hearts would be set firm
and their fears abated
1890 while awaiting this pestilence.
In Ely where the abbey
had been built and chartered,
Saint Audrey, a woman of nobility
through her holiness and strength,
1895 ran the convent honorably
and kept it well all her life.
We will tell you of a great conflict
that developed
        between King Egfrid
1900 and the archbishop Saint Wilfrid
whom the king removed from his episcopal see.
[Because of it] Wilfrid stayed with Saint Audrey

Treis anz com[ë] en exil fu:
Ceo est par seint Bede coneu.
Sainte Audree enveia a Rome   1905
Pur lur bosoignes ce seint home
Pur lur abbeïe amender
Et lur dignitez comfermer.
Com seint Wolfrid de Rome vint,
Par Suxesse son chemin tint: 1910
Cel païs par u cil passa
A crestïenté atorna.
Saint Wolfrid quant fu veneü
En Ely fu bien receü.
Tel previlege i aporta   1915
Ke tut tens iert et durera.
En meïsme cel an finy
Seinte Audree ke tint Ely.

Le mal dont la dame moreut
Fu d'une enfleüre ki creut   1920
Soz la gorge, entur le col fu,
Dont la dame a tel mal eü
K'ele jeut et fu en langor.
Tant fu grevee en la dolor
Ke tuz furent dese[s]peré   1925
De sa vie et de sa saunté.
La virge en oroison manoit,
Sa char dantoit et destroinoit.*
A Deu rendi grace et merci
De la dolur qu'ele sueffri.   1930
Ele entendi ke Deu flaele
Ceuz k'il eime et ke il repele.
Les riches homes sunt tant mari
Et les povres tut autresi.
Les riches pur lur seingnorie,   1935   fol 114v col 2
Les povres pur lur grant aïe
De ceo ke lur donoit suvent
Ses asmones mut largement.
La seinte virge ert mut heitee
Et de son mal joieuse et lee   1940
Et dist sovent, par son deserte,
Li ert ceste dolur aperte
Pur les nuesches k'ele portoit
D'or, ou sovent se delitoit.

the three years he was in exile.
This fact is known by Saint Bede.
1905 Saint Audrey sent the holy man to Rome
for what they needed:
to get support for the abbey
by having their status confirmed.
When Saint Wilfrid returned from Rome
1910 his route took him through Sussex.
As he passed through that region
he converted it to Christianity.
When Saint Wilfrid arrived back
in Ely, he was well received,
1915 for he had brought back to them a privilege
of rights guaranteed to last forever.
In that same year Saint Audrey,
abbess of Ely, died.

The cause of the lady's death
1920 was a large swelling which grew
on her throat and spread around her neck.
The lady suffered so much pain from it
that she lay down quite ill.
She was so overcome by the pain
1925 that everyone despaired
for her health, even for her life.
But the virgin prayed continually.
so that she could [again] overcome and repress the flesh.
She even gave thanks and praise to God
1930 for the pain she suffered.
She knew that God chastises
those whom He loves and calls to Himself.
Rich men are burdened
and so are the poor:
1935 the rich because of their noble duties,
the poor because of their heavy taxes
often imposed by the very one who gives them
generous alms.*
The saintly virgin was joyously happy
1940 and pleased about her illness,
and often said that it was her own fault
that this suffering was visible on her
because of the gold necklaces she once wore
in which she took such delight.

Entur son col crut seinte Audree,   1945
Ke par cel malfeit fust grevee,
Mes ele espera et creï
Que par cel mal [ele] espeni
Le suerfait et la vanité
De l'or qu'elë avoit porté.   1950

Iceste virge glorïuse
Ke tant digne est et precïuse
Coveita et out grant desir
K'a son seigniur peüst venir.
Pur la dolur ke tant l'enpire   1955
Li firent venir un bon mire,
Kinefrid estoit cil nomez,
En fisique ert mut alosez.
Comandé li ont k'il ovreist
L'enfleürë et hors en mist   1960
L'humur ke dedenz ert atreite,
Et il i ha la plaie faite.
Par deuz jurs il essüaja
Cele enferté et aleja*
Par quei tuz eurent esperance   1965
Ke vie eust et deliverance,
Mes al tierz jur fu seinte Audree
De cele plaie si grevee
K'ele senti sanz nul resort   fol 115r col 1
Ke s'enferté traoit a mort.   1970
Ses compaignes fist assembler,
Tant com ele pooit parler,
Devant li pur reconforter
Et pur la vertu Deu mustrer.
Tute mist s'entente et sa vie   1975
En ymnes et en psalmodie
Ke Deu son esperist mist
En son regne et garde preïst
De li et de la compaignie
K'en son servise out establie.   1980
Son cors receut et puis fini,
En sa garde s'alme rendi.*
Granz dolurs menerent en plurs
Et les freres et les sorurs.
La sue alme boneüree   1985
Fu des angles en ciel portee.

1945   Saint Audrey believed that she suffered ill
around her neck because of that sin,
but she hoped and believed
that through her pain she expiated
the excess and vanity
1950   over the gold she had worn.

This glorious virgin
of such worth and esteem
wanted so much
to go to her Lord.
1955   Because the pain greatly worsened
they had a good doctor come to her.
His name was Kynefrid.
and he was well revered in the field of medecine.
They asked him to lance
1960   the swelling and let out
the humor which was filling it,
so he made an incision in it.
For two days the pain eased
and she felt better.
1965   As a result everyone hoped
that she would live and be healed.
But on the third day Saint Audrey
began to suffer so from the incision
that she felt she had no recourse,
1970   that she was dying of this infirmity.
She assembled her community
so that she might address them
to reassure them
and to demonstrate the power of God.
1975   She made every effort and used her remaining energy
to sing hymns and psalms.
Then she asked God to place her spirit
into His kingdom and to take care
of her and also of the community
1980   which she had established in His service.
She received His body [the host] and then died
commending her soul into His care.
Both the brothers and the sisters
expressed their profound grief in many tears.
1985   Her blessed soul
was borne to heaven by angels

Entre les virges fu asise
Et en lur compaignie mise.
A reïnes fu bien venue
Et des autres bien receüe.   1990
De juin la noveime kalende,
Bien est ke chacun i entende
Savons sa mort et son obit
Si com nos trovom en escrit,
Puis le sezeime an ke maistresse   1995
Avoit esté et abb[e]esse.
Entre ses compaignes fina,
Si com ençois le devisa,
Car ele avoit prié sovent
K'eles li fuessent en present.   2000
En un sarcu k'il eurent quis
De fust, la ont cel seint cors mis.
Setante nef anz sont passés   fol 115r col 2
Et sis cenz puis ke Deu fu nés
Kant la roïne, seinte Audree,   2005
Devia et fu enterree.
En tens Aldulf, si com j'entent,
E Loer ky fu roy de Kent
La roïne Audree moreut
Seintement si com faire deut.   2010
Seint Bede mostre une aventure
K'en sa char n'out corumpeüre:
Aprés sa mort ne k'en sa vie
N'est entamie ne blemie.
A sa tombe ont plusurs eüe   2015
Santé des mals et receüe.
Par avision li plusur
I sont garriz de lur dolur.
Les dïebles de plusurs cors
[A sa tombe sont issis hors.]*   2020
De totes manieres des maus
Garit Deu plusurs et fist saus
Et les simples furent oÿ
Qui crïerent a Deu merci
Ky vit et regne et regnera   2025
In seculorum secula.

Seint Hunus le servise fist
Et l'abb[e]esse en terre mist

and was seated in the company
of the virgin saints.
She was welcomed by queens
1990   and well received by all.
Everyone should know
that the ninth [day] of the kalends of June,*
is the date of her death,
as it is so recorded.
1995   After six years*
of being mistress and abbess,
she expired amid her companions,
just as she had always wanted it,
for she had often prayed
2000   that they be present with her [at her death].
They had sought out a wooden sarcophagus
in which they placed that holy body.
Six hundred and seventy-nine years had passed
since the birth of God [Christ]
2005   when the queen, Saint Audrey,
passed away and was buried.
I believe it was during the time of Aldulf,
when Hlothere was king of Kent,
that Queen Audrey died
2010   in the saintly way that she merited.
Saint Bede relates a story
[which indicates] that her flesh did not decay.
After her death, just as in her life
she was neither tainted nor blemished.
2015   At her tomb many received
cure from their ills;
many had visions of her at the tomb
and were healed of their sufferings.
[At her tomb] devils
2020   [came forth] out of many bodies.
God healed people of all kinds of diseases,
making them whole again.
And simple folk who cried to Him for mercy
were heard by God
2025   who lives and reigns and will reign
forever and ever.

Saint Huna performed the service
and placed the abbess in the ground

En la compaignie de ceus
K'ele out tenu pour ses feeus: 2030
En un sarcu de fust l'ont mise
En cimiteire de l'eglise.
N'i out orgueil d'argent ne d'or
Ne piere a mettre cel tresor.
Granz [genz] out a cel assemblee,*   2035
Viez et jofnes de la contree
A ky ele out mut grant bien fait.
Saint Hunus cel estre leit,   fol 115v col 1
En un sotil liu s'en ala
Ke l'em puis Humeie apella.   2040
De son non Humeie receut
Le non par ceo qu'il i esteut.
Solitaire vie mena
Pur Deu tant com il i dura.
Aprés sa mort dist de cestui   2045
Ke Deu fist miracle pur lui.
Plusurs genz en urent santé
Et garrirent d'enfermeté.
Icil ky les miracles virent
Celeement les os cuillirent,   2050
Dedenz un sarcu les poserent,
A Thorneie les aporterent,
Car il avoient bien espoir
Ke vers Deu lur peüst vale[i]r.

L'an ke sainte Audree moreut   2055
Et que Jhesu Crist la receut,
Unkes si grant miracle avint
Ke la gent a merveillie tint
D'un sergant ke l'avoit servie
Dementiers k'ele fust en vie.   2060
Seint Bede moustrë a la gent
Pur ceo ke profist i entent.
Eg[el]frid qui out [a] espose
Seinte Audree la glorïuse
Gueroia le roy Edelreit   2065
Ke Merchenelande teneit.
Ou lur granz hoz ke il banirent
Delez Trente se combatirent,
La fu Alwines occis,
Frere Eg[el]frid et ses amis.   2070

in the presence of those
2030 whom she considered her faithful ones.
They buried her, in the wooden coffin,
within the church cemetery.
There was no proud silver or gold
nor precious stone to adorn this treasure.
2035 There were a great many people in that assembly—
old and young alike from the area
for whom she had done so much good.
Saint Huna abandoned the life he was living
and went away to a solitary place
2040 which since then has been called Huneya.
Huneya got its name from him
because that was where he lived.
He led a solitary life
for God as long as he lived.
2045 After his death it was said
that God performed miracles through him,
A number of people had their health restored,
having been healed of some infirmity.
Those who witnessed these miracles
2050 secretly gathered his bones,
placed them inside a sarcophagus,
and carried them to Thorney,
for they fervently hoped
this gesture would be of value to them before God.

2055 The year that Saint Audrey died
and was received by Jesus Christ,
one particular miracle occurred,
which caused people to marvel.
It concerned a servant who had been in her service
2060 while she was alive.
Saint Bede relates it to the people
so that they might profit from it.
Egfrid, who [once] had glorious Saint Audrey
as his wife,
2065 went to war against King Ethelred
who held Mercia.
The great armies they had both raised
fought beside the river Trent.
Egfrid's brother Alwin
2070 and his friends were killed in the battle.

Edelreit, cist devant dit roys,
Dont li livres parla einçois, fol 115v col 2
Il avoit Hostride esposee,
Lur soreur, ky li fu donee.
Entre les autres fu tüez 2075
Un hom, Yma ert apellez.
Tut le jur jeut si com occis,
En demein fu trové tut vifs.
Ses plaies estreint et benda,
Aler s'en vout, tant s'enforça. 2080
Mes tost aprés l'out coneü
La gent Edelreit et l'out tenu.
Le menerent a lur seigniur,
Un conte de [mut] grant valur.
Il le receut, si s'entremist 2085
A son pooir qui le garist.
Kant il comença a garir,
Sil vout lïer pur li tenir.
Kant cil ky l'avoient lïé
De li estoient enloignié, 2090
Deslïé se trovoit et seins
Des piez, des jambes et de[s] meins.
Hom li enquist coment ceo fu
Ke li lïen ne l'out tenu.
Cil lur repondi que il out 2095
Un frere abbé qui conversout
A Toncestrë en l'abbeïe.
Prestrë estoit de seinte vie.
Tunnus a non cil Dieu amis:
« Il quida ke je fuesse occis. 2100
Messes ha chantees por mei.
Pur ceo sui deslïé, ceo crei. »
Pur vendre a Londres ont mené
Cestui, Fresus l'a achaté
Mes mut feisoit a merveillier 2105
Ke nul ne[l] pout si ferm lïer fol 116r col 1
A l'hore ke Tunnus chantast
Ke delïé ne se trovast.
Come Fresus iceo entent,
Si l'en a [pro]mis par serment* 2110
K'en brïef terme a lui vendra,
Et sa raünson li dorra.
Al roy Loher ky ert en Kent

King Ethelred,
whom the book mentioned before,
had been given in marriage Ostryth,
Alwin's and Egfrid's sister.
2075 Among the others killed in the battle
was a man named Yma.
All day he lay as if dead,
but the next day he found himself alive.
He closed and bound his wounds
2080 and tried to get away as best he could.
But right away Ethelred's men
recognized him and captured him.
They led him to their lord,
a very worthy count
2085 who received him; thus he [Yma] submitted himself
to the power of this man who could offer him protection.
As he began to get well, the count had him tied up
     to keep him from getting away again.
Whenever the men who had bound him
2090 distanced themselves somewhat from him,
Yma became loose, with no harm
to his feet, legs, and hands.
When they asked him how it could be
that the ropes did not hold him,
2095 he answered that he had
a brother, an abbot, who lived
in Tonchester at the abbey,
a priest who led a holy life.
This friend of God was named Tunna.
2100 "He thought that I had been killed,
so he chanted masses for me.
I do believe that is why I became unbound."
Then they took him to be sold in London.
where Fresus bought him.*
2105 But it was greatly marveled
that no one could bind him securely enough
so that at the hour when Tunna chanted
he would not become unbound.
Once Fresus was made aware of this,
2110 Yma swore to him
that in a short time he would come back
and give him the necessary ransom money.
So he went right away

S'en ala cist hastivement.
S'aventure li a contee, 2115
Le roy Loher li ad donee
Sa raünson, et cil ala
A Fresus, si s'en aquita.
Cist fu botellier seinte Audree
Kant Eg[el]frid l'out esposee. 2120
Loher fu fiz de sa soreur,
Pur ceo fist a cestui honur.
A son frere est alé Ysma,
Tut en ordre le reconta
Coment et en quel hure avint 2125
Ke lïens n'anieus ne li tint.
Ceo sout bien et creüt Tunna
Ke ceo est a l'heure k'il chanta.
Par la prïere de cestui
Avindrint autres biens a lui. 2130
Essemple en pristrent par raison
D'amones faire et d'oreison ·
Plusurs ky l'oïrent conter
Pur lur bons amis delivrer.
Cist Ysma ne fu mie suls 2135
Ke Deus, li peres glorïus,
A plusurs en fist aïe
Ky sainte Audree eurent servie*
Si com de Huna et d'Oswy,
Et d'un Elger ki la servi 2140 fol 116r col 2
Dont nos aprés devom parler.
Il ne feïst a oblïer.

Cele seinte virge honoree
Ki remist aprés seinte Audree
En Ely, Werborc out a non: 2145
Mut fu de grant religion.
Rey Edelred, son uncle, oÿ
La seintee et le bien de ly.
De deuz covens la fist maistresse
Et benesquist a abb[e]esse.* 2150
A Wintringham li menerent
Et [a] Hamborc li comanderent
Ou mut out seinte compaignie
Des dames et riche abbeïe.

to King Hlothere of Kent,
2115 and told him the whole story.
The king gave him the ransom money,
he returned to Fresus,
and thus he regained his freedom.
Yma had been Saint Audrey's butler*
2120 when she was married to King Egfrid;
Hlothere was the son of Audrey's sister [Seaxburga],
and that is why he honored the man's request.
Yma went to his brother [the abbot]
and recounted to him all the events, one after another,
2125 how and at exactly what time it happened
that neither cords nor chains could hold him.
Tunna believed his story and realized
that the unbinding occurred at the very hour he chanted.
Through Tunna's prayers
2130 other good things came to Yma.
Many who heard this story
rightly took it as an example
to give alms and to pray
for the deliverance of their good friends.
2135 Yma was not the only one,
for God, the Glorious Father,
helped many people
who had served Saint Audrey,
such as Huna, Ovin,
2140 and a certain Elger who also served her,
but we will speak of him later,
for he must not be forgotten.*

The holy honored virgin
named Werburga
2145 remained in Ely after Saint Audrey passed away.
She was very devoutly religious.
King Etheldred, her uncle, hearing
about her saintliness and goodness,
made her mistress of two convents
2150 and ordained her as abbess:
she was sent to Wintringham
after which she was placed in Hanbury
where there was a very saintly community
of ladies and a wealthy abbey.*

Aprés le decés seinte Audree   2155
Fu seinte Sexborc apellee
Par Deu et par election
Qu'ele gardast cele maison
Et cele seinte compaignie
Ky en Ely fu establie.   2160
De Deu fu Sexborc espiree
Par les merites seinte Audree.
Essample prist de sa sorur,
Le covent tint a grant honur.
Ceste dame dont nos parlom   2165
De Deu out inspiration
De voir les os seintë Audree
Et qu'ele feüst remuee.
Mettre les vout honestement
Et garder les puis dignement.   2170
Meint miracle out sovent veü
A la tombe ou ele a geü:
Lur establi de visiter
Cel seint tresor et regarder.   fol 116v col 1
Au covent le mostra et dist   2175
[Et] mut loërent Jhesu Crist.

De ses freres aparaillia
E pur quere les enveia
Sarcu de pierre covenable
A mettre cel tresor mirable,   2180
Car n'en aveit nul en Ely.
Par la Deu grace avint issi:
A Grantecestre ou il alerent
En Armesworde une en troverent
Delés le mur de la cité.   2185
De blanc marbre l'ont avisé.
Les veisins mut se merveillierent.
Il ne surent ne ne quiderent
Qu'onques tel piere fu veüe.
. . . .*   2190
Distrent ke Deu l'out tramise
Pur la virge ki leenz ert mise.
Un covercle ont desus trové
De colur et de quantité
Autre tiel com li sarcu fu   2195

2155   After the death of Saint Audrey
       Saint Seaxburga was called
       by God and by election
       to maintain the house
       and the holy community
2160   that was established in Ely.
       Through the will of God Seaxburga was inspired
       by the merits of Saint Audrey
       and followed her sister's example
       of governing the convent most honorably.
2165   This particular lady
       was led by God
       to view the bones of Saint Audrey
       and to have her body moved.
       She wanted to put the bones in a worthy place
2170   and keep them in more appropriate manner,
       for she had seen many a miracle occur
       at the tomb where her sister was laid to rest.
       She directed her people to go
       and look at that holy treasure.
2175   She showed the body and spoke at the monastery,
       and they all greatly praised Jesus Christ.

       She appointed some of the brothers
       to go in search of
       an appropriate stone sarcophagus
2180   in which to place this marvelous treasure,
       for there was nothing suitable in Ely.
       By the grace of God this is what happened:
       they went to Cambridge
       and found one made of white marble
2185   beside the city wall
       in Armsworth.*
       The inhabitants were amazed,
       for they did not believe
       that such a stone had ever been seen there.
2190   . . . .
       They said that God had sent it
       for the virgin who would be put inside.
       Near this place where God had led them,
       they found a lid
2195   of the same color and dimensions

Ou par Deu furent aveneu.
Cil furent lez, Deu mercïerent
Ensemble ou eus l'en aporterent.
Bon orree eurent et bon vent,
En Ely vindrent leement.   2200
Le sarcu portent a l'eglise
Ou la seinte reïne ert mise.
Seinte Sexborc grant joie en fist
[Et] Deu et ses seins benesquist.
Granz gens de malades i out   2205
Que Deu pur la virge sanout:
Ky le sarcu eurent sivi,
Deu lur dona santé pur li.*   fol 116v col 2
La novele fu espandue
Par tute Engleterrë et sue   2210
Del remuement seinte Audree.
Mut i out granz genz assemblee.

Le jur vint qui estoit nomé
Ke cil seint cors fu remüé.
Sesze anz out en terre geü.   2215
Mut i a grant pople venu
A icele sollempnetee.
De toz doit estre confermee
Ceo qu'il ont veü et oÿ
A la translation de ly.   2220
Seint Wolfrid l'erceveske dist,
Noneine velee le fist:*
En quel conseil ele out esté
Testimoine li a porté
K'ele out virginité gardee   2225
Pur quanqu'ele fust esposee,
Et bien garda tot son aage
Virginité et puceleage.
Kinefrid i fu qui conta
De l'enfleure dont la taillia   2230
Ke il vit sa vie et sa mort
Dont plusurs ont joie et efort.
Le pople par devotion
Alerent a procession
Ou psalmes et ou melodie   2235
La u ele estoit enfoïe.
Kant le sarcu eurent overt

as the sarcophagus.
They rejoiced, thanking God for it;
then they left with the objects.
The winds were favorable
2200 and they arrived happily in Ely.
They carried the sarcophagus into the church
where the holy queen was to be placed.
Saint Seaxburga expressed great joy,
blessing God and his saints.
2205 Quite a number of sick people
who had followed the sarcophagus
were healed by God through the virgin:
God gave them health because of her.
The news about the translation
2210 of Saint Audrey spread
throughout all England.
and a crowd of people assembled there.

The appointed day came
when that holy body was to be moved.
2215 It had lain in the earth for sixteen years.
A great many people came to Ely
for this solemn occasion.
All those present can confirm
what they saw and heard
2220 at Saint Audrey's translation.
Saint Wilfrid, the archbishop,
who had been her counselor, spoke saying
that he had veiled her as a nun,
and he affirmed the fact
2225 that she had kept her virginity
even though she was married,
that, indeed, throughout her entire life
she had kept her maidenhood.
Then Kynefrid told
2230 about the tumor that he lanced for her
and said that he had observed her life and death,
both of which brought joy and strength to many people.
Singing psalms and hymns
out of devotion for her,
2235 people went in procession
to the place where she was buried.
When the sarcophagus was opened,

Le cors virent tut en apert
Si entier et en tel semblant
Come d'une femme dormant.   2240
A grant merveillie l'unt tenue
Ki ont la virge itel veüe.   fol 117r col 1
Onkes mes n'oïrent parler
Ke cors peüst entier durer.
Pur ceo qu'ele out son cors gardé   2245
Pur Deu et sa virginité
Et fu por li et chaste et pure,
L'a gardé Deu d'entameüre.
La plaie k'avoit sainte Audree
En son col fu tute sanee   2250
Ke Kenifrid li fist aperte.
A sa mort fu uncore overte.
La vertu Deu omnipotent
Fu clere en cel remuement.
Cil ke fist le boisson ardoir,   2255
Et en clere flambe aparoir,
Si qu'il nen art [ne] n'enpira,
Et [cil] qui Daniel delivra
De la fosse ou il fu geté,
Ke de lionz [ne] fu[st] devoré,   2260
Cil garda ce cors de porir
Et d'[em]pirer et de blesmir.

O reverence ou honesté
Cel seint cors ont bien lavé;
En novel souaire l'unt mise   2265
Si l'en porterent en l'eglise.
En sarcu k'il ourent trové
Par Deu et illuec aporté
Mistrent icel seintime cors.
Uncore i gist cist chier tresors,   2270
La atendra l'avenement
Del rey de gloire omnipotent.
Merveillie ont del sarcu veü
Qui a tel mesure fu
N'en lé n'en long plus [ne] manoit   2275
Fors autent [qu']au cors covenoit.   fol 117r col 2
Kant le cors ont en sarcu mis
Le covercle ont desus asis.
Le[s] pierres ensemble se pristrent

they clearly saw the body
completely whole, resembling
2240　a woman sleeping.
They considered it a great miracle
to have seen the virgin like that,
since they had never heard
that a body could remain intact [after death].
2245　But because she had kept her body
and virginity for God
and had remained pure and chaste for Him,
God prevented her from decomposing.
The wound that Saint Audrey
2250　had in her neck, the one that Kynifrid had opened,
and that at her death was still open,
was now completely healed.
The power of Almighty God
was clear in this change.
2255　He who made the bush to burn
and to appear in bright flames
so that it was neither consumed nor damaged,*
and He Who saved Daniel
from being devoured by lions
2260　in their den where he was thrown,*
He was the One Who kept Saint Audrey's body from rotting,
losing its freshness, or fading.

With reverence and propriety
they carefully washed that holy body,
2265　wrapped it in a new shroud,
then carried it into the church.
They put the most holy body
into the sarcophagus that they had found
and brought there through God's help,
2270　where this cherished treasure yet lies.
There she will await the coming
of the omnipotent King of Glory.*
Those who saw the sarcophagus marveled
that its measurements were such
2275　that it was neither longer or wider
than necessary to accommodate the body.
After they had placed the body in the sarcophagus,
they fitted the lid on top.
Then the stones began to fuse together,

Et si joinstrent et [si] asistrent 2280
Ke nul ne pooit veir jointure
N'ou avoit esté l'overture.
Merveillieus ert cil enginieres
Ky si fist joindre les deuz pierres:
Cist sire qui l'iaue envoia 2285
As fiz Israël et dona
Et la fist au pople commune
Pout faire de deuz perres une.
Cist Deu ke fist l'habitement
Par meins d'angles a seint Clement 2290
En la mer ou deut gesir
Lur fist icel sarcu polir
A l'oez la virge seinte Audree
La roïne bon[e]üree.
Sis cenz et setante nef anz 2295
Et sesze, seint Bede e[s]t disanz,
Puis l'incarnation Jhesu
Quant ceste translation fu
Erent passés et acomplis,
Si com nos mostre[nt] les escris. 2300

Granz miracles e granz vertuz
De la virge sont avenuz
Ke nos ne devom pas celer
Mes avant dire et reconter.
Ceo nos reconte l'escripture 2305
K'autre[tiel] fu sa vest[e]üre
Si juieus, si fresche, si bele
Com[e] le jur ke la pucele
I out esté ensevelie:
Nule chose ne fu blemie. 2310   fol 117v col 1
Li plusur par atochement
De dras eurent delivrement
De l'enemi ki les travaillia,
Et les ydropiques sana.
Cils ky a sa tombe venoient 2315
De lur granz mals gariz estoient.
De ce ne nos merveilliom mie:
El le deservi en sa vie.
Grant entente mist de saner
Les malades et visiter. 2320

2280 and join and seal
       so that no one could detect the seam
       where the opening had been.
       Marvelous was the Engineer
       who joined these two stones!
2285 The same Lord who sent water
       to the children of Israel
       and made it available to all His people*
       could certainly blend the two stones into one.
       The same God who through the hands of angels
2290 made a dwelling place for Saint Clement
       in the sea where he lay*
       commanded the angels to smooth out the sarcophagus
       used for the virgin Saint Audrey,
       the blessed noble queen.
2295 Saint Bede says that
       six hundred seventy-nine years plus sixteen
       had passed
       since the incarnation of Jesus
       when this translation took place,
2300 just as the writings show us.

       Great miracles and demonstrations of power
       came from the virgin;
       we will certainly not conceal them
       but continue to tell more about them.
2305 The writing tells us
       that her clothing was exactly the same—
       as bright, as fresh, as beautiful
       as the day the maiden
       was buried in them.
2310 Nothing had faded.
       By touching her linens
       several people were delivered
       from the devil who was tormenting them,
       and she cured people afflicted with dropsy.
2315 Those who came to the tomb
       were healed of their terrible illnesses.
       We are not at all surprised by this,
       for she merited it during her lifetime:
       she made a great effort to visit
2320 the sick and to cure them.

Del sarcu de fuest nos redist
Ou el jeut, ke nul ne le vist
Qui de ses ieus n'eüst santé
S'il i eüst enfermeté.
Ki dedenz peüst mettre son chief   2325
Ja n'i eüst dolur si grief
K'il ne fuest gariz sanz demure:
Sein s'en ala en un pou d'heure.

Ke la verité veut enquerre:
De[l] liu ou le cors jeut en terre,   2330
Sourt de duce ewe une fontaine
[A] merveillies sanable et seine.
Plusurs i ont eü santé
Ky en beivent et sont arosé.
Cunoïst cil qui fist l'escrit   2335
Que il a reconté et dist
Ceo qu'il out oÿ et veü
Et par autre genz entendu,
Et si requier nostre Seigniur
Par sa pitié et sa duçur   2340
Ke de li deigne merci aver,
Et que li doint force et poër
De miracles dire et conter
Et de son livreson finer   fol 117v col 2
Qu'il en hait guerdon et grié   2345
De la seintime Trinité.

Quant la roïne seinte Audree
De cel siecle fu trespassee
Sodeinement, ç'avons oÿ,
Bien fu confesse et bien [fini]*   2350
Devant le covent de l'eglise.
Ke fu a faire icel servise
Sexborc ki mut ert vertueuse
En Deu servise et glorïuse.
Cele dame ert suer seinte Audree.   2355
Li out la [cure] delivree
Et mis en garde le covent
El les treita mut seintement.
Deu mostra bien k[e] il amout
Son servise quant il li plout   2360
Ke le cors sa sorur veïst.*

Concerning the wooden sarcophagus where she had lain,
we are told that anyone who looked on it
was healed of any infirmity of the eye
that he might have had.
2325 Anyone who put his head inside it
would have immediate relief
no matter how bad the headache,
and he would go away cured in a short time.

For the benefit of those seeking the truth:
2330 from the place where her body had lain in the ground
there springs forth a fountain of fresh water
wonderfully curative and pure.
A number of people have been healed there
when they drank the water and or were sprinkled with it.
2335 The author of the book must know this to be true,
for he recounted
what he himself had both seen and heard
and also what he had heard through other people.
And he beseeches our Lord
2340 through His pity and kindness
to have mercy on him,
and to give him the strength and ability
to relate the miracles
and complete his presentation
2345 so that he might receive recompense and grace
from the Most Holy Trinity.

When Queen Saint Audrey
passed suddenly from this world,
as we have heard,
2350 she was properly confessed and her life ended well
in the presence of the church community.
So Seaxburga, who was quite virtuous
and glorious in the service of God,
was next to perform the service [as abbess].
2355 She was the sister of Saint Audrey
who had handed over the convent to her,
placing it in her charge.
Seaxburga governed them in a most holy manner.
God showed that he indeed esteemed
2360 her service to Him when it pleased Him
to let her see the body of her sister.

En [un] novel sarcu le mist
Kant cist seint cors fu regardé
Autresi entier fu trové
Com[e] le jur qu'ele fini   2365
Et quant hom l'ad enseveli.
Kant seinte Sexborc out vescu
Long tens, icel covent tenu,
La seinte dame enmaladi
En bone vielliesce fini.   2370
Bien sout le jur k'elë iroit
A son seigniur et fineroit.
Delez sa sorur l'enfoïrent,
Glorïeus sepulcre li firent.
Grant miracle fist Deu pur li   2375
Kar a plusurs santé rendi.
Seinte Ermenild fu aprés li,
Sa fillie, abb[e]esse en Ely.   fol 118r col 1
Le siecle haÿ et despi[s]t
En povreté pur Deu se mist.   2380

Si com nos reconte l'estoire
Ke saint Bede mist en memoire,
Seinte Sexborc en Sepie
Receut le veil et fu veleie
De l'erceveske Thederi   2385
Et puis s'en ala en Ely.
Sa fillie Ermenild i lessa
Et icel liu li comanda.
Quant seinte Sexborc i fini
Si s'en ala ceste en Ely.   2390
En son liu a sa fillie mise,
Werborc, pur governer l'eglise.
Kant ceste dame fu finie
Pres de s'aunte l'ont sevelie.
La mort de li fu precïuse   2395
Et en Jhesu Crist glorïuse.

Aprés sa mere a receü
Le covent d'Ely et tenu
Ceste virge, seinte Werborc,
Mes ele transi en Emborc;   2400
Mes puis fu son cors remüé
D'eluec et a Cestre porté.

She put it in a new sarcophagus,
and when the holy body was placed on view,
it was found to be completely whole,
2365 just as it was the day she died
and was buried.
When Saint Seaxburga had lived her life
and held the convent for a long time,
this holy woman fell ill
2370 and died at a fine old age.
She was well aware of the day that she would die
and go to her Lord.
They buried her beside her sister
and made her a splendid sepulcher.
2375 God performed great miracles through her,
for she restored health to many people.
After Seaxburga, her daughter Ermenilda
was made abbess in Ely.
She disdained the world,
2380 and became poor for the sake of God.

Just as the story
recorded by Saint Bede tells us,
Saint Seaxburga entered orders in Sheppey
and was veiled
2385 by Archbishop Theodore,
then later went to Ely.
She left her daughter Ermenilda there [at Sheppey],
entrusting the place to her keeping.
Then, when Saint Seaxburga died,
2390 her daughter went off to Ely,
and in her place Ermenilda left her daughter
Werburga to govern the church.
When Ermenilda died,
she was buried near her aunt, Saint Audrey.
2395 Her death in Jesus Christ
was precious and glorious.

After her mother, this virgin,
Saint Werburga, received
and held the convent at Ely,
2400 yet she died in Hanbury;*
but then her body was removed
from there and carried to Chester.

Aprés le decés seinte Audree
Et puis Sexborc ke fu finee
Et seinte Ermenild et Werborc,   2405
Ky fu ensevelie a Emborc,
Dura la congregation
D'Ely et la religion
De[s] dames ki remises furent
Et ki en l'eglise aresteurent   2410
En pes et en grant seinteté
Et bien eurent lur digneté,   fol 118r col 2
Deskë Ingar vint en la terre
Et Hubbe pur la gent conquere.
Hulf et Alfdene i sont venu   2415
Ou grant defforz com ont eü.
Ensemble ou eus treis reis menerent,
Tote Bretaignie environerent*
Hosteng et Baseng et Gintron,
Si eurent les treis rois a non.   2420
Par ces fu le regne gardé
Ke ge vos ai ici nomé.
Tant ont par le païs alé
K'il sont en Ely arivé.
L'yle gastirent et maumistrent   2425
Totes ses noneines occistrent.
Le moster ont ars et robbé
Et tot l'avoir ont enporté.

A ceste gent un home avoit
Ky serjant au d[ï]eble estoit.   2430
Cil vint au sarcu seinte Audree,
La roïne bon[e]üree:
Tresor quida trover dedenz
Et ke ceo fust or ou argent.
Ou sa hache feri desus,   2435
Si qu'il i fist un grant pertus.
Mes Deu en meïme l'eure
De sa vengance ne fist demeure.
Pur la merite seinte Audree
I a [sa] puissance moustree.   2440
Les ieus perdi et puis mureut
Malement, si com faire deut.
Aprés long tens a cele eglise
Vindrent ses clers a Deu servise.

After the death of Saint Audrey
and then the demise of Seaxburga,
2405 Saint Ermenilda, and Werburga
who was buried in Hanbury,
the congregation of Ely continued
and so did the religious life
of the ladies who had been placed there.
2410 They lived in the church community
in peace and great holiness
and kept their privilege
until Ingwar and Ubba came to the area
to conquer its people.*
2415 Ulf and Halfdan also came there
to do as much violence as they could.
Three kings who went all over Britain
came with them:
Haesten, Bagsecg, and Guthrum
2420 were their names.
The kingdom was held by these three
whom I have just named for you.
They went all through the land
until they arrived in Ely
2425 where they laid waste the island, wrought great destruction,
and killed all the nuns.
They burned and pillaged the church
and carried off all the possessions.

Among these people there was a man,
2430 a servant of the devil,
who came upon the sarcophagus of Saint Audrey,
the blessed queen.
He believed he would find some treasure inside
and thought that it might be gold or silver.
2435 He struck the top of it with his ax so hard
that he made a great hole in it.
But as soon as he did, God
did not delay His vengeance.
Because of Saint Audrey's worth,
2440 He demonstrated His power:
The man lost his eyes and then died
in a terrible manner, as indeed he should have.*
Much later clerics in the service of God
came to this church

En cel liu ont tant demoré   2445
K'Edrez fu rois en poësté,   fol 118v col 1
Mes pur iceo ke il ne furent
De tel vie cum estre durent
Ne reverence n'ont portee
Al glorïus cors seinte Audree,   2450
Furent getez de la maison
Et perdirent lur mansion.
Ci conte ke li maistres d'eus
Sovente foiz dist a iceus
K'il descreï que pas ne fust   2455
Iluec le sèint cors ne g[e]üst.
S'ele i fust remise, ce dist,
Plusurs miracles i veïst.
Un de ses compaignions li dist
Un grant miracle par respit: 2460

Une dame qui pres estoit
Contreite ert k'el ne se movoit.
Ses mains ne pooit avant traire
Pur li seignier ne la croix faire.
A ouit homes se fist porter   2465
Desqu'a l'eglise et amener
Devant le fiertre seinte Audree:
En tut fut garie et sanee,
S'en i ala ceste a maison
Glorifiant Deu et son non.   2470

D'un home conte ki manoit
A Bradeford, [cil] muz estoit:
Set anz avoit issi esté
Que il n'avoit nïent parlé.
Ses parenz le menerent ci,   2475
Sa parole out, sachez de fi.
Devant toz dist ke seinte Audree
Sa parole li out donee.

Une pucele avuegle nee
Sa veüe had recovree.   2480   fol 118v col 2
Diz anz avoit quant ele i vint
Et quant cist miracles avint.

Un bachelier ne fu pas seins

2445   and stayed there as long as
        King Edred was in power.
        But because they did not lead
        the kind of life that they should have,
        nor did they revere
2450   the glorious body of Saint Audrey,
        they were turned out of the house
        and lost their living quarters.
        It is said that their master
        often told them
2455   that he did not believe
        that the holy body lay there.
        If she had been laid to rest there, he said,
        he would have seen a number of miracles.
        One of his companions in the community told him
2460   of a great miracle as a cautionary exemplum:

        A lady who lived nearby
        was so stiff that she could not move.
        She could not even bring her hands forward
        to make the sign of the cross.
2465   So she had herself carried by eight men
        all the way to the church and brought
        before the shrine of Saint Audrey.
        She was completely healed,
        and went home
2470   glorifying God and His name.

        He also told him about a man
        living in Bradford who was mute.
        For seven years,
        he had not spoken a word.
2475   His parents brought him to the church
        where, be assured, he received his speech.
        He declared before all that it was Saint Audrey
        who restored his ability to speak.

        A maiden born blind
2480   recovered her sight.
        She was ten years old when she came there
        and this miracle occurred.

        A young man was not sound of body—

Einz ert contrait d'une de[s] meins.
Ici vint, la tombe atocha   2485
Ou cele mein, sein s'en ala.

D'un prestre dit ke sa quisine
Out comandé a sa meschine.
En un di[e]meine le dist
Devant tierce ke chous cuillist.   2490
Par destresce la fist aler
Et un pel en sa mein porter,
Pur foïr les chous mist en terre.
Le pel mes a sa mein li serre,
Ne l'en poeit partir ne hostir,   2495
Au provere le vait mostrir,
Mut en fu tristes et dolenz:
Merveillie fu a meinte genz.
Le pel ont de deuz pars coupé,
Issi a suenc anz demoré.   2500
« A un convive la venimes
Et cele aventure veïmes.
Nos disimes a cel proveire
Ke cil vousit promettre et creire,
Et la cheitive fust menee   2505
Desquë al fiertre seinte Audree,
K'elë avroit pitié de lui,
Si li f[e]roit grace et merci.'
Einz ke mangissomes, alames
Al fiertrë et pur li priames.   2510
Deu pur la virge fist vertuz:
Hors de sa mein chaÿ li fuz.
Mut en furent l[i]ez sy parent
Et li autre communaument.   fol 119r col 1
Pur ceo, maistre, ceo lo en fey   2515
Ke les biens de la virge crey.
Si les biens ne creis de la dame
Ton cors le comperra et t'amme. »*
Cil est veirs li mut corociez
Si a quatre homes envoiez   2520
Et comanda ke il ovrissent
Lou sarcu et le cors veïssent.

Issi com en cest escrit truis
En sarcu avoit un pertuis

one of his hands was paralyzed.
2485 He came here, touched the tomb
with that hand, and went away whole.

He told about a priest who commanded
his servant girl to prepare his meal.
He told her to pick some cabbages
2490 one Sunday before terce.
Authoritatively he made her take
a stick in her hand and go.
In order to dig the cabbages she put the stick
into the ground, but it stuck in her [closed] hand,
2495 and she could not get it out.
She showed it to the priest
who felt very sad and sorry about it.
Many people were puzzled by this.
Finally they cut off the two ends of the stick,
2500 and her hand stayed like that for five years.
"We went to share a meal there
and saw this amazing thing.
We told the priest
that he should be willing to act on faith,
2505 and have the poor girl taken
to the shrine of Saint Audree
who would take pity on her
and accord her grace and mercy.
So before we ate, we went
2510 to the shrine and prayed for her.
God, for the virgin's sake, did a miraculous thing:
the stick fell out of her hand.
Her parents were overjoyed by this,
as was everyone else.
2515 For this reason, master, I declare in faith
that I believe in the good deeds of the virgin.
If you do not believe in the lady's beneficent power,
then your body and your soul will pay for it."
The master became quite angry with him,
2520 and commanded four men
to go open
the sarcophagus and view the body.

I learned from the book that
there was a hole in the sarcophagus

K'un Denois ou sa hache fist   2525
Dont Jhesu Crist vengance prist.
Quant li Danois et si compaignion
Destruierent sa terre environ,
Clers, noneines et autre gent
Occistrent tut comunaument   2530
Fors les jefnes k'il amenerent,
En cheitivesons les livrerent.
Un home [i] ert de Normandie
Ki mut enprist grant estotie:
Seur le sarcu set foiz feri,   2535
Les ieus perdi et puis fini.
Aprés la grant destruction,
Si com en cronike trovom
Dit, [li] clers ki s'en furent fuï ·
Revindrent ariere en Ely.   2540
Li malurez prestres i vint
Ki ou eus compaignie tint.
Al sarcu seinte Audree alerent:
Ou crocs de fer ke il porterent
Voleient acrocher le cors   2545
Et auscun de dras mettre hors.
Li uns dist a ses compaignions:
« Pur nïent [nos] en duterons   fol 119r col 2
K'enter ne soit le cors de li
Si com le jur qu'ele fini.   2550
Ceo verrez vos hastivement,
Deu en prenge grief vengement. »
Li prestre di: « Ge pris mut poy
Des vieus les essamples ke g'oy.
Ore verrai si sa vesture   2555
Est bien entiere et uncor dure. »
Ou une chandeile qu'il tint
Al pertuis de la tombe vint.
De cel seint cors voleit savoir,
Mes il n'en pout mie veoir.   2560
Dedenz le sarcu li chaoit
La chandeile ke il tenoit.
Ardant i fu si longement
Ke merveillie fu a la gent
Ke les dras ne furent bruliez   2565
Et le cors de li entamez,
Car bien fu lur apparissant

2525   made with an ax by a Dane
        on whom Jesus Christ took vengeance.
        When the Dane and his companions
        destroyed the land in the area,
        they killed clerics and nuns
2530   and other people as well,
        except for the young whom they carried away
        and made slaves.
        There was a man from Normandy*
        who acted with foolish boldness:
2535   He struck the sarcophagus seven times,
        lost his eyes, and then died.
        After the great destruction,
        as we find written in the chronicles,
        clerics who had fled
2540   came back to Ely.
        The unbelieving priest also came
        back with them.
        They went to the sarcophagus of Saint Audrey
        carrying iron hooks,
2545   for they wanted to hook the body
        and pull out some of the clothing.
        One of them said to his companions:
        "We should in no way doubt
        that her body is intact,
2550   just as on the day she died.
        You will see that right away.
        God may take terrible vengeance on us for this."
        The priest said: "I set very little store
        by the tales I've heard from old people.
2555   Now I shall see for myself if her clothes
        are in one piece and have lasted."
        With a candle in his hand
        he approached the hole in the tomb,
        wanting to know more about that holy body.
2560   But he could not see anything.
        Then the candle he was holding fell
        into the sarcophagus.
        It continued to burn for a long time,
        and the people were amazed
2565   that the clothing did not catch fire
        and destroy the body,
        for they could clearly see

La chandeile dedenz ardant.
De totes pars li ont crié
Ke mal a fait, mal a ovré.   2570
Onkes pur le cri de la gent
Ne lessa son porposement:
Sur une verge out un croket
K'al pertuis de la tombe met.
De fer estoit li crocs devant,   2575
Oit feiz [i] ala en turnant.
Il voleit traire les dras hors
Dont estoit covert cist seint cors.
Quatre bacheliers appela
En s'aïe, si lur rova   2580
A traire le drap k'il out pris,
Et il [i] ont lur poër mis.   fol 119v col 1
Un petitet estraist en sous
A grant force desk'au pertus.
Puis ke seinte Audree senti   2585
Ke l'em hostoit se[s] dras de li,
Si com li prestres reconta:
A sey les trait et resembla
A tel force, lur fu avis,
Com si mein d'home i eüst mis.   2590
Et parla la virge dedenz
Si que bien oïerent les genz,
Et dist: « Vos n'avez mie espase
Ne de Deu ne de moi la grace
Ke vos depecez mon suaire.   2595
Vos en avrez peine et contraire. »
Ke vos en diroue [je] mes?
Ne demora gerres aprés
K'as maisons ke li prestres tint
Grant mal et pestilence avint.   2600
Sa femme moreut malement
Et ses enfanz hastivement,
Et tut le plus de sa menee
En fu destruite et enpiree;
Et il meïsmes s'enfuï   2605
Sanz repentance si fini.
As diebles out son refuï
Qui receurent l'ame de li.
Deuz des autres ki ou li furent
Al sarcu malement morurent.   2610

the burning candle inside.
All the people around cried out
2570 that he had acted badly and done something evil.
But despite the protest of the people
he did not relinquish his purpose.
He attached an iron hook
to the end of a rod
2575 then stuck it into the hole of the tomb.
He twisted it in eight times
trying to pull out the clothing
with which that holy body was covered.
He called four young men
2580 and asked them
to help him pull out the clothing he had hooked,
and they put their strength to the task.
With great effort he drew out
a little piece from inside.
2585 Since Saint Audrey felt
that someone was pulling her clothes from her—
and this was just as the priest recounted it—
she drew them back and readjusted them
with such force that it seemed to them
2590 as though a man's hand had done it.
Then the virgin inside spoke aloud
and the people could hear her quite well.
She said: "You do not have the right
or permission from either God or me
2595 to pull apart my shroud.
You will be punished for this."
What more can I tell you?
Not long afterwards
a terrible plague struck
2600 the domains held by the priest.
His wife died in a terrible manner,
his children died soon thereafter,
and all the rest of his household
was destroyed or brought to ruin because of this.
2605 The priest himself fled
and died without repenting,
thus taking his refuge with the devils
who received his soul.
Two of the others who were with him
2610 at the sarcophagus died in a wretched way.

Le tierz fu sergant de l'eglise,
Confés se fist de cele enprise,
Mes tant out par la mesprison,
Kant [il] venoit a la meison,
K'il ert devez et enragez,   2615
De force de sen desveiez.   fol 119v col 2
Li quart fu prestre, Alfelin nomez;
Cil fu de grant mal enfermez.
Cil fu plein de paralisie:
Oit mois entiers ne levoit mie,   2620
Mes ses parens ki mut l'amerent
A seint' Audree le porterent
Ou luminaire et ou grant don
Et pur li firent oreison.
Pur la repentance k'il out   2625
La virge santé li donout.
Pur icel fait, com ge vos di,
Cil ke le miracle ont oï
Greigniur reverence ont portee
A la virge et plus honoree.   2630

Edrez, li nobles, li bons reis,
Ky estoit sire des Engleis
Dis anz regna et puis moreut,
Et Edwines aprés receut
Le regne: al quart [an] fu finiz   2635
Et a Wincestre ert enfoïz.
Edgar, un hom de grant parage,
Al seizime an de son aage
Al regne aveir fu appellez
Et de seint Donstan [fu] sacrez.   2640
Cist fu bon rei et Deu ama
Et les eglises restora.
Edgar fu rei de [mut] grant pris
Et de[l] linnage Kenegis.
Bones leis tint et bonement   2645
Treita le regnë et la gent.

Par rei Edgar dont je vous dy
Fu refeite en l'yle d'Ely
Et par l'eveske de Wyncestre
Edelwold, ky donc [i] est maistre   2650   fol 120r col 1
L'eglise ke destruite fu

The third one was a servant of the Church
who confessed his misdeed,
but because it was so great a sin,
when he returned home
2615   he went insane and remained
devoid of his right mind.
The fourth was a priest named Alfelin.
He became severely afflicted
with paralysis;
2620   for eight full months he could not even stand up.
But his parents, who loved him very much,
took him to Saint Audrey.
They brought her candles and fine gifts
and prayed for him.
2625   Because he had repented,
the virgin restored his health.
As a result of the event I have just related
those who heard about this miracle
began to display greater reverence
2630   and honor toward the virgin.

Edred, the good and noble king,
who was lord of the English,
reigned ten years before he died.
And after him, Edwy received
2635   the kingdom; after his fourth year as king he died
and was buried in Winchester.
Then Edgar, a man of great lineage,
was consecrated by Saint Dunstan
and became king
2640   when he was sixteen years old.
He was a good king who loved God
and restored His churches.
Edgar, who was a descendant of Cynegils,
was a king of great merit,
2645   for he enacted good laws
and ruled the kingdom and its people with justice.

This particular king, Edgar,
together with Bishop Ethelwold
of the See of Winchester,
2650   restored the church on the isle of Ely
which the Danes had destroyed

Ou li Danois furent venu.
Aprés la grant destruction
K'il firent et l'occision
Avoit esté long tens, ceo dist,   2655
Kant le rei Edgar la resist.
Moines i mist et bone gent
Et estora un grant covent.
De Wyncestre un bon moine i mist,
Simeon, et prior l'en fist.   2660
Icist prior par sa queintise
Comença une noble eglise.
Mes einz ke il la peut parfaire
Li estovit a sa fin traire.
Moine d'eluec, Richard out non,   2665
Ke fu receu par Symeon
Fu fait prior aprés cestui:
La cure fu baillie a lui.
Mut s'entremist, mut se pena
De faire ceo k'il comença.   2670
Une descorde avint issi
Entre li et le rey Henri
K'il de l'eglise entrelessa
L'ovraine et a Rome en ala.
A l'apostoile ad tot mustré,   2675
Sa cause et sa necessité,
Et li apostoile li fist
Voluntiers quank'il li requist.
En Engleterre est revenuz
En s'eglise est bien receüz.   2680
Seinte Audree en ha mercïé,
Si ha s'ue[v]re [re]comencé.
Tant ha ovré k'il la fina,
Et en son quer se porpensa   fol 120r col 2
K'il f[e]ra le cors remüer   2685
De la virge et dedenz porter.
Ci com nos fait ici entendre,
Essample de Joseph vout prendre
Ky le cors son pere porta
En Chanaan et remua.   2690
L'erceveske de Canterbire
Requist le prior com[e] pere,
Seint Anseüm, qu'il [i] alast
Et de ses compagnions menast.

when they came.
But it is said that the restoration by King Edgar
took place quite a long time
2655 after the great destruction
and slaughter.
King Edgar placed monks and good people there
to establish a great monastic community.
He took a good monk from Winchester
2660 named Simeon and made him prior.
This prior, through his wise governance,
began to build a magnificent church.
But he died
before he could complete his work.
2665 One of the monks named Richard,
whom Simeon had taken into the monastery,
was made prior after him:
The responsibility was turned over to him,
and he busied himself, working hard
2670 to complete what Simeon had begun.
But there arose a disagreement
between him and King Henry
so he set aside the work of the church
and went to Rome.
2675 He presented
his entire cause and need to the pope
who willingly granted
everything he requested.
When he returned to England,
2680 he was welcomed by his community.
He thanked Saint Audrey for his success
and took up his work again.
He worked so hard that he completed the church,
and began to contemplate
2685 having the body
of the virgin moved and brought inside.
As we understand it,
he wished to take example from Joseph
who removed his father's body
2690 and carried it into Canaan.*
The prior asked
    the archbishop of Canterbury,
Saint Anselm, as father [of the church], to come
and bring some of his companions—

Teus com li vendroit a pleisir,   2695
Si fetement les fist venir.
Li eveske de Norwiz i fu
Alwine, ceo hay entendu,
Ky fu abbes de Rameseie
E Gonter qui fu de Thorneie   2700
L'abbé de Persore, Guion,
Geforei, le tressorer par non,
De Wincestre et seigniur de Nichole,
L'arcediacne de Nichole.
Il fist le erceveske aler   2705
A icel seint cors remüer.
E clers et lais comunaument
Out mut a cel remüement.
Ou grant procession et bele
De la viel ovre a la novele   2710
Porterent le cors seinte Audree,
La roïne bon[e]üree.
Hautement ou duz chant l'ont mise
Pres del haut autier en l'eglise.
Mes une merveillie ont veüe   2715
Ke suer le cors fu avenue.
D'une chandeile ke fu arse
La flamesche virent esparse.   fol 120v col 1
Unkes n'i out blemeüre
Ne de feu nule entameüre   2720
Suer le drap k[y] entor lui fu,
Ç'ont il apertement veü.
Par un prestre i fu jadis mise
La chandeile ardant et enprise
Ky fu honiz et sa meison   2725
Et tote sa possession.
Si avint, ceo trovom escrist,
Com de seint Estevene dist,
Kant li seint cors fu remüez,
Tonerre i vint et granz orrez,   2730
Tens ke checun bien quidoit
Ke la virge nïent ne ple[oi]t
Le remüement de son cors
Ne k'ele feüst porté hors.
Et seinte Sexborc, sa sorur,   2735
Et seinte Hermenild par honur
Ceo jur me[ï]mes remüerent

2695   as many as he would like.
And Saint Anselm joyously had them come:
the bishop of Norwich was there,
Alwin, so I heard,
who was abbot of Ramsey,
2700   Gunter, abbot of Thorney,
Guyon, abbot of Pershore,
a man named Geoffrey, treasurer
of Winchester and lord of Lincoln,
and the archdeacon of Lincoln.
2705   The prior had the archbishop himself come
to move the holy body.
There were many clerics
and lay folk as well at this translation.*
In a grand and beautiful procession
2710   they carried the body of Saint Audrey
the blessed queen
from the old building to the new one.
With great honor and sweet song they placed her
near the high altar in the church.
2715   Then they witnessed a miracle:
They saw a flame
from a burning candle
spread out to her body;
yet from the fire
2720   there was not the least damage
done to the fabric that enveloped her.
They saw this in plain view.
The flaming candle
had been placed there by a priest
2725   who was dishonored for doing so, as was his family
and all his possessions.
Then it happened, we find recorded,
(as is also told of Saint Stephen)*
that when the holy body was moved,
2730   there were great thunderstorms
which made everyone think
that the virgin was not pleased
to have her body moved
or taken outside.
2735   Both Saint Seaxburga, her sister,
and Saint Erminilda
were moved the same day

En le eglise reporterent.
Pres de seint' Audree les mistrent
En beus sarcuz k[e] y[l] lur quistrent.   2740

Quant seinte Withburc fu trovee
Et le sarcu [fu] remüee,
Une dure aventure avint
Ke checun a merveillie tint,
Que li sarcu fust defendi   2745
K'hom poöit veir le cors de li.
Plusurs distrent ke Deu voleit
Ke l'em veïst quele ele estoit.
Richard pur la dame honorer
Un autre sarcu fist ovrer   2750
A la mesure, a la longur
De l'autre et tut a la leür.*   fol 120v col 2
Kant il eurent apparaillié,
Plus curt le troverent d'un pé.
Pur c'entendunt comunaument   2755
Ke la virge ne vout nïent
K'e[n] nul autre sarcu fuest mise,
Si ont la piere ariere rasise.
Ensemble se joinst et serra;
Onkes puis nul n'i adesa.   2760
Li eveske Herbert en apert
Vit cel seint cors a descovert
Et li abbes de Westmostier
Ki en ce livre non ha Garnier.*
Tant fu hardiz k'il apresma   2765
Le piez et les meins mania;
Et plusurs autres ont veü
Le seint cors si com [il] einz fu.
Donc le porterent en l'eglise,
Pres des autres la virge ont mise.   2770
Sovent sunt iluec avenuz
Granz miracles et granz vertuz.
Cil bon prior enmaladi,
Seinte Withburc k[e] il servi
Vint devant li visablement,   2775
A li parla mut ducement,
Si qu'il le dist a son covent:
« Seigniurs, veez ci en present
Seinte Withborc devant mei ci.

and carried with honor into the church.
They were placed near Saint Audrey
2740   in beautiful sarcophagi that had been sought especially for them.

When Saint Withburga['s grave] was located
and the sarcophagus moved,
a terrible event took place
that caused everyone to marvel:
2745   the sarcophagus broke open,
exposing her body.
Some said that God wanted
people to see what she was like.
To honor the lady, Richard
2750   had another sarcophagus made
to scale, exactly the same
width and length of the other.
But when it was ready,
they found it a foot too short.
2755   By this they all understood
that the virgin did not want
to be placed in another sarcophagus.
So they put the stone back together,
and it joined and sealed itself.
2760   No one ever touched it again.
Bishop Herbert clearly saw
that holy body when it was exposed,
and the abbot of Westminster,
by the name of Garnier in the book,
2765   was so bold as to approach
and touch her feet and hands.*
Many others saw the holy body
intact as it was before she died.
Then they took it into the church
2770   and put this virgin near the others.
Great miracles and wondrous occurrences
have often taken place there.
When the good prior grew infirm,
Saint Withburga, whom he had faithfully served,
2775   appeared in a vision
and spoke to him very sweetly,
He told his monks:
"Gentlemen, Saint Withburga
is here before me.

De mei cheitif li cri merci. »   2780
Aprés ceo k'il avoit ce dist,
Si li rendi son esperit.
Enfoïz fu dedenz l'eglise
Ou duz chant et ou Deu servise.

Par grace de seint Esperit   2785
Et par prophecie redit   fol 121r col 1
Les miracles de seinte Audree,
Dont la vie avom translatee.*
Oÿ avom ke de richesce
Se fist povre et mist en destresce.   2790
Sa char danta et nuit et jur
En servise son creatur:
Les riches dras tuz deguerpi
Et de la heire se vesti.
Ele deguerpi sa contree   2795
En estrange liu est alee:
Granz miracles fist Deu pur li
Taunt com[ë] ele s'en fuï.
Li angle Deu la conforterent:
Lur parente ert et mut l'amerent.   2800
Parent[e] ert as angles del ciel*
Ke meine vie angeliel.
Li aposteles nos devine
Ke virginité est roïne
Sur tutes les vertuz ki sont   2805
En ceus qui habitent en mond.
Ce ke la virge seinte Audree
Fu entiere en sarcu trovee,
Esprove et si testimonie
Ke virge fu tote sa vie.   2810
Pur ce ne pout le cors suffrir
Ke enpirer deut ne blemir:
Bonë est ceste marchandise
Ke la virge ha de Deu conquise,
Ke pur li danter et destreindre   2815
Puet a la gloire Deu ateindre.

Entre les miracles dirom
D'un paën cruel et felon
Ke par fol hardement feri
Suer la tombe et iluec fini.   2820   fol 121r col 2

2780 I cry to her for mercy on this wretch that I am!"
      After he had said this,
      he rendered his spirit to her.
      He was buried within the church
      with the sweet singing of a beautiful mass.

2785 By the grace of the Holy Spirit
      and by divine guidance we now give an account of
      the miracles of Saint Audrey
      whose life we have translated.*
      We have heard how she gave up her wealth
2790 and made herself poor and needy.
      She subdued the flesh both night and day
      in order to serve her Creator:
      Laying aside all her fine clothes
      she dressed in a hair shirt.
2795 She left behind her own country
      and made her way to a distant place,
      and God performed great miracles for her
      as she fled.
      God's angels comforted her;
2800 She was their kin, and they loved her very much.
      She was kin to the angels in heaven*
      for she lived an angelic life.
      The apostle teaches us
      that virginity is the queen
2805 of all virtues found
      in those who inhabit this world.*
      The fact that the virgin Saint Audrey
      was found incorrupt in her sarcophagus
      demonstrates and proves
2810 that she was a virgin all her life.
      For this reason her body could never suffer
      deterioration or damage.
      Good is the merchandise
      which the virgin conquered for God:
2815 for by restraint and control of it
      she may attain the glory of God.

      Among the miracles we will tell
      of a cruel and wicked pagan
      who fool-heartedly struck
2820 the tomb and died there.

Par tant li autre s'aparceurent
Coment la dame honorer durent.
Et d'un moine nos dist ici,
Aceo avoit non, si ert d'Ely.
Chaet ert en grant maladie 2825
Si fu mis [en] enfermerie.
En sa dolur ha reclamee
La glorïuse sainte Audree
K'elë eüst de li merci.
La nuit aprés kant il dormi 2830
Vint la virge devant cestui,
Ducement a parlé a lui.
La virge li ad demandee
« Cunois me tu ? Tu as santé.
Di a tes frieres k'il s'amendent 2835
Et k'a moy honorer entendent
Mieus k'il n'ont fait ou, si ce non,
Il en averont mal guerdon.
Hastivement sanz nul resort
Seront tochez de cruel mort. » 2840

Edgar le roy reconte ici
Ky restora le liu d'Ely.
Cent anz un meins erent passé
Ke Danois i eurent esté
Et faite la destrucion 2845
Et de noneines l'occision.
Le roy Edgar mist a l'eglise
Grant terre et dona grant franchise.
Einz fu l'eglise governee
Par la roïne seinte Audree, 2850
Par seinte Sexborc, sa so[r]ur,
Et par seinte Ermenild meint jur.
Bones dames l'eglise tindrent
De si ke li Danois [i] vindrent. fol 121v col 1
Roy Edgar il refist cel estre, 2855
[Et] Edelwold, cil de Wincestre:
Le roy par comandement,
[Et] l'eveske par prechement.
Grant entente checun i mist
Et grant biens a l'eglise i fist. 2860
Deuz eveskes vindrent au roy
Et chacun le requist par soy,

Because of this, others realized
that they must honor the lady.
Then we are told of a monk
of Ely named Acca
2825 who fell seriously ill
and was put in the infirmary.
In his pain he called on
glorious Saint Audrey
to have mercy on him.
2830 The next night, while he slept,
the virgin came before him.
She spoke gently to him
asking him:
"Do you know who I am? You are healed.
2835 Now tell your brothers to amend their ways
and to be more attentive to honoring me
better than they have, or, if not,
they will be punished for it:
suddenly, without any recourse,
2840 they will suffer a cruel death."

Now we are told about King Edgar
who restored the site of Ely
almost one hundred years
after the Danes had been there,
2845 destroyed it,
and slaughtered the nuns.
King Edgar granted considerable land
and large tax exemptions to the church.
Previously the church had been governed
2850 by the queen Saint Audrey,
by her sister Saint Seaxburga,
and by Saint Ermenilda.
For a long time good ladies held the church
until the Danes came.
2855 King Edgar and Ethelwold of Winchester
reestablished monastic life there:
the king gave orders,
and the bishop preached sermons.
Each of them put much effort into it
2860 and made sizeable donations to the church.
Two bishops named Sidelwald and Thurstan
came to the king,

Sidelwold et Thorstan par non,
Ke de Ely lur fist le don.
Checun voloit cel liu avoir   2865
Et par cointise et par avoir.
Uns hom qui fu de Dalehan
Ke l[i] em apelloit Wolstan
Mut del roy ert, ceo dist, privez
Par Deu estoit a lui alez   2870
Si l[i] ad dist que gra[a]nter
Ne fait a ces deuz ne doner
L'eglise qu'il ont demandee:
Contre lou Deu serreit donee.
Tant ad cil le roy conseillié   2875
Qu'il ad pur l'eveske envoié,
Edelwold, que fu de Wincestre.
Si l[i] ad mostré de cel estre,
Par son conseil ad estably
Ke moines mettra en Ely.   2880
Et requist li mut bonement
K'il soit maistre de cele gent.
Li eveskes quant l'entendi
A Damnedeu graces rendi.
Les clers ke i furent hosta,   2885
Moines profés i assembla.
De Brithnoth, un home sené,
Seur ceo covent [il] fist abbé.   fol 121v col 2
Terres et rentes i dona
Li eveskes et conferma   2890
Par le privilege le roy
Edgar, ke Deu ama en foy.
Li eveskes par seinte Audree
Ad l'eglise bien aornee
Pur aveir l'aïue de li   2895
Et que Deu ait de li merci.
Kanque le roi pot de franchise
Dona et mist a cele eglise
Par tesmoigne de cel escrit
Ke seint Bede reconte et dit.   2900
Kanque le rois i out doné
Si en a Rome confermé
Seur excommunication
K'il l'hosteroit de la maison.

each requesting
that Ely be given to him,
2865 and each hoping to obtain it
through flattery and bribes.
A man from Delham,
named Wulstan, who, it is said,
was among the king's close friends,
2870 was led by God to go to the king
and tell him not to give
to either of these two
the church they were asking for:
it would be given contrary to the will of God.
2875 He advised the king so insistently
that the king sent for the bishop,
Ethelwold of Winchester
and Ethelwold explained the situation to him.
Following his [Ethelwold's] advice the king agreed
2880 to put monks in Ely.
He then requested most properly
that Ethelwold himself become master of those monks.
When the bishop heard this,
he gave thanks to the Lord God.
2885 He ousted the clerks who were there
and assembled professed monks in their place.
He made Brithnoth, a prudent man,
abbot of the monastery.
The bishop also gave them lands and great revenues
2890 which he confirmed
by a privilege of
King Edgar who truly loved God.
On behalf of Saint Audrey, the bishop
had the church well decorated
2895 hoping to have help from her,
and mercy from God.
As much as he possibly could, the king
gave tax exemptions to that church,
according to the testimony in the written record
2900 told and recounted by Saint Bede.
Whatever the king gave the monastic house—
and this was confirmed by Rome—
only upon excommunication
would he take it away.

Une aventure mostrerons,   2905
Dont bon testimonie avons,
D'un home ki out non Leffi,
De Leflad sa femme autresi,
Ki en Cantebrige menoient
Et terre[s] a Donham avoient.   2910
Une marchandise firent
A l'eveske, si li vendirent
Deuz ydes qu'il achata;
Quinze livres lur en dona
Par Lefwine, ki les porta,   2915
Son moine, et a eus les baillia,
Et cele terre avoit donee
Li eveskë a seinte Audree.
Mes quant li roy Edgar fini
Iceo Leffi se repenti   2920
De la terre que il vendi:
Partie de l'avoir rendi   fol 1221 col 1
Et partie lur reveia,
Et la terre lur deforça.
Sovente fois en plais fu mis,   2925
Par la bone gent del païs
Fu ateint, mes tuz jurs tenoit
Si qu'amender ne se voloit.
Seinte Audree justise en fist
Et de mort subite l'occist: 2930
Li et sa femme si moreurent
Maveisement com faire durent.

De Wigar avint veraiment
Ki a l'eveske par covent
Vendi quinzë ydes de terre   2935
A Brandonë et Livresmere.
Pur vint livres k'il en dona
Et le[s] cent souz li envoia
Par un home ki out non Wine
Et par son moine Lefwine.   2940
En poy de tens Wigar fini;*
Yngulf Brandonë lur tolli,
Mes puis ne buit ne ne manga
De si que le quer li creva.
Sa femme et ses enfanz morurent.   2945
Dedenz l'an peine et mort receurent.

2905 We will now tell a story
      of which we have a good account,
      about a man named Leffi
      and his wife Lefta
      who lived in Cambridge
2910 but also owned land in Downham.
      They struck a deal
      with the bishop: they sold him
      two hides of land which he bought*
      for fifteen pounds
2915 through his monk Lewine,
      who brought the money and handed it over to them.
      Now the bishop had given this land
      to Saint Audrey.
      But when King Edgar died
2920 Leffi regretted
      having sold the land.
      Part of the money he returned,
      and part he withheld,
      and retained the land illegally.
2925 Several times he was taken to court over it;
      he was accused by the good people of the country,
      but he always held out,
      unwilling to make amends.
      However, Saint Audrey rendered justice:
2930 she slew him with sudden death.
      He and his wife both died
      in a terrible manner, as indeed they should have.*

      Concerning Wigar it is true
      that through an agreement he sold
2935 the bishop fifteen hides of land
      at Brandon and at Livermere.
      The bishop paid twenty pounds for it
      plus a hundred pence that he sent to him
      through a man named Winna
2940 and through his monk Lewine.
      Shortly thereafter, Wigar died;
      Ingulf took the Brandon land from them,
      but afterwards he could neither eat nor drink
      because his heart gave out.
2945 His wife and his children also died.
      Within the year they all received the penalty of death.

Siward ha mut grant doul heü
Pur son frere qu'il ha perdu.
Sanz [le] conseil de ses amis
Et des hauz homes del païs   2950
Pur la vengance seinte Audree
Cele terre [ha] quite clamee.

En cel livre reconte ici
D'un moine ki del sen issi.
A complie fu ou l'abbé   2955
Kant li dïeble l'ha tempté   fol 122r col 2
Einz [que] l'ure fuest parfinie
S'en ala hors par deverie.
Edwines fu cil [hom] nomez.
Droit a la table en est alez,   2960
Ferue l'eüst vereiment.
Siward i vint ki li defent.
Un moine out leenz de Wincestre,
Godriz out non de mut seint estre.
Cil vit li diable venir   2965
Ke le moine fist hors issir:
Com un noir enfes prist celui,
Hors le mena ensemble ou lui.
Par commun consel del covent
Ariere ameinent cel dolent: 2970
Devant la virge seinte Audree
[Ceus] pur li ont merci crie[e].
Aprés ceo qu'il avoit dormi,
Son conseil [dit] et descovri
Ke il se vout aler eiser,   2975
Son ventre voleit espurger.
Li diable[s] ert descenduz
En son ventre et del quer issuz.
As necessaires l'ont mené
Tant i a li moines esté   2980
Ke li diable veirement
S'en issi par le fundement.
Tote la cort vileinement
En fu puiant si durement
K'a peine le pout nul suffrir,   2985
Einz se voloient tuz fuïr.
En tel manere seinte Audree
Ha a cestui santé donee.

[Abbot] Siward felt deep sorrow
over the brother he had lost,
so without consulting his friends
2950   or the officials of the country
he declared the land free
because of the vengeance of Saint Audrey.

The book tells next
about a monk who went out of his mind.
2955   At compline he was with the abbot
when the devil tempted him.
Before the hour of compline had ended
the monk, whose name was Edwin,
went outside completely insane.
2960   He went straight to the [refectory] table.
and would certainly have struck it
if Siward had not prevented him.
There was inside the church a monk from Winchester
named Godric who led a holy life.
2965   He saw the arrival of the devil
who made the monk leave the service:
Resembling a dark child, he took the monk
and led him outside with him.
By common consent of the community
2970   they brought this poor man back [into the church]
and before the virgin Saint Audrey
begged for mercy on him.
After he had slept for a while,
he spoke up and said
2975   that he wanted to go ease himself—
he wanted to empty his bowels.
The devil had left his heart
and had descended into his intestines.
So they took him to the latrines;
2980   the monk stayed there long enough
to allow the devil
to come out through the bottom.
The whole courtyard
stank of such intense vileness
2985   that the monks could hardly bear it,
they all wanted to flee!
That is how Saint Audrey
restored this man's health.

Puis cele heure ke ge vos di
N'i out diable si hardi   2990   fol 122v col 1
Ki le mur osast assaillier
De cel covent ou enz venir
Ke autresi ne fust geté
Com sis compains ki i out esté.

Issi avint de deuz müez,   2995
Li un fu Ulf, li autre Ailrez:
Ceo deuz vindrent a seinte Audree,
En lur quers ont merci crïe[e].
Ulf recovra delivrement
Sa parole tot pleinement,   3000
Meis Ailrez fu baubeiant
Issi com emfes apernant.
En ces deuz fu tel demostrance
K'il n'ourent mie ouele creance.

En icel livre nos reconte   3005
K'en Cantebrige out un vesconte,
Picot out non, Normanz estoit.
Mut fu crüel, granz mals fesoit.
Dedenz la terre seinte Audree
A sovent mise et demandee   3010
Male costome et male assise
Tel ke onkes mes n'i out mise.
Plusurs distrent k'il mefesoit,
Ke vers la dame mespernoit,*
Et par orguil [il] respondi   3015
Ke il ne savoit rien d'Ely.
Puis si avint k'il fu perduz,
Ne sout nul k'il fu devenuz.
Li uns distrent k'il fu raviz
Et de cors et d'ame periz   3020
Si com Datan et Abiron
Ki alerent en Achiron.
Li autre distrent ke müez
Est en beste et transfigurez   fol 122v col 2
Com Nabugodonosor fu   3025
En qui Deu mostra sa vertu.

Un hom de mut grant felonie
Par Picot receut la baillie

Since this occasion,
2990   there has been no devil so bold
        as to dare assail the wall
        of that monastery or come in among the monks
        lest he, too, be ejected
        the same way his companion had been.

2995   This is what happened to two mutes
        named Ulf and Ailred.
        Both of them came to Saint Audrey.
        and cried in their hearts to her for mercy.
        Ulf promptly recovered
3000   his speech completely,
        but Ailred babbled
        like a child just learning [to talk].
        These two demonstrated
        that they did not at all have equal faith.

3005   The book tells us
        that in Cambridge there was a Norman sheriff
        named Picot
        who was very cruel and did great harm.
        He often imposed
3010   heavy taxes and assizes
        such as had never before been levied
        on the lands belonging to Saint Audrey.
        Many said that he was doing wrong,
        that he was mistreating the lady Saint Audrey;
3015   to which he haughtily answered
        that he knew nothing about Ely.
        Then he simply disappeared,
        no one ever knew what became of him.
        Some said that he was snatched away
3020   and perished body and soul
        like Dathan and Abiram*
        who went into the river Acheron [of Hades].
        Others said he was changed
        and transformed into a beast,
3025   as was Nabuchadnezzar
        on whom God demonstrated his power.*

        A terribly wicked man
        received the governance

De cel païs et cel contee.
Kant diable l'eurent menee   3030
Cist a mut la gent sainte Audree
Damagee et a mal tornee.
Trop sovent les acheisona
Et a grant tort les enpleida.
Si nul seinte Audree noma   3035
Celui prist et enprisona.
Cil se pleignoient mut sovent
A seinte Audree et a covent
Et distrent ke c'ert pur lachesce
De lur abbé et pur peresce   3040
K'il ne voloit le purchacier
N'a lur bosoignes ceus aider.
Agardé fu comunaument
Et de l'abbé et del covent:
L'endemain a Gerveis ira,   3045
De par la virge li dira
Ke peis leist aveir a sa gent.
Pur li fist prïere le covent.
La nuit devant k'aler devoit
Li abbes et parler voloit,   3050
A Gerveis est avenue
Une grant merveillie sue:
Seinte Audree devant li vint
Et un bordon en sa mein tint.
Ses deuz so[r]urs ou li estoient,   3055
Bordons portoient et tenoient.
Celui apella seinte Audree
Ki tant avoit la gent grevee: fol 122r col 1
« Cheitif, » dist ele, « malsenez
Ky mes hommes as tormentez !   3060
Tu en avras mal gueredon. »
En cors le fert de son bordon
Et les autres le ront fereu
Et cil cria qui blescé feu.
Ses hommes sont venu corant.   3065
Cil lur dist tut en oïant
De la seinte virge qui fu
A lui, si l'a a mort fereu.
V[e]oir la peurent; ce lor dist,
Atant rendi son esperit.   3070
La novele fu tut contee

of this shire through Picot.
3030 Once the devils had brought him there
he did much damage
to Saint Audrey's people.
He often falsely accused them
and wrongly prosecuted them.
3035 If anyone even mentioned Saint Audrey
he was taken and imprisoned.
The people frequently lamented
to Saint Audrey and to the monastery,
saying that because the abbot was
3040 cowardly and lazy
he refused to pursue the matter
or to attend to their needs.
Finally it was mutually decided,
both by the abbot and the community,
3045 that the next day he would go to Gervase [the wicked man]
and on behalf of the virgin he would tell him
to leave her people in peace.
He had the monastics pray for him.
The night before the abbot
3050 was to go and speak his mind
it is widely known that
a miraculous thing happened to Gervase:
Saint Audrey appeared before him
holding a staff in her hand.
3055 Her two sisters were with her;
they, too, carried staves.
Saint Audrey called out to this man
who had done such harm to her people:
"Miserable, evil-minded man," she said,
3060 "You who have harassed my people!
You will now receive a terrible recompense."
She struck his body with her staff
and so did the others.
The wounded man screamed
3065 and his men came running.
He told them all about
the holy virgin who had come
to him and struck him a death blow.
He claimed they should be able to see her; and having said that,
3070 he then rendered up his spirit.
News spread everywhere

De la vengance sainte Audree.
Li abbes remist a meison,
N'i avoit puis rien se bien non.
Nul n'osa puis ce di retraire,   3075
Grever ses hommes ne mal faire.

Si nos reconte de Godriz,
Un moine ke mut fu parfiz:
Cil estoit del covent d'Ely
Entre les moines autresi   3080
Com en orbe maison chandeile
Ou dedens niule e[st] clere estoile.
Une nuit aprés le servise,
Kant il out oré en l'eglise,
Lassez fu, si s'ert endormiz.   3085
Par avision fu raviz:
En ciel devant Deu vit ester
Seinte Audree et forment plurer.
Pur ses servans crioit merci,
Kar vers l'abeïe d'Ely   3090
Vit une sïete encochie[e]
De traire tute aparaillie[e].   fol 123r col 2
Une persone l'arc tenoit
Ke l'eglise ferir voloit.
Par la prïere seinte Audree   3095
Fu la sïete trestornee.
Le prudhome tot espanté,
Eveilliez est et effreé.
La nuit aprés en oreison
Pur ceste grant avision   3100
Remist a mostier et ora.
Vers le grant autier esgarda,
Si vit ma dame seinte Audree
Ke de sa tombë ert levee.
Ou ses so[r]urs et sa nï[e]ce   3105
Par le quer ala une pece
Jesk'a l'enfermerie vint;
Une toaile en sa mein tint,
As malades k'ele trova
Et ieus et vis lur essüa.   3110
Godriz le moines les siwy.
Et quant ele s'en departy,
Si s'est vers le moine tornee

about Saint Audrey's vengeance.
The abbot remained at the monastic house,
where there has been nothing but good ever since.
3075   Since that day no one has dared to take
her men away, disturb them, or treat them badly.

Here we are told of Godric,
a monk who was perfect in every way.
He lived at the monastery of Ely
3080   among the other monks,
like a candle in a dark house
or a bright star in a cloud.
One night after the service,
when he had stayed to pray in the church,
3085   he was so tired that he fell asleep
and was caught up in a vision
in which he saw Saint Audrey in heaven
crying bitterly before God.
She was begging for mercy on her servants,
3090   for toward the abbey of Ely
Godric saw an arrow cocked and
ready to be released.
The person holding the bow
was aiming at the church,
3095   but through the prayer of Saint Audrey
the arrow was turned aside.
The good man woke up
terrified.
The next night during prayers,
3100   because of this great vision,
he again remained in the church and prayed.
He looked toward the high altar
and saw milady Saint Audrey
who had risen from her tomb
3105   with her sisters and her niece.
She walked a ways through the choir
and came to the infirmary.
Holding a towel in her hand
she wiped the eyes and faces
3110   of the sick people she found there.
The monk Godric followed the women.
As she was leaving,
she turned toward the monk

E li dist k'ele ert sainte Audree
K'il vit en ciel en oreison 3115
A Deu pur cele maison.
Cil rendi graces et merci
A Deu, et ele s'envani.
Seue chose est ke l'endemein
Son[t] li moine gari et sein. 3120
Avoit de Deu grace et vertu
Uns de[s] moines ki gari fu.
Gocelin out non ; mout amoit
Vies des seins k'il translatoit.
Par la santé k'out recovree, 3125
Al loënge de sainte Audree   fol 123v col 1
Fist une prose ou melodie
Ke uncore est en l'abeïe.

Ci conte de l'abbé d'Ely
Ki par une nuit s'endormi: 3130
Del conte de Warenne vit
Ke cele nuit out son obit.
Des dïebles fut entreprise
Sa alme k'en enfer ont mise.
Au ter jur vint sa femme la, 3135
En Ely cent sous aporta
Que il li avoit devisé,
Mes n'i out moine ne abbé
Ke[s] vousist recevoir ne prendre.
A la dame firent entendre 3140
Coment li abbes out veü
Sa fin et quele heure ce fu
Et coment les dïebles vindrent
Et s'alme enporterent et tindrent
Pur la virge [a] k'il out tollue 3145
Terre k'ele out long tens tenue,
Et avoit a lay fié tornee
Ceo qu'en aumone fu donee:
Mut en receüt mal guerdon.
Guilliames out cist cuens a non. 3150

Long tens aprés ke seinte Audree
Fu de ce siecle trespassee,
Chaÿ fudre seur le eglise:
Seint Piere fu del feu enprise.

and told him she was Saint Audrey
3115 whom he had seen in heaven praying
to God for this house.
Godric gave thanks and praise
to God, and she vanished.
In fact, the next day
3120 the monks were well and healthy.
One of the monks who was healed
by the grace and power of God
was named Goscelin. He especially loved
the saints' lives, which he had translated.
3125 Because he had recovered his health,
in praise of Saint Audrey
he wrote a sequence with melody*
that is still in the abbey.

Next we are told about an abbot of Ely
3130 who went to sleep one night
and dreamed that the Count of Warren
would die that very night
and that his soul would be taken by devils
and put in Hell.
3135 Three days later the count's wife came to Ely
bringing one hundred pence
which he had bequeathed to the abbey.
But there was not a monk or abbot
who was willing to take [the money].
3140 They explained to the lady
how the abbot had seen
his demise, what time it happened,
how the devils came,
carried away his soul, and kept it
3145 for the sake of the virgin, for the count had confiscated
and that the virgin had owned for a long time
and he had turned into a secular fief
that which had been given as alms.
He had received an ill recompense for doing so.
3150 The count's name was William.*

A long time after Saint Audrey
had departed this life,
lightning struck the church.
[The tower of] Saint Peter was burned;

Par la prïere seinte Audree 3155
L'eglise ki fu enbrasee
Fu recossee contre nature.*
Ore oëz par quel aventure.
Charbon et fer et plumb chaÿ
Seur la gent ke nul ne peri. 3160 fol 123v col 2
Ou lur meins treistrent le merien
Ke del feu ne sentirent rien.
Del feu de Babiloine dist
Ke Deu par ire lur tramist
Ke tote la cité gasta, 3165
Mes Deus cestui ensüaga:
Par la prïere seinte Audree
I a Deu sa pieté mostree.

En sezime an le roy Henri
K'il out regné vint en Ely 3170
Un home, a Chateriz manoit.
Brustan out non, riches estoit.
Pur poür de mort se vout rendre.*
Robert Malarteis le fist prendre,
Par gage et par plege le mist. 3175
Lierres le roy estoit, ce dist,
De son tresor k'il out emblé
Et longement l'avoit celé.
A Hontedone le menerent,
A Raol Basset le mostrerent; 3180
Par agart de la court le pristrent,
A Londres en prison le mistrent.
Cienc mois i fu, forment lïez,
De feim, de froid miseisïez.
Treis jurs et treis nuiz jeüna 3185
K'il ne beüt ne ne manga.
Seint Beneït requist ou plur
Et seinte Audree par duçur
Ke par eus fuest reconfortez
Et de cele prison getez. 3190
La nuit aprés issi avint
Ke dedenz la gaole vint
Seint Beneït et seinte Audree,
Cele virge bon[e]üree.   fol 124r col 1
Devant Brustan, ou grant clarté, 3195
Ducement ad a lui parlé.

3155   But through the prayer of Saint Audrey
the church, which was heavily enflamed,
was spared in an unnatural manner.
This is the way it happened:
coal, iron, and lead fell
3160   on the people, but no one perished.
They pulled away the [burning] wood with their hands,
yet they did not feel the fire at all.
Concerning the fire of Babylon it is said
that God in anger sent it upon them
3165   and destroyed the entire city.*
But God mitigated this fire
through the prayer of Saint Audrey.
thus showing His compassion in this instance.

In the sixteenth year of King Henry's
3170   reign, a man who lived in Chatteris
came to Ely.
His name was Brustan, and he was wealthy.
Afraid he was dying, he had decided to become a monk.
But Robert Malarteis had him seized
3175   and placed under guarantee and pledge,
accusing him of being a thief
who had stolen from the king's treasury
and had concealed it for a long time.
They took him to Huntingdon,
3180   and presented him before [judge] Raoul Bassett.
By order of the court he was taken
to London and put in prison
where he remained tightly bound for five months,
suffering from hunger and cold.
3185   He fasted for three days and nights
during which he neither drank nor ate.
In tears he called upon Saint Benedict
and also softly called to Saint Audrey
hoping to receive help from them
3190   and release from prison.
Then the following night
into the jail came
Saint Benedict and Saint Audrey,
the blessed virgin,
3195   appearing in great radiance before Brustan.
She spoke to him sweetly.

Ele dist k'ele ert seinte Audree
Ke il avoit tant reclamee:
Or li deïst sa volenté
Et il li a merci crïé: 3200
Ke hors de prison le meïst,
Il rendroit ce ke li promist.
La virge regarda et dist
Seint Beneït que il feïst
Le comandement Jhesu Creist. 3205
Seint Beneït les anieus preist,
Ou ses deuz meins les despesça
Contre le parei le[s] geta.
Tel noise firent al hurtier
Ke cil ki devoient garder 3210
A la gaole i sont coreu,
Si sont cel miracle veü.
Tut esbahi et esmaié
Demandent ke l'a deslïé.
Un hom qui fu lïé a lui 3215
Les respondi devant cestui
Et dist k'il out dame vïue
Ou grant clarté leenz venue
Et un moine quel deslia
Et qui les boies depesça. 3220
La novele ert ne pas cele[e],
A la roïne fu contee,
A bone Maud[e] ki estoit*
A Londres ou ele manoit.
Elë envoia l'endemain 3225
Pur li Raol, son chapelein
[Ky] par devant li l'a mené.
Quant ele en sout la verité, fol 124r col 2
Les seins comanda a soner
Par la cité et Deu loër. 3230
A Westmoster procession
Li firent ou devotion
Et receurent joieusement.
La roïne hastivement
L'en ad envoié en Ely 3235
Ou il s'ert renduz et
    rendi.*
La roïne aprés i ala
Et les buies ou li porta.

saying that she was Saint Audrey
on whom he had called,
and that he should tell her what he wanted.

3200   He begged her to be merciful,
and said that, should he be freed from prison,
he would give [himself] to her as he had promised.
The virgin looked at Saint Benedict
and told him to do

3205   as Jesus Christ commanded.
Saint Benedict took the chains,
tore them apart with his two hands,
and threw them against the wall.
They made such a racket when they hit

3210   that the prison guards
came running
and saw this miracle.
Amazed and baffled,
they asked who had unchained him.

3215   A man who had been bound to him
answered them before Brustan could
and said that he had seen a lady
of great radiance come into the jail
with a monk who unfettered him

3220   and tore the chains apart.
News of this could not be kept a secret.
It was told to the queen,
good Queen Maude, who was
there in London where she lived.

3225   The next day she sent
Raoul, her chaplain, for him,
and he brought Brustan before her.
When she learned the truth [of the matter],
she commanded that the bells be rung

3230   throughout the city and that God be praised.
With great devotion they staged
a procession to Westminster in his honor
and he was received joyfully.
The queen immediately

3235   sent him away to Ely and he became a monk
there where he had intended
    to take orders.*
Later the queen went there,
bringing the chains with her,

Graces rendi a seinte Audree
De la pitié k'ele out mostree.   3240

Un hom manoit, ce dist ici,
Delez l'abbeïe d'Ely.
Si fort avoit la dent dolur
K'il n'out repos ne nuit ne jur.
A un fevre en la vile ala   3245
De son dent traire lui preia.
Ses tenaillies le fevre i mist,
Es joues remist le motist.*
Donc par fu il tuz enragez
De anguissë et tormentez,   3250
Heula et cria com un tors:
Cil le mist de sa forge hors.
Le cheitif ke anguiseus fu
Se purpensa qu'il out veü
Les buies Brustan al moster,   3255
La vout aler sa dent tocher:
Avis li fu de verité
Ke de tochier avra santé.
As buies coreut delivrement
De l'anel atocha sa dent,   3260
En meïmes l'eure gari.
Cist miracles avint issi.   fol 124v col 1

Mestres Raos de Donewiz,
Ce nos reconte li escriz,
Chaï en tel enfermetez   3265
Ke chief et cors out tut enflez.
Tant est s'enfermeté creüe
K'il perdi memoire et veüe.
Par peché et par orde vie
Li avint ceste maladie,   3270
[Ne] nul ne voit ke ja quidast
Ke il garist ne repassast.
Tuz li plusurs de ses parenz
Estoient entur lui dolenz,
Et ses amis et ses voisins   3275
Ne attendirent for la fins.
Quant sa compaignie vint avant*
Seinte Audree merci criant,
Et li promist, si li pleüst

and gave thanks to Saint Audrey
3240 for the compassion she had shown.

It is told that a man lived
beside the abbey of Ely.
He had such a bad toothache
that he had no rest night or day.
3245 He went to a blacksmith in town
and begged him to pull his tooth.
So the blacksmith put his tongs in,
sticking the instrument between his cheeks.
The man went completely beserk
3250 from the pain and torture.
He screamed and bellowed like a bull so much.
that the blacksmith threw him out of his forge.
The miserable man, who was in such pain,
remembered that he had seen
3255 Brustan's chains in the church
and decided to go there to touch his tooth [to them].
He was convinced that
by touching them he would recover.
He ran at once to the chains
3260 and touched his tooth to a link.
At that very moment he was cured,
and that is how this miracle occurred.

Master Ross of Dunwich,
so the writing tells us,
3265 became so ill
that his head and whole body swelled.
His infirmity increased to the extent
that he lost his memory and his sight.
This sickness had come upon him
3270 as a result of a vile and sinful life.
No one who saw him could believe
that he would ever recover.
All of his many relatives
gathered around him grieving,
3275 and his friends and neighbors
expected nothing but his death.
Then his wife came forth
begging for mercy from Saint Audrey,
and promised that, should it please her

Ke icist clers santé eüst,   3280
Lui et li rendroit a s'eglise
Et tuz jurs mes en son servise.
Kant cele promesse avoit faite
Et devant tuz dite et retraite,
En sa lange premerement   3285
Creva le mal hastivement.
Par tuz les membres autresi
S'en coreut le mal et issi,
Et quant le mal fu issu hors,
Si li laverent tot le cors.   3290
Sein fu, en Ely s'en ala
Et sa compagnie ou li mena,
Et puis escrit en l'abeïe
Tut l'ordre de sa maladie.

D'un miracle dirom la somme.   3295
A Berningham out un home.   fol 124v col 2
Suspris fu de grant maladie:
Veüe out perdu et oïe,
La parole et tote l'entente.
De vie n'i out nule atente;   3300
Mes [que] tut ne peut il parler,
En son quer prist a remembrer
De seinte Audree et de sa vie
Ke a meinte home a feit aïe,
Et pensa que si il pooit,   3305
A s'eglise le requeroit.
En cest miraclë un recont
K'une dame out a Seint Edmund
A cui la virge s'aparut:
Par devant li vint, si estut.   3310
Cele dame si s'eme[i]lloit
K'el [ne] dormeit ne ne voloit.
Sainte Audree l'aresona
Et dit que l'endemain ira
A Berningham a marché: 3315
Lefmar trovera dehaité
Et tut apresmé a la mort.
A ses parenz face confort
Et lur die qu'a limillion
Mesurent son lit environ: 3320
De scire le facent emplir,

3280   to restore health to this clerk,
        both he and she would give themselves to her church
        and be henceforth in her service.
        Once she had made this promise
        and reiterated it before everyone,
3285   the sickness quickly subsided
        first in his tongue,
        then it flowed out
        from all of his limbs as well.
        When the disease was completely gone,
3290   they bathed his whole body.
        Healthy again, he went to Ely
        and took his wife with him.
        There in the abbey he wrote down
        the whole story of his illness.

3295   We will give a complete account of another miracle:
        At Barningham there was a man
        who was taken quite ill.
        He lost his sight, his hearing,
        his speech, and all ability to understand.
3300   There was no hope for his life.
        Although he could not speak at all,
        in his heart he began to recall
        Saint Audrey, her life story,
        and how she had helped many people.
3305   So he thought that if possible
        he would pray to her in her church.
        This miracle story goes on to say
        that there was a lady in Bury Saint Edmunds
        to whom the virgin appeared
3310   and stood before her.
        The lady was so unnerved
        that she could not sleep nor did she want to.
        Saint Audrey talked with her
        and told her to go the next day
3315   to the marketplace in Barningham:
        there she would find Lefmar ill
        and very near death.
        She should comfort his loved ones
        and tell them to measure around his bed
3320   with a candle mesh.
        They were to complete the candle with wax,

Lui meïmes facent venir
En Ely, si li offera
Et sa santé recevera.
Si tot com il ont mesuré.　　　　3325
Recovra Lefmar sa santé.
Kant gariz fu, a seinte Audree
Ad Lefmar s'offrende portee.

Pres d'Arondel manoit un hom
Robert de la Rive out [a] non.　　　　3330　　　　fol 125r col 1
Par peché out tel maladie
Ke nul en lui quida [la] vie.
Tel manere out d'enfermeté
Ke les sens l'eurent en vilté:
De sa vie eurent tuz ennui.　　　　3335
Un jur parla sa femme a lui
Et li dist que s'il requeroit
Seinte Audree que il garroit.
Chandoilë et don li promist
Et en Ely [il] la requist.　　　　3340
Al tierz jur que ele out loé
Vint a celui en volunté:
Si del mal poeüst trespasser
Ke sa chandeile iroit porter
A la roïne seinte Audree.　　　　3345
Mul[t] l'a en son quer reclamee,
Promist qu'il iroit en Ely.
En pensé qu'il avoit de li,
Par une fenestre est venue
Seinte Audree k'il a veüe.　　　　3350
Vestue fu mut noblement:
Tut furent blanc si vestement.
A celui dist que ele estoit
Seinte Audree k'il requeroit.
Ore feïst ce qu'il promist　　　　3355
Et il avroit santé, ce dist.
Cil salli sus, si se leva
Tut sein. En haste se chauça.
Tus crïerent k'il se
　　seignast
Et quidoient qu'il se devast.　　　　3360
Cil ad sa chandoile atornee,
Si l'ad aporté a seinte Audree.

have Lefmar come
to Ely to offer it,
and he would regain his health.
3325   As soon as they had measured,
Lefmar recovered.
After his healing, Lefmar
carried his offering to Saint Audrey.

Near Arundel there lived a man
3330   named Robert de la Rive.
Because of sin he was so sick
that no one thought he would live.
His illness was of such a nature
that his loved ones were repelled by him
3335   to the extent that they all wanted him to die.
One day his wife talked with him
and told him that if he called on
Saint Audrey he would get well.
He should promise her a candle and gifts
3340   and pray to her in Ely.
Three days after his wife had counseled him,
he made up his mind that,
if indeed it would overcome his illness,
he would take his candle
3345   to the queen Saint Audrey.
He implored her in his heart,
and promised that he would go to Ely.
While he was thinking of her,
he saw Saint Audrey
3350   come through a window.
She was quite nobly dressed:
all her clothing was pure white.
She told him that she was
Saint Audrey whom he was beseeching.
3355   Should he do as he promised,
he would regain his health, she said.
He jumped up completely well
and quickly put on his shoes.
Everyone cried to him that he should make the
        sign of the cross,
3360   for they thought that he might be losing his mind.
He prepared his candle,
took it to Saint Audrey,

Grace et loënge li rendi
De ce k'ele l'avoit gari. fol 125r col 2

Del roy Anne nos dist ici 3365
K'un oratorie establi
En l'honorance de seinte Audree
Sa fillie k'il a mut amee.
En Merchenelande l'asist,
Pur Deu servir autier i fist. 3370
Issi avint k'un riches hom,
Herbert de Forches avoit non,
Il et sa gent illuec passa.
Une bone dame i trova
Que li pria qu[e] il entrast 3375
En la chapelë et orast.
Il ne voloit nïent entrer,
La dame i ala pur orer.
Quant en la chapele est venue,
Si a une dame veüe 3380
Devant l'autier en oreisons*
Et en mut granz afflictions.
Un sautier et un cierge ardant
Tenoit, et cele ala avant
Et demanda que ele fu. 3385
La dame li ad respondu:
« Je sui, » dist ele, « seinte Audree.
Ne seiez nïent effree[e].
Estez en sus, si escotez
Le servise ke vos orrez. » 3390
Cele dame si trait ariere,
Si s'apuia a la meisere.
Dames [i] unt a grant plenté
Ki en chantant ont Deu löé
Ou melodië angeliel 3395
Com ci fuessent angles del ciel.
Ele issi hors, si apella
Herbert et entrer li rova fol 125v col 1
Pur oïr cele melodie.
Cil dist ke il [n']avoit oïe. 3400
Il entra enz et s'en reissi
Treiz foiz, meis nïent ne l'oï.
Mut en fu tristes et dolenz
Et ses compaignions et sa genz.

and gave her thanks and praise
because she had cured him.

3365   Concerning King Anna we are told
that he established an oratory
in honor of Saint Audrey,
his daughter whom he loved dearly.
He built it in Mercia
3370   and included an altar for celebrating mass.
It so happened that a rich man
named Herbert de Forches
came through the area with his people.
He met a good lady there
3375   who invited him to enter
the chapel to pray,
but he had no desire to go in,
so the lady went in to pray.
When she came into the chapel,
3380   she noticed a lady
agonizing in prayer
before the altar.
She was holding a psalter and a burning candle.
The first lady went forward
3385   and asked who she was.
The lady answered her:
"I am Saint Audrey," she said.
"Do not be afraid.
Come up here and listen
3390   and you will hear the mass."
Then the lady drew aside
and leaned against the wall.
There were a great number of ladies
praising God in song
3395   with angelic melody,
as if they were angels from heaven.
She went outside, called
Herbert, and asked him to come in
to hear this melody.
3400   He said that he had not heard it.
He went in and came back out
three times, but he heard nothing.
He was quite sorry and disappointed,
as were the people with him.

A Honbern l'ont dolent conté   3405
Ky ert priur de Davintré.
Cist ert de grant auctorité
Et coneüs de grant bonté.
Reconter ala en Ely
Ce miracle dont ge vos di.   3410

En Coventré un hom manoit,
Halfdene out non. Cil revenoit
D'une feire ou il out esté.
Maveise gent l'ont encontré.
A Kinildesworde le menerent.   3415
Grant raençon li demanderent.
Mut le destreindrent malement
Et lïerent trop durement,
Ke li quir del chief li rompi
Et le sang tut cler en issi.   3420
Meis il ne vout a eus finer
Ne sa foi [ne] vout afier,
Car il ne pooit mie rendre
La raençon, ne l'out ou prendre,
Si voloit mieuz iluec morir   3425
Ke il deüt sa foy mentir.
En ses tormenz li remembra
De Brustan ke Deu delivra
De la prison par seinte Audree,
Cele virge bon[e]üree.   3430
Il la requist, si la promist,
Si de prison hors le meïst,   fol 125v col 2
Que son hom lige devendra
Et tuz jurs meis le servira.
Hastivement sont despecïez   3435
Les lïens dont il ert lïez:
Issi est Halfdene eschapez.
Deskes au bois s'en est alez;
A chiens et a hu l'ont siwy.
En cros d'un chene se tapi.   3440
Cil ne[l] peurent mie trover,
Ariere les covint aler.
Halfdene ala a sa maison.
En Ely par devotion
Ala ce miracle conter   3445
Et seinte Audree mercïer.

3405   They told this story sadly to Honbern,
        prior of Daventry,
        a man of much authority
        known for his great goodness.
        He went to Ely to recount
3410   the miracle I have just told you.

        In Coventry there lived a man
        named Halfdene. He was returning
        from a fair he had attended
        when some evil people encountered him,
3415   took him away to Kenilworth,
        and demanded a large ransom.
        They restrained him in a cruel manner,
        binding him so tightly
        that his scalp broke open,
3420   and bright blood flowed out.
        Although he did not wish to die at their hands,
        he refused to pledge his faith,
        since there was no way he could pay
        the ransom, for he did have it nor could he get it.
3425   He preferred to die there
        rather than to swear falsely.
        In his torment he remembered
        Brustan whom God delivered
        from prison through Saint Audrey,
3430   the blessed virgin.
        He prayed to her and promised her
        that if she would get him out of prison,
        he would become her liegeman
        and serve her from now on.
3435   Immediately the cords with which
        he was bound broke apart.
        Thus Halfdene escaped.
        With shouting men and dogs in pursuit of him,
        he got as far as the woods
3440   where he hid himself in the hollow of an oak tree.
        They were unable to find him
        and gave up the search.
        Then Halfdene went home.
        Out of devotion he went to Ely
3445   to recount this miracle
        and to thank Saint Audrey.

Aprés la mort d'un bon abbé,
Symeon, si l'avom nomé,
Remistrent en Ely ses moines
Dont cist livres est temoines.　　　　　3450
Cil cuillierent l'or et argent
Ne lesserent aornement.
Le chief seint Botolf enporterent
Et les reliques que y erent,
Une cortine ot merveillieuse,　　　　　3455
Onque puis n'i out si precieuse.
Ou cel avoir k'il enporterent
A Geldeford tut droit alerent.
En un hostiel se herbergierent.
Trop i beurent et trop mangerent.　　　　　3460
La meson fu arce la nuit
Et quanqu'il porterent destruit.
La nuit fu arce la cortine
K'il emblerent a la roïne.
L'endemen a Wincestre alerent,　　　　　3465
Lur felonie reconterent.　　　　　　　　　fol 126r col 1
El liu dont i[l] furent veneu
Ont le larrecin reconeu.
Seinte Audree crïent merci,
Puis le manderent en Ely.　　　　　3470
Puis n'i out home si hardy
Ki emblast ou moster d'Ely.

A Ciringcestre avint, ce dist,
Un miracle ke truis escrist:
Une vesve femme i manoit　　　　　3475
Que une bele fillie avoit.
Cele vesve dont nos parlom
A Walingford prist baron,
Ranulf a non, qui l'esposa
Et a sa maison le mena.　　　　　3480
Sa fillïe ad ou li menee,
Noble pucele et ascemee,
Mes ke sa mere contredist
Et contralia et despist.
Une nuit se geut et dormi,　　　　　3485
Une femme vint devant li.
De sa mein en vis la feri
Ke de son nes sang li issi.

After the death of a good abbot,
named Simeon,
his monks remained in Ely
3450   (of which this book is an attestation).
These monks gathered up all the gold and silver,
not leaving a single ornament.
They carried off the head of Saint Botulf
and other relics that were there.
3455   There was a marvelous tapestry—
never has there been one so precious.
Carrying away all these valuables
they went straight to Guildford,*
took lodging at an inn,
3460   then drank and ate too much.
That night the inn burned,
and all that they brought was destroyed.
That night the tapestry they had stolen
from Queen Audrey was burned.
3465   The next day they went to Winchester
and confessed their wickedness.
In the place from whence they had originally come [Winchester]
they admitted the theft
and begged for mercy from Saint Audrey.
3470   Then it was made known in Ely.
Ever since, there has been no one so bold
as to steal from the church at Ely.

They tell of a miracle, which I have also found in writing,
that occurred in Cirenchester
3475   where there lived a widow
who had a beautiful daughter.
This particular widow
married a nobleman from Wallingford
named Ranulf,
3480   who took her into his home.
She brought her daughter along with her,
a noble and well-attired maiden,
yet one who opposed,
despised, and argued with her mother.
3485   One night as she lay sleeping,
a woman appeared before her.
With her hand she struck the girl on the face
so that blood ran from her nose.

La pucele s'en enveillia.
Mut se dolut et mut greva. 3490
Vers un des ieus li descendi
Le cop si que l'on l'en tolli.
De l'autre conte ici le voir
K'ele n'en peut mie bien voir.
Tant par fu de cel mal grevee 3495
K'a la mort estoit atornee.
A la roïne seinte Audree
Ad sa mere merci crïee
Pur sa fillie piteusement
Ou lermes la requist sovent 3500   fol 126r col 2
Ke ele eüst pité de ly.
Une nuit avint issi
K'une femme li vint devant,
Si l'apella tut en oiant.
Demanda li si el dormoit. 3505
Cele [li] dist que non fesoit.
« Promettez, » dist ele, « a aler
Et vostre chandeile a porter
En Ely desqu'a seinte Audree,
Si serez de vos ieus sanee. » 3510
Cele dame se departi,
L'autre le mist tot en obli.
Par trois fois [i] vint, si li dist
Ke sainte Audree requeïst.
Cele li dist k'el ne porroit 3515
Car sa mere ne le seuffreit.
Nepurquant el parla a lui
Et la mere li respondi
Ke fantasme ert k'ele out veüe,
Dont s'est la pucele teüe, 3520
Mes tost aprés ou la veüe
Ravoit la parole perdue.
Seinte Audree la glorïuse
Requist la mere doleruse.
A la pucele est revenue 3525
La dame k'ele out einz veüe,
Si la reprist a apeler:
Cele ne pout a lui parler.
La dame en la buche li mist
Une fleur et parler la fist.* 3530
Dist li k'a seinte Audree alast

The maiden awoke
3490   in pain and terrible suffering.
The blow fell so near one of her eyes
that it knocked the eye awry.
The writing states clearly that out of the other eye,
she could barely see.
3495   She seemed so devastated by this injury
that she was ready to die.
Her mother cried so desperately
for Queen Saint Audrey
to have mercy on her daughter,
3500   weeping as she called out,
that Saint Audrey took pity on her.
One night
a woman appeared before the girl
and called aloud to her,
3505   asking if she were asleep.
The girl replied that she was not.
"Promise," the woman said, "to go
take your candle
to Ely, all the way to Saint Audrey;
3510   then your eyes will be healed."
The lady departed,
but the girl forgot all about it.
Three times the lady came and told her
what Saint Audrey had requested of her.
3515   The girl explained her that she could not do it
because her mother would not allow it.
Nevertheless, she spoke to her mother about it,
and the mother told her
that it was only an illusion that she had seen.
3520   So the daughter said no more.
But soon after, along with her sight
she lost her speech.
Then the grieving mother prayed
to glorious Saint Audrey.
3525   The lady whom the maiden had seen before
came back to her
and began to call her;
but the girl was unable to answer.
Then the lady put a flower in her mouth
3530   that enabled her to speak.*
She told her to go to Saint Audrey

Et sa chandoile li portast.
Cele promist joieusement
Ke ele iroit hastivement,　　　　　　　　　fol 126v col 1
Mes kant ele fu bien sanee,　　　　　　3535
Si ad sa promesse oblïee.
Autre foiz cele dame vint,
Une maceue en sa mein tint
De fer ; sur le front li asist
Si ke le sang issir en fist.　　　　　　　3540
Cele remist tot refre[ë]e,
Si quida bien estre tuee.
L'autre nuit vint saintë Audree
Le front li tert, si l'a sanee.*
Ou un blanc drap k'ele tenoit　　　　　3545
Li terst le front, si li desoit
Ke pur sa mere itel servise
Li fist ke l'en avoit requise.
Sa chandoile face et s'offrende
En Ely voise, si le rende,　　　　　　　3550
Et li dist k'ele ert seinte Audree
Ki sa mere out tant reclamee.
Cele leva seine et heitee,
A sa mere est aparaillie[e].
En Ely amedeuz alerent　　　　　　　3555
Et lur chandoiles i porterent.
A seinte Audree les offrirent,
Mercis et graces li rendirent.
Cele fu de ses ieus sanee,
Ariere vont en lur contree.　　　　　　3560
De l'oil torleus et del meilliur
Fu seine, onc puis n'i out dolur.

A Borewelle un hom manoit*
Gefroi out non. Sa femme avoit
Entur le col un' enferté　　　　　　　3565
Dont nul ne li promist santé.
Enflé ert si resplendissant
Com[e] charboucle reluisant.　　　　　　fol 126v col 2
Bons mires i firent venir.
Tuz distrent k'el fu al morir.　　　　　3570
En cele grant enfermeté
Li sovint et ad remembré
De seinte Audree la roïne,

and take her a candle.
The girl promised joyfully
that she would go right away.
3535   But when she was completely well,
she forgot her promise.
Once more the lady appeared
this time holding an iron club in her hand.
She struck such a hard blow on the girl's forehead
3540   that blood flowed out.
The girl was left badly frightened,
and thought she had been killed.
The next night Saint Audrey herself appeared to her,
stroked her forehead, and cured her.
3545   With a white cloth in her hand
she wiped the girl's forehead and told her
that it was for her mother's sake that
she rendered this service, for the mother had requested it in prayer.
The girl should prepare her candle and her offering,
3550   and go to Ely to present it.
Then she told her that she was Saint Audrey
to whom her mother had prayed so much.
The maiden arose, healthy and happy.
With her mother she prepared herself,
3555   and both of them went to Ely
bringing their candles
which they offered to Saint Audrey,
giving her thanks and praise,
for the girl was cured in both eyes.
3560   They went back to their own country.
In her crossed eye and in the better one
she was made whole and had no more pain.

In Burwell there lived a man
named Geoffrey whose wife had
3565   an infirmity around her neck*
for which no one offered her a cure.
It was so swollen and bright,
shining like a carbuncle stone.
They had fine doctors come there,
3570   and all of them said that she was about to die.
During this terrible illness
she remembered
Saint Audrey, the queen,

Qui a tans cheitifs est mescine.
Piteusement merci li crie;   3575
Meïsme l'heure fu garie.
En Ely ala mercïer
La dame ki la vout saner.

Un hom de Colecestre ala
Ou sa magnee k'il mena   3580
Jesk'en Ely a seinte Audree,
Si a sa offrende portee.
Nichole requist, le porter,
Ke il le deut herbergïer
Et il se fist en sa maison,   3585
Si com en ceste escrit trovom.
A mie nuit enmaladi
Cil hom, la parole perdi. .
Jesk'a primes a issi jeü.
Sa compaigne ke ou li fu   3590
Et les autres ki li gardoient
Nïent de vie ne quidoient.
Sa femme com[e] forcenee
Parla issi a seinte Audree:
« Dame, roïne glorïuse,   3595
K'a forfait ceste dolereuse?
Par quel peché m'est avenu
Ke mon baron m'avez tollu?
De nostre contre[e] venimes
Et jesk'ici vos requeïmes.   3600
Ne deüsses mie sofrir
K'ariere ne peüst venir.   fol 127r col 1
S'en nostre contree moreüst,
[Et] entre ses amis geüst,
La moitié ne me pesast mie   3605
Ke vos requeroit mes aïe
Et a nos tenoit hom aidable
Et pie et duce et socurable.
S'ore ai ci mon baron perdu,
Certes il iert par moi seü   3610
En quel liu ke je jamés vienge,
Ke nul pur dame [ne] vos tienge
Ne ke mes nul ne vos requere
Par offrende ne par prïere. »
Com[e] la femme se desroit   3615

who for so many sufferers had been the remedy.
3575 Piteously she cried to her for mercy,
and at that very moment she was cured.
She went to Ely to thank
the lady who was willing to heal her.

A man from Colchester
3580 took his family
all the way to Ely
to bring an offering to Saint Audrey.
He sought out Nicholas the porter,
who was to give him lodging,
3585 and settled into his home,
according to the written account.
At midnight the man fell ill
and lost his speech,
and remained like that until prime.
3590 His wife who was with him
and all those hosting him
did not believe that he would live.
His wife, as if she were a mad woman,
spoke thus to Saint Audrey:
3595 "Lady, glorious queen,
what wrong has this sorrowful woman done?
What sin has caused you
to take my husband away from me?
From our homeland we have come
3600 all this way pray to you.
You should not allow him
to be unable to return.
If he were to die in our own country
and be buried among his friends,
3605 it would not bother me half as much.
People have always implored your aid,
and considered you helpful,
pious, sweet, and merciful.
But now if I lose my husband here,
3610 I will certainly know
that I should never again come to this place,
nor in any way regard you as my lady,
nor ever again make requests of you
either by offerings or by prayers."
3615 While the woman thus argued

Et vers seinte Audree tençoit,
Cil leva sus sein et heitié
Com de songe fuest enveillié.
Donc se est la feme escrïee,
Graces rendi a seinte Audree.   3620
Devant sa tombe sont alé,
Si li ont promis et voué
Ke chescon an la requeront,
Lur offrende li porteront.

Une femme d'ydrope emflee   3625
Vint a la tombe seinte Audree,
A la virge criout merci.
Desuz la tombe s'endormi,
Mes quant ele fu esperie,
Tote rendi l'ydropesie.   3630
Tant s'en delivra ke li prestre
Ou l'encensïer ne pout estre
Devant l'autier por encensier
S'il ne feïst estreim getier.
De ce miracle furent cert   3635
La gent kil virent en apert.   fol 127r col 2

D'un moine avom l'escrit veü
Ki de Glastingebire fu.
Mut fu nez de maveise gent.
Vilein furent tut si parent,   3640
Et il fist tut jurs maveisté
Et de ordesce et de peché.
Fel fu et par maveise vie
Ala il hors de s'abbeïe.
L'ordre reneia et despist,   3645
En pechés del siecle se mist
Ke des pechés est corumpuz
Et des maveises genz issuz.
Ne say de quel part li venist,
Ke Deu ovrast ne bien feïst.   3650
Cist reneiez, dont ge vos di,
Ranulf, ke son ordre geurpi,
A l'eveske d'Ely ala,
Il le receut et mut l'ama.
Ranulf fu fel et encusere   3655
Et de gent sudoire fu lere

and reproached Saint Audrey
her husband got up well and healthy,
awakened as if from a dream.
Then the woman cried out,
3620 giving thanks to Saint Audrey.
They both went to her tomb
and there promised her
that every year they would come pray to her
and bring her an offering.

3625 A woman swollen with dropsy
came to the tomb of Saint Audrey,
cried to the virgin for mercy
and fell asleep at the tomb.
But when she woke up
3630 the swelling had broken open.
So much fluid poured forth
that the priest could not continue
to perfume the altar with his censer
until he had spread straw around to absorb it.
3635 The people were convinced of this miracle
which they personally witnessed.

We have read a story about a monk
from Glastonbury.
who was born of very wicked people.
3640 In fact, all his relatives were evil,
and he was always getting involved in some wickedness,
foulness, or sin of some sort.
He was cruel, and because of his wicked life
he left his abbey,
3645 renounced and scoffed at his order,
indulged himself in worldly pleasures.
In short, he was begotten of wicked people
and corrupted by sin.
I do not see how it could ever happen
3650 that God could work or do any good through him.
This deserter I am telling you about,
Ranulf, who left his order,
went to the bishop of Ely
who received him and loved him dearly.
3655 Ranulf was a cruel man, a denouncer,
and a dishonest person who could deceive people

Par mentir et par losangier,
Dont il se sout trop bien aider.
L'ama l'eveske durement
Et mut creüt son loement.   3660
Son senescal et son bailli
Fist Ranulf, tant [il] le creï,
Et cil colvert tuz jurs haÿ
L'eglise et les moines d'Ely.
A l'eveske les encusa   3665
Et la maison mut enpira.
Dist li ke il erent beveur
Et de male vie et lecheur,
Et dist k'il n'erent mie digne
De manoir en cel liu benigne.   3670   fol 127v col 1
Uncor le dist k'il ne poit faire,
Si com les moines oi retraire,
Nule franchise ne nul don
Ne nul otrei si par eus non.
Ne demora pas longement   3675
Ke li eveskë ou grant gent
Ala en autre region,
Si comanda a cel felon
L'eglise d'Ely a garder
Et l'evesché a governer.   3680
Onkes plus tost n'out la baillie
K'il ne vousist par felonie
Avoir destruit tut le covent
Et l'eglise mise a nïent,
Si ne feust par la renomee   3685
Ke a l'eveske en fu portee.
Un prior out en la maison,
Frere Williamus out a non.
A l'eveske fu mut amis,
Cel an meïsmes l'i out mis.   3690
Li et les autres ad hostez
Et de lur mestier deposez:
Les natureus serjans hosta
Et estranges i amena.
Les moines destreut et leidi   3695
Et lur viande lur tolli.
Tant le[s] fist destreindre et garder
Ke nul ne pooit hors aler
Pur faire pleinte ne mostrance

through lies and flattery,
which he knew all too well how to use to his advantage.
The bishop loved him dearly
3660   and had complete faith in his counsel
to the extent that he made Ranulf
his seneschal and his bailiff.
All the while this perfidious man
hated the church and the monks of Ely.
3665   He falsely accused them to the bishop,
which did great harm to the whole house.
He told him they were drunkards
who led an evil and lecherous life
and that they were not worthy
3670   to live in this good place.
He also said that the monks had told him
that he could not
give any privileges, gifts, or permissions
to the church except through them.
3675   Not long afterwards
the bishop with a large entourage
went to another region
and left this evil man
the charge of the church of Ely
3680   and the governance of the diocese.
No sooner did he have the authority
than he perversely would have had
the whole convent destroyed
and the church reduced to nothing
3685   were it not for the fact that rumor of it
reached the bishop.
There was a prior in the house
named Brother William,
a good friend of the bishop,
3690   who had placed him in the monastery that same year.
Ranulf removed him and the other monks,
divesting them of their posts.
He took away the regular servants
and brought in new ones.
3695   He tormented and mistreated the monks
and even deprived them of food.
He had them so strictly guarded
that no one could get out
to complain or protest

A nuli de lur mesestance. 3700
Deuz anz suffrierent en covent
Ceste peine et ce marrement,
Tant que priv[e]ement prïerent,
Seinte Audree ou lermes requerent, fol 127v col 2
Ke par sa pitié lur aidast 3705
Et de Ranulf les delivrast.
Lur prïere oÿ seinte Audree;
Tost fu la novele portee
A l'eveske ke mut peisa
Et de revenir se hasta. 3710
L'eveskë oÿ bien parler
De deuz serjanz et reconter,
Raol et Henri sont nomé,
Par cui Ranulf avoit ovré.
Icist destruient la maison 3715
Et en avront mal guer[re]don.
L'eveske vint hastivement,
De plusurs fist grief vengement
Ke de la gent Ranulf estoient
Et qui ou li le mal fesoient. 3720
Ranulf et Henri s'en alerent
Ou tant d'avoir com amenerent.
Cil ki remistrent furent pris,
Li lay et pendu et occis,
Li clerc erent tot en chatié 3725
Et hors del païs exilié.
Raol li Borgondois s'en fui,
A la virge crïout merci
Et reconout s'iniquité,
Que malement avoit ovré. 3730
N'i out puis clerc n'official
Ke as moines feïst nul mal.
Pur la vengance ke de ceus
Fist seinte Audree, eurent pes d'eus.

En tens N[e]el, l'eveske, avint* 3735
K'une cheitive femme vint
De Coteham, envogle estoit,
Trois anz devant veü n'avoit. fol 128r col 1
A la feste [ele] fu menee
La glorïuse seinte Audree, 3740
Sa chandoile offri et dona,

3700   to anyone about their terrible situation.
       For two years those in the monastery
       endured this pain and oppression.
       Finally they began to pray secretly
       and in tears asked Saint Audrey
3705   to help them out of pity
       by delivering them from Ranulf.
       Saint Audrey heard their prayer.
       When the news reached the bishop
       he was terribly upset by it
3710   and hastened to return.
       The bishop had been told
       about two servants
       named Raoul and Henry,
       through whom Ranulf had worked.
3715   They were the ones who wrecked the house
       and would surely receive punishment for it.
       The bishop came back immediately.
       and took heavy vengeance against
       those among Ranulf's people
3720   who were involved with him in this evil.
       Ranulf and Henry left
       with as many possessions as they could carry,
       but those who remained were captured.
       The laymen were hanged,
3725   while the clerics were all punished
       and exiled from the country.
       Raoul the Burgundian fled,
       but then begged for mercy from the virgin
       admitting his sin
3730   and acknowledging that he had done wrong.
       Since then no cleric or official
       has done any harm to the monks.
       After the vengeance that Saint Audrey
       took on Ranulf's people, they lived in peace.

3735   In the time of Bishop Nigel, it so happened
       that a poor woman came
       from Cottenham. She had been
       completely blind for three years.
       She had to be led to the feast day
3740   of glorious Saint Audrey.
       She gave her candle as an offering

Desus la tombe demora.
A la virge cria merci
Et que ele out pité de li.
La seinte virge, Deu amie,   3745
Ad sa prïere bien oÿe.
Ses yeus sana et [les] ovri
Et sa veüe li rendi.
Cele que eins i fu menee
Tote seine s'en est alee.   3750
Ceo seürent tuz veraiment
Et clerc et lay communaument.

D'un prestre dit k'il mut ama
Seinte Audree, si comanda
Ke ses parochiens feïrassent   3755
Sa festë et li honorassent.
Un en i out qui respondi
K'il n'en savoit nïent de li,
Dont ele ert ne ki ele estoit
Ne il nïent ne feireroit.   3760
Le jur meïme ala ovrer
En champ; si com il deut passer
Un[e] haie pur issir hors,
Si li entra un pel en cors.
Par grant « aï » l'en rasacha,   3765
Mes la pointe dedenz brisa.
Tut l'an i fu, mult li greva,
De jur en jur li enpira.
Al chief de l'an tut si parent
Li loërent comunaument   3770
Ke a la feste deut aler
Seinte Audree merci crïer.   fol 128r col 2
Il i ala et si offri,
Le jur et la nuit attendi,
Veillia, et si cria merci.   3775
Seinte Audree pas ne l'oï.
Triste et dolent le ont mené
Cil qui ou li furent alé.
Dehors la vile en un beu pré
Le cochent, si l'ont reposé.   3780
A prime oÿ les seins soner.
Vers l'eglise prist a orer
Et dist: « Dame, de grant pité,

and remained at the tomb
crying to the virgin for mercy
asking her to take pity on her.
3745 The holy virgin, friend of God,
did indeed hear her prayer.
She healed her eyes
opening them so that her sight was restored.
She who at first had been led there
3750 went away completely whole.
Everyone knew this for a fact,
both clergy and lay people alike.

Concerning a certain priest it is said that he dearly loved
Saint Audrey; so he ordered
3755 his parishioners to honor her
by celebrating her feast day.
But one of the parishioners answered
that he knew nothing about her,
where she was from or who she was,
3760 so he refused to celebrate her feast.
That very day he went to work
in the fields; while passing through
a hedgerow in order to get out [to the fields]
a twig stuck into his body.
3765 With a loud scream of "Ouch!" he pulled it out,
but the tip broke off inside.
It stayed there all year, causing him great pain.
Day by day the pain grew worse.
At the beginning of the year all his relatives
3770 in agreement advised him
to go to the feast
of Saint Audrey to plead for mercy.
So he went there and presented himself.
Day and night he waited,
3775 keeping vigils and crying for mercy,
but Saint Audrey did not hear him.
Those who had come with him
led him away, sad and grieving.
Outside the city in a beautiful meadow
3780 they laid him down and let him rest.
At prime he heard the bells ring
and began to pray toward the church
saying: "Lady of great mercy,

Pur un seul jur si t'ay peché
Ne deüssez si prendre a ire.   3785
Mut en ay suffert grant martire.
Dame, pur Deu regardez moy.
Je te promet en bone foy
Ke tut jurs mes te serveray
Et vostre feste garderay.   3790
A tuz ceus le f[e]ray feirer
Ke m'amerunt et avrunt cher. »
Kant il out s'oreison finie
Seinte Audree li fist aïe.
En liu ou le pel li feri   3795
Creva, la pointe s'en issi
Del pel dont il estoit feruz.
Tost sein est a meison venuz.

D'un frere dist de la meison
Ke prechout, Brithmar out non,   3800
A ponz fairë et relever
Soleit le[s] reliques porter
Et la chemise seinte Audree
Dont meint bien [...] est ovree.
En une vile ou il entra   3805
Chiés un prodome herberga.   fol 128v col 1
En berz gesoit enfanz petiz
Si durement enmaladiz
K'il ne quidoit si la mort non.
Brithmar feist pur lui oreison   3810
A la reïne seinte Audree.
La chemise k'il out portee
Mist sur l'enfant, si l'en covri
Et il ad veire tot garri.
Einz le tierz jur beut et manga   3815
Et fu tot sein ke mal n'en a.

De Thomas dit une aventure,
Un clerc ke sout mut lettr[e]üre.
Pur la scïence k'il savoit
Orguillius ert, sovent fesoit   3820
Tel chose ke [n']avenoit mie
Ke clerc deüt mener tel vie.*
Par li meïme avons oÿ
K'en grant maladie chaÿ

for only one day did I sin against you.
3785 You should not be angry over it,
for I have suffered great misery because of it.
Lady, for God's sake, look upon me.
I promise you in good faith
that from now on I will serve you
3790 and keep your feast day.
I will make all those who love me
and hold me dear honor it."
When he had finished this prayer
Saint Audrey came to his aid.
3795 At the place where the stick had pierced him
[his skin] opened up and out came the tip of the stick
that had wounded him.
He returned completely whole to his home.

The book tells about a brother of the house
3800 named Brithmar, who was a preacher.
To make and illustrate his points
he had the habit of carrying around the relics
and the chemise of Saint Audrey
through which much good has come about.
3805 He went into one particular town
where he lodged in a good man's home.
Lying in a cradle there was a small child
So gravely ill
that Brithmar suspected it was dying.
3810 He said a prayer for it
to the queen Saint Audrey,
then took the chemise he carried
and covered the child with it,
and the boy was completely healed.
3815 By the third day he drank and ate
and was quite healthy, for he was no longer ill.

It also tells a story about Thomas,
a clerk who knew much about books.
Because of the knowledge he possessed
3820 he was haughty and often did things
that did not suit
the life of a clerk.
Directly from him we heard
that he fell so seriously ill

K'il ne peut parler de treis jurs.   3825
De vie n'atendoit socurs
Le mire, ne cil kil gardoient
Neule santé ne esperoient.
Kant vit k'il ne pooit garir,
Ses amis fist a lui venir,   3830
Par devant eus se fist confés.
Enolliez voloit estre aprés,
Mes ses amis et si veisin
Li loërent, ge[s]qu'au matin
Attendi[s]t et Deu reclamast   3835
Par sa pité k'il li aidast.
Par lur conseil [a] attendu
Thomas, se li est sovenu
De la reïne precïuse,
Seinte Audree la glorïuse.   3840   fol 128v col 2
Devotement l'a reclamee:
« Reïne, » dist il, « seinte Audree,
A ce besoing, dame, vos pri
Ke vos de moy aiez merci.
Si torner puis a gareison,   3845
[Et si de vos avoir pardon,]*
Pur dame vos reconostrai
Et tuz jurz mes vos serverai,
Et si amender[a]i ma vie
Et lerray estre ma folie. »   3850
Il avoit ja ouit jurz geü.
La nuit li est si avenu
K'avis li fu k'en une eglise
Ke duz chant [ot] et beau servise
Cume de voiz angelïel   3855
Ke de la sus venist del ciel.
Dedenz l'eglise out un autiel
De marbre, il ne vit unkes tel.
Une bele dame en estant
I vit et ele oiroit devant.   3860
Avis li fu qu'a Deu oroit
Pur li et [ke] merci crioit.
Puis vint a lui, si li hostoit
Ou un blanc drap k'ele portoit
La poudre k'il out sur son vis.   3865
[Monda le lit, s'envanit puis.]*
Bien sout ke c'estoit seinte Audree

3825   that he could not even speak for three days.
        The doctor did not expect him to live
        nor did those taking care of him
        have any hope for his health.
        When he realized that he could not get well,
3830   he called his friends to him
        and in their presence made his confession.
        After that he wished to receive extreme unction.
        But his friends and neighbors advised him
        to wait until morning
3835   and to call upon God
        to help him through His mercy.
        Following their advice Thomas waited;
        then he remembered
        the precious queen,
3840   glorious Saint Audrey.
        Out of devotion he called on her:
        "Queen Saint Audrey," he said,
        "in my need, lady, I beg you
        to have mercy on me.
3845   If I can return to health
        [and receive pardon from you]
        I will acknowledge you as my lady
        and will serve you forever.
        I will amend my life,
3850   and forgo my foolish ways."
        He had been in bed for eight days
        when, one night,
        he dreamed that he was in a church
        hearing a beautiful mass
3855   sung as though with angelic voices
        that came from heaven above.
        Inside the church there was a marble altar
        the likes of which had never seen.
        All at once he saw a lovely lady
3860   praying before this altar.
        He believed she was praying to God
        and crying for mercy on his behalf.
        Then she came toward him;
        with a white cloth she was holding
3865   she wiped the dust off his face.
        [She cleaned his bed, then disappeared.]
        He was certain this was Saint Audrey

A qui il out merci crïe[e].
De l'avision s'enveillia
Thomas, a sa gent le conta.　　　　3870
Cil li dïent k'il est gariz
De ce soit tuz seürs et fiz.
Il garri bien et trespassa,
D'iluec en avant s'amenda.
Puis s'en ala a seinte Audree;　　　　3875
De sa santé l'a mercïee.
Il meïsmes fist cest escrit
Del miracle k'avons redit.

fol 129r col 1

D'un jofne moine redit ci
Ke [en] enfermeté chaÿ　　　　3880
Tel k'il ne se pooit aider
Ne pez ne mains a lui sacher.
Dosze anz out si com nos trovom.
Simple fu mut, Johan out non.
Seinte Audree le visita.　　　　3885
Del pan de son mantel hosta
La poudre ke suer li trova.
Et puis aprés li comanda
K'al martir seint Edmund alast
Et pur son amor li priast　　　　3890
Ke il le dout saner pur ly.
Le moine leva et garry.
A l'autier seinte Audree vint,
Congïé prist, son erre tint.
A Seint Edmund s'en est alez,　　　　3895
La fu tut gari et sanez.
Al covent de lieenz conta
Com seinte Audree l'enveia
A seint Edmund pur garrison.
Il mercïerent le baron　　　　3900
Et la virge pur qui ce fu
Dont ont le miracle veü.

D'un bachelier redit ici,
Rechard out non, si fu d'Ely.
En tel maladie chaÿ　　　　3905
Ke le cheitif del sen issi,
Si fu devez et enragiez
K'il ne pooit estre lïez.

on whom he had called for mercy.
Thomas awoke from the dream
3870 and related it to his people.
They told him that he had been healed,
for they were all convinced of it.
He indeed got well and completely recovered.
From then on he changed his ways.
3875 He went to Saint Audrey
and thanked her for his health.
He himself wrote about
this miracle we have recounted.

It tells the story of a young monk
3880 who fell so ill
that he could not take care of himself
nor move his hands or feet.
We are told that he was twelve years old,
that he was simple-minded, and his name was John.
3885 Saint Audrey visited him
and with the hem of her garment wiped away
the dust she found on him.
Afterwards she told him
to go to Saint Edmund the Martyr
3890 and ask him through love
to provide healing for her sake.
The monk got up and felt better.
He went to Saint Audrey's altar,
took his leave, and made the journey.
3895 He went to Bury Saint Edmunds,
where he was completely cured and restored to health.
He told the monastics living there
how Saint Audrey had sent him
to Saint Edmund for his healing.
3900 They all thanked the good man [Saint Edmund]
and the virgin, for whose sake it was done,
for the miracle they had witnessed.

Now here is the story of a young man
named Richard, who was from Ely.
3905 He became so ill
that the wretched man went out of his mind.
He was so insane
that he could not even be bound.

Par totes les rues aloit
Criant et la gent travaillioit.   3910   fol 129r col 2
Une nuit aloit par la rue,
Si ad une dame veüe.
Ses vestemenz, li fu avis,
Resplendi come feu espris.
« Cheitif, » dist ele, « que fais tu? »   3915
Mut ad grant mal et a heü.
Il demanda ke ele fu
Et la virgë ad respondu:
« Je sui, » dist ele, « seinte Audree,
Dame de cel liu sui nomee. »   3920
Le malade quant il oÿ,
Si li cria pur Deu merci.
La dame vers li ala, ce dist,
Sa manchë entur le chief mist.
En l'eglise le fist aler   3925
De sa santé Deu mercïer,
Et dist li k'il estoit gariz.
Il en rendi griez et merciz.
Il fist ce k'ele comanda:
En mostier vint et si oura   3930
Devant la tombe seinte Audree,
Puis a s'aventure contee.

De l'eveskë en dist ici
Ke durement enmaladi.
Tant out la maladie fort   3935
Ke tuz jugeient a la mort.
Une femme avoit en Ely
Ke mut ama Deu et servi.
Les moines pur Deu [la] peisseient
Pur le grant bien k'en li v[e]eient.   3940
Une nuit quant ele dorm[o]it
Li fu avis que ele estoit
Dedenz l'eglise pur orer.
Si vit une noneine ester   fol 129v col 1
Devant l'auter, vers li ala.   3945
Deriere un des uis la trova
Et dist k'ele ert a li venue,
Si li mostroit une maceue
De fer k'ele avoit aportee
Dont ele venjoit seinte Audree   3950

He went all through the streets
3910   yelling and disturbing people.
One night he was going along the street
and he saw a lady.
It seemed to him that her garments
shone as if they were on fire.
3915   "Poor fellow," she said, "What are you doing?"
In his great pain he cried out,
asking who she was;
and the virgin answered him:
"I am Saint Audrey," she said,
3920   "I am known as the lady of this place."
When the sick man heard this,
he begged her for God's mercy.
The story goes on to say that the lady approached him
and placed her sleeve around his head.
3925   She bade him go into the church
to thank God for his health,
for she told him that he was cured.
Expressing his gratitude, he thanked her
and did what she commanded:
3930   he went into the church and prayed
before the tomb of Saint Audrey,
then he told his story.

The story is told of a bishop
who became gravely ill.
3935   The illness was so serious
that everyone expected him to die.
There was a woman in Ely
who dearly loved God and faithfully served Him.
The monks fed her out of charity
3940   because of the great goodness they saw in her.
One night while she was sleeping,
she dreamed that she was
praying inside the church
when she saw, standing in front of the altar,
3945   a nun who came toward her
and found her behind one of the doors.
The nun told her that she had come to see her,
then showed her a club
of iron that she had brought
3950   with which she avenged Saint Audrey

De ceus ke vers li meperneient
Et amender ne se voleient
E qui lui erent tol[e]ür
[Et] meffeisant et destruieür.
La femme demanda son non   3955
Et s'ele osoit la vision
A nuli dire ne conter,
S'el li voloit congé doner.
« Withbourc, » dist ele, « sui nomee
Et si sui suer la seinte Audree.*   3960
A un moine, Aüstin a non,
Contez icest' avision.
A le eveske voit mostrier,
Si li conseil de s'amender
Ou il vendra a male fin.   3965
Bien li mandez par Aüstin,
As autres le die autresi
Ke sovent unt meffeit a li. »*
La povre femme s'enveillia
Si fist ce qu'ele comanda.   3970

En cest escrit avom trovee
De ceus ke eurent meserré
Vers seinte Audree et vers sa gent,
Com ele en prist grief vengement.
Des clers, de[s] moines nus retrait   3975
Et des lais ki li ont meffait:
D'Adam ke conestable fu,
Del boiteillier ay entendu,   fol 129v col 2
D'Alisandre ki li mesfist,
Henri li Estrange meprist,   3980
Williame de Selford vos nom,
De Ricard de seint Pol trovom,
L'arcediacne de l'eglise.
Williame, ci com ci devise,
Ky en un pleit reconte ci   3985
Et sen et memoire perdi,
Et tut li autre compaignion
Alerent a perdition.
Et de l'eveske nos devise
Ke un jur se fist en l'eglise   3990
Et fesoit ses devisions
De terres dont il fist ses dons.

against those who had wronged her
and did not wish to amend their ways:
against thieves,
evil-doers, and destroyers.
3955 The woman asked her name
and said that she dared not
recount this vision to anyone
unless she would give her leave to do so.
The nun replied, "Withburga, is my name,
3960 and I am Saint Audrey's sister.*
Recount this vision
to a monk named Augustine.
He in turn should reveal it to the bishop
and advise him to amend his ways
3965 or else he will come to a bad end.
Make clear to him through Augustine
that he tell it as well to other people
who have often wronged Audrey."
The poor woman woke up,
3970 and did as Withburga had commanded

We have found in this writing
[stories] about people who have done wrong
to Saint Audrey and to her people,
and about how she took severe vengeance on them for it.
3975 We are told about clerks, monks, and lay people
who have acted improperly toward her:
I have heard about Adam who was a constable,
about a butler,
about Alexander who wronged her,
3980 and Henry the Strange who defied her.
I will also mention William of Shelford to you,
and Richard, the archdeacon
of Saint Paul's church.
William, so it is told
3985 in one of these stories,
lost his faculties of reason and memory;
and all the others in this company [of wrong-doers]
went to perdition.
We are also told about a bishop
3990 who one day set himself up in church
and started dividing up its lands
to bestow as his personal gifts.

Feru fu de paralisie
Et porté [en] enfermerie.
Iluec murut hastivement,   3995
Ne vesqui mie longement.
Ceste vengeance est acertee
Ke ce fist Deu pur seinte Audree.

Un hom de Hantone out langui,
Tant geut en mal k'il acorbi: 4000
Ne se pout drescer ne lever.
En Ely vint merci crïer.
Seinte Audree merci cria.
Bien longement il demora.
Les moines leenz le peisseient   4005
Ke la maladïe ennoient.
Devant la tombe un jur ora
Et la virge le redresca.
A haute voiz s'est escrïez
Devant trestuz k'il ert sanez.   4010

Si nos conte de Julïen,
Un clerc ke mut avoit grant bien.   fol 130r col 1
Mut sout des ars, bien fu lettrez,
Et mut fu de l'eveske amez.
Puis ke il primes s'acointa   4015
L'eveske N[e]el mut l'ama.
Il dist a l'eveske N[e]el
Ke bien fuest ke li jovencel
Ke moine estoient apreïssent
Et en devine page leïssent.   4020
Meuz en savreient Deu servir
Et honestement contenir.
Le eveske se assenti:
Deuz jefnes moines de Ely
Pur endoctriner li baillia,   4025
Et il a Londres les mena.
Le plus jefnes fu fol, ce dist.
Pur foler son ordre despist.
Son compaign fu de grant bonté
Et de bone moralité.   4030
Mes si avint que poi dura:
Sa fin le prist et tost fina.
L[i] autre une nuit se dormit.

He was struck with paralysis
and was carried to the infirmary
3995   where he soon died—
he did not live for very long!
It is certain that this vengeance
was taken by God for the sake of Saint Audrey.

A man from Southampton had suffered
4000   and had been lying ill for so long that he was bent over
and could not stand up straight.
He came to Ely to beg for mercy
and began crying out to Saint Audrey.
He stayed in Ely such a long time
4005   that the monks living there started feeding him
to help combat the illness.
One day he was praying before the tomb,
and the virgin raised him up straight.
He cried out in a loud voice
4010   in front of everyone that he was cured.

There is a story about Julian,
a very wealthy clerk
who was well educated and skilled in the arts,
and he was dearly loved by the bishop.
4015   Ever since he first came to know him,
Bishop Nigel was quite fond of him.
Julian told Bishop Nigel
that it would be good for the young men
who were monks to learn
4020   to read the Holy Scriptures.
As a result, they would know how to serve God better
and how to conduct themselves honorably.
The bishop consented
and gave him two young monks from Ely
4025   to instruct.
So he took them to London.
We are told that the younger one was imprudent
and disregarded his vows in order to behave foolishly,
whereas his companion was full of goodness
4030   and respectable morality.
But, as it turned out, the latter had only a short life,
for he died soon thereafter.
One night the other one was asleep

Avis li ert ke il le vit
A Seint Pol devant le mostier,   4035
Mes il n[e] osoit aprismier.
Cil li [dist] qu'il s'asseürast:
N'ert mie mort, a lui parlast.
Puis li dist k'il avoit veüe
Seinte Audree et reconeüe   4040
Devant Deu, et tint un sautier
Et si l'oÿ pur li prier.
Kant ce out dist, si s'envani,
Ses compainz e[s]t tost esperi.
D'iluec en avant s'amenda: 4045
Prodom devint et Deu ama.   fol 130r col 2
S'avision ad recontee
Come ma dame seinte Audree
Par la grant merite de li
De ses pechiez l'out departi.   4050

A Grettone un prodom manoit
Ke de son labur droit vivoit.
Une nuit dormi et sompnia
K'une voiz vint, si li rova
Ke a Seint Edmund deut aler*   4055
Et a l'abbé Ording parler,
Et li deïst k'il ert mandez
Ke garni fuest et atornez
K'a Grettone peüst venir
Et un seint home deffoïr.   4060
Mes ert seinte Audree par non
K'out veü en avision.
En honeste liu li meïst.
Aillïez out a non, ceo dist.
Le prodom vint hastivement,   4065
Fist bien icest comaundement.
A Seint Osmon tost s'en ala.*
A l'abbé Ording le mostra.
Li abbes a Deu mercïé
Ke ceo lui avoit demostré.   4070
Tant fu d'autre fere encombrez
Ke dunc n'i poëit estre alez.*

Un povre home, ci dist, estoit
Ke en la contre[e] manoit

and dreamed that he saw his companion
4035 standing in front of Saint Paul's church,
but he did not dare to approach him.
His companion told him to be reassured:
he was not dead, and the two of them should talk.
Then he told him that he had seen
4040 Saint Audrey
standing before God and holding a psalter
and had heard her praying for him.
When he had said this, he disappeared,
and his companion woke up immediately.
4045 From then on he changed his ways:
he became a good man who loved God.
He recounted this vision
and told how the lady Saint Audrey
through her great merit
4050 rid him of his sins.

In Gretton there lived a good man
who earned his living directly from his labor.
One night he lay sleeping and dreamed
he heard a voice telling him
4055 that he should go to Bury Saint Edmunds
and speak to Abbot Ording
and tell him he had been sent
so that the abbot might make preparations
and come to Gretton
4060 to exhume a holy man
and put him in a more appropriate place.
Now it was Saint Audrey herself
whom he had seen in his dream.
She said that the holy man's name was Ailliez.
4065 The good man quickly
carried out this command.
He went immediately to Bury Saint Edmunds
and revealed everything to Abbot Ording.
The abbot thanked God
4070 that the good man had related this to him,
[but] he was so burdened with other matters
that he would be unable to go at that time.*

There was a poor man, so it says,
who lived on the outskirts

De Norantone, ou il fu nez.   4075
Maladis ert et tuit emflez.
N'ert pas mortel s'enfermeté,
Mes Deus voloit ke sa bonté
E la merite seinte Audree
Fust par son mal signifie[e].   4080   fol 130v col 1
Une nuit la ou il se just*
Une dame lui aparust
Et li dist qu'alast en Ely,
Sa garison avroit par ly.
L'endemein cil s'est esmeüz   4085
Et je[s]k' en Ely s'est venuz.
A tiel hure vint a mostier
Com les moines deurent mangier.
Un serjant ke clöeit les uus
Li rova qu'il alast en sus.   4090
Cil fu egres de uus fermer
Et le malade de l'entrer.
Pur Deu li requist ducement,
Cil le feri par mal talent:
Li enferm plora e gemi,   4095
Et li serjant s'en repenti,
Pensa ke mal li avoit fait,
Si a [a] son mestier retrait.
Li uus ovri et cil entra
Et pur l'amur Deu li pria   4100
K'a la fonteine le menast
Et de cele ewe li donast.
Cil li [dit] qu'il n'i out vessel
Hanap ne jouste ne seiel.
« Alez, » fait il, « et si veez   4105
Et hastivement repeirez. »
Cil est alez a la fonteine
Si com s'aventure le meine.
Parfonde ert, ne poit avenir,
Et il s'en ai[d]eit a partir:*   4110
Piteusement l'ad esgardee.
L'ewe est encontre li montee,
Par tut le pavement coreut.   fol 130v col 2
Il se leva et si en beut.
Meïme l'heure fu gariz,   4115
Tut desenflé et agreilliz.
Le serjant, quant il a veü

4075   of Northampton where he was born.
He was sick and all swollen,
but his illness was not terminal,
for God willed that the goodness
and the merit of Saint Audrey
4080   be manifested through it.
One night, there where he lay,
a lady appeared to him
and told him that should he go to Ely
where he would receive healing through her.
4085   The next day this man awoke
and went all the way to Ely.
He came to the monastery at the hour
when the monks were scheduled to eat.
A servant who was locking the doors
4090   asked him to go away,
for he was as eager to close the door
as the sick man was to enter.
The sick man implored him kindly for God's sake,
but the irritated servant struck him.
4095   The sick man began to cry and moan,
and the servant repented,
thinking he had injured him
and had neglected his duty.
So he opened the door to him and the man came in,
4100   begging him for the love of God
to take him to the fountain
and give him some of the water.
The servant told him there was no vessel,
cup, bowl, or skin at the fountain.
4105   "Go," he said, "see for yourself,
and come back quickly."
Then the sick man went to the fountain,
as he was destined to do,
but the water was so deep that he could not reach it,
4110   and he prepared to leave.
Sorrowfully he looked at the water,
and as he did it rose toward him,
flowing over the pavement stones.
He got up and drank from it,
4115   and at that very moment he was cured,
thin, with all the swelling gone.
When the servant saw him,

Et le miracle aparceü,
A covent l'ad tost reconté
Et il en [ont] Deu mercïé   4120
Et la roïne sein[t]e Audree
Ki sa poissance i a mostree.

Une femme i fu ja menee
Ke longement ert aveuglee.
Ses ieus lava de la fonteine   4125
Sa veüe out, tote fu seine.

D'une mechine avom oÿ
Ki en la fonteine chaÿ.
Son vessel [el] voloit puisier,
Si li estoit a trebuchier.   4130
Treis heures i fu, s'i neia,
Si que nul ne l'en releva.
Ricard et Stephene par non
L'en trestrent sus. Par oreison
Ke il firent a seinte Audree   4135
Estoit cele resuscitee.
Les clers ki le miracle virent
A Damnedeu graces rendirent.

En tens le roi Edgar trovom
K'out une grant assension   4140
De seculers clers de la terre
Envers ceus ke voloient querre
K'il fuissent en religion.
Edelwold l'eveske par non,
Ke tenoit le sé de Wincestre,   4145
Et Wolstan de Wireceste   fol 131r col 1
Et Brithnode, abbé de Ely,
Checun de ces s'i assenti
D'hostier les seculers chanoines,
Et as eglises firent moynes.   4150
Ky ne voudroit l'ordre tenir,
Si l'en feïst hom departir.
Les clers au roy Edgar alerent
Et de cel hovre se clamerent.
Distrent k'il erent deposé   4155
Et de lur eglises geté
Sanz reison et sanz jugement.

he recognized the miracle,
immediately reported it to the monastery,
4120   and they all thanked God
and Queen Saint Audrey for it,
for in this she had shown her power.

A woman was brought there
who had been blind for a long time
4125   She washed her eyes in the fountain,
and received her sight; she was completely cured.

We have also heard about a young girl
who fell into the fountain.
She wished to dip in her vessel
4130   but lost her balance.
She was in the fountain for three hours and drowned,
for no one lifted her out.
Finally men named Richard and Stephen
pulled her up. Through the prayers
4135   they made to Saint Audrey
the girl was revived,
and the clerks who witnessed the miracle
gave thanks to the Lord God.

In the time of King Edgar we learn
4140   that there was a great revolt
of the secular clerks of the land
against those who were insisting
that clerks should be members of a religious order.
The bishop named Ethelwold,
4145   who held the See of Winchester,
Wulfstan of Worcester,*
and Brithnoth, abbot of Ely,
all agreed
to remove the secular canons
4150   and place monks in the churches:
any clerk who did not wish to take holy vows
would be made to leave.
The clerks went to King Edgar
and complained of this act.
4155   They said they were being deposed
and unreasonably and unjustly
thrown out of their churches.

Le roy en out grant maltalent.
Pur iceste chose amender
Fist tost son conseil assembler   4160
De clers, de barons, ce me semble,
En un mostier vindrent ensemble.
Lur Edgar fesoient issi
Ke les clers fuissent reseisi.
Une crois de perre out asise   4165
Ancïenement en l'eglise
Ke dist en haut si com l'oÿ:
« Je ne voil pas k'i soit issi. »
Deuz foiz le dist. Espö[e]ntez
En fu le roy et les barnez.   4170
Pur ce pout bien le roy oïr
K'a Deu ne vint mie a pleisir
Ke les moines fuissent hosté
Ne des eglises remüé.
Les eveskes s'en departirent   4175
A Damnedeu graces rendirent.
Ceo miracle fu bien seüz
Par Engleterre et entenduz.

De l'abbé Brinoth mostre ici   fol 131r col 2
Com il fist venir en Ely   4180
Seinte Wythborc k'il remüa
De Der[e]ham ou la trova.*
Al roy Edgar se conseillia
Par son conseil genz assembla,
Eveskes, moines, et abbez.   4185
A Der[e]ham les ad menez.
La nuit veillia en oreison
Devant lui par devotion
A mie nuit la tombe ovri,
De la terre la descovri.   4190
La virge trova en tel guise
Com le jur ke ele fu mise.
Salua la, si la requist,
Si li pleut, ke ele sueffri[s]t
Ke il l'en peut faire porter   4195
En Ely pur li honurer.
Ses compaigniuns a apellez
Ou tut le cors s'en sont alez.
Seur eus s'aparut une estoile

The king was very upset by all of this.
To take care of the matter
4160 he immediately assembled his council
of clerks and barons, so I am led to believe,
who gathered in the church.
Then Edgar addressed them saying
that the secular clerks should be reinstated.
4165 A stone cross that had been standing
since ancient times in the church
spoke aloud, and he heard it say:
"I do not wish it to be like that."
It spoke these words twice. The king
4170 and his barons were frightened by it,
but because of it the king realized
that it did not at all please God
for the monks
to be removed from the churches.
4175 The bishops left
giving thanks to the Lord God.
This miracle was well known
and heard throughout England.

Concerning Abbot Brithnoth the book tells
4180 how he removed [the body of] Saint Withburga from Dereham
where he found her
and brought her to Ely.
He had sought the advice of King Edgar
and, following his counsel, assembled the people—
4185 bishops, monks, and abbots—
and led them to Dereham.
Out of great devotion, he spent the night
in prayer before her [tomb].
At midnight he opened the grave
4190 and recovered her from the earth.
He found the virgin in the same state
as the day she was placed in the grave.
He greeted her and asked her
if she would please permit him
4195 to have her carried to Ely
in order to honor her.
He called together his companions
and left with the body intact.
A star appeared over them,

Plus clere ke nule chandoile.   4200
Par cele clarté ont veüe
La droite veie et coneüe.
A Brandone ou le cors alerent,
A icel rivagë entrerent.
Kant i fu jur cil s'aparceurent   4205
Des païs ke garder la deurent:
Ou lur armes aprés li vont,
Tristes et dolenz, grant doel font.
Kant il virent k'ele s'en vait
Par ewe, si s'en son[t] retrait.   4210
Ariere vont, mes ceus d'Ely
A joie alerent contre ly.   fol 131v col 1
A Tidbricheseie ariverent,
Li moine encontre li alerent,
Grant procession ordenerent.   4215
Le cors seinte Audree i porterent
Et seinte Sexborc, sa so[r]eur;
Autre reliques par honeur
Furent le jur porteez hors,
Si fu receü cist seint cors.   4220
Ou duz chant et o beu servise
Le porterent dedenz l'eglise.
Devant le fiertre seinte Audree
Mistrent cele virge honoree.
Graces rendent al creatur   4225
Ke del porter lor fist honur.

En un miracle dist ici
D'un parent l'eveske d'Ely.
Chevaler fu, Adam out non.
Le quer out crüel et felon   4230
Et [ert] queites de gaain faire.
A la feire, com oi retraire,
De Norhantone un borgois prist,
En Ely en prison le mist.
Tant le destreint et tormenta   4235
Par ouit jurs ke cil se feia
De rendre li sa raençon.
Son fiz mist pur li en prison.
Li vallez tut enanelez
Checun jur fu acostumez   4240
D'aler requerre seinte Audree,

4200 brighter than any candle,*
   and by its light they could
   discern the right path.
   They arrived in Brandon with the body,
   where at the riverbank they entered [the water].
4205 When it was daylight, the local people
   who were supposed to guard Withburga saw [what had happened].
   Sad, mourning, and making a great lament
   but armed with weapons, they went after them.
   When they saw that she was being taken away
4210 over the water, they retreated.
   While they were going back home, people from Ely
   joyously set out to meet her.
   When they arrived in Turbutsey,
   the monks came to meet her.
4215 They organized a great procession
   carrying the body of Saint Audrey
   and her sister Saint Seaxburga.
   In honor of the occasion other relics
   were carried outside that day
4220 when the holy body was received [in Ely].
   With the sweet singing of a beautiful mass
   they carried her into the church
   and placed the honored virgin
   before the shrine of Saint Audrey.
4225 Then they thanked the Creator
   for having given them the honor of translating [the body].

   One miracle story tells
   about a relative of the bishop of Ely,
   a knight named Adam
4230 who was evil and cruel-hearted,
   always seeking his own gain.
   I heard that at the fair
   he took a citizen of Northampton
   and put him in prison at Ely.
4235 He tormented him
   for eight days until the man pledged
   to pay him his ransom and agreed
   to have his son take his place in prison.
   The boy, draped in chains,
4240 began to go every day
   to pray to Saint Audrey,

La roÿne boneüree:*
Par sa pitié la conseilliast
De la prison le delivrast.
Un jur la virge s'appareut   4245   fol 131v col 2
A l'enfant la ou il esteut
Deriere l'autier et orant.
A lui parla se li dis[t] tant:
« Emfes, demein delivre estras*
A ceste heure, ne dotez pas. »   4250
L'endemain a cele heure avint
Ke cil ke en prison le tint
Fu par diable forcenez
Ke li estoit ou cors entrez.
En cele devision fina.   4255
Li enfes quites s'en ala.

De l'eveske N[e]el nos dit
D'un miracle ke truis escrit
Ke au roi Estefne ert mellez
Et enpirez et encusez.   4260
Tant pardona l'ire et l'enui
L'eveske k'il fina a lui:
Avoir li dona et promist
Et grant tresor en gage mist
K'en Ely prist dedenz l'eglise.   4265
La croiz le roi Edgar a mise,
Ke il dona en la maison,
En gage a un gïu felon.
Cil gïu ke sovent veoit
Cist volt, durement le haoit.   4270
Un jur prist un cotel ageu,
En un des geus l'en a fereu.
Aprés le cop le sang issi
De l'oiel ke tot le volt covri.
Le geïu mut se repenta.   4275
A Damnedeu merci cria.
Cel grant miracle ad reconté,
Ne pooit mie estre celé.   fol 132r col 1
Merveillie estoit ke de dur
     fust
Ke sanc pur cop issir deüst.   4280
La croiz rendue fu en Ely,
Puis n'i out gïu si hardy

the blessed queen,
beseeching her in her mercy
to deliver him from prison.
4245 One day the virgin appeared
to the child there where he stood
praying behind the altar.
She spoke to him and said:
"Child, tomorrow at this hour
4250 you will be free, fear not."
The next day at that very hour it so happened
that the man holding him in prison
went mad because the devil
had entered into his body,
4255 and in this state he died.
The child went away free.

There is a miracle recorded
concerning Bishop Nigel:
he was on unfriendly terms with King Stephen,
4260 who had both blamed and denounced him.
The bishop stayed the anger and ill-will of the king
by making an arrangement with him:
he promised to give him money
and pledged great treasures
4265 which he took from inside the church of Ely.
King Stephen took the cross which King Edgar
had donated to the monastery*
and gave it in pledge it to a wicked Jew.
This Jew, who often saw
4270 the face [of Christ on the cross], hated it bitterly.
One day he took a sharp knife
and struck it in one of the eyes.
After the blow blood came forth
from the eye and covered the whole face.
4275 Then the Jew deeply repented
and cried to the Lord God for mercy.
He recounted this great miracle,
for it could not be concealed.
It was truly miraculous that from the hard
      wood
4280 blood should flow out as the result of a stab.
The cross was returned to Ely,
and since then there has been no Jew so bold

Ky osast puis croiz manïer
Ne desus prester nul denier.

A Londres vint un'enfertez   4285
Dont li plusors sont enfermez:
Fevres anguissouses prenoient
Et mut sovent en i moroient.
Long tens i fu la maladie
K'il n'eurent socurs ne aïe,   4290
Mes neporuec bien lur avint:
De seinte Audree lur sovint.
Ducement merci li crïerent
Et mut sovent la reclamerent.
La nuit la virge s'apparut   4295
A un fevre la ou il jut
Et dist ke l'endemein alast
A sa forge, si regardast,
Sur s'oncleume avroit un dener
Dont il achateroit acier.   4300
Anelez petiz en feroit
Et as malades les dorroit.
Kiconkes l'anel porteroit
De sa fevre garriz serroit.
Ja mes n'en sentiroit doleur   4305
Ou il moroit einz le tierz jur.
Le fevre al matin se leva
Et fist ce k'el li comanda.
Le denier a issi trovee,
Si en ad asier achatee.   4310
Anelez a fait et donez,   fol 132r col 2
Li malades furent sanez.
Kant il n'out mes plus de l'acier,
Si s'entremist autres forgier
De fer, et iceus departi   4315
As malades, si sont gari.
Brithmar de Averille avoit
Si fort cel mal k'il s'en moroit.
A seinte Audree ala orer,
Si oy d'une femme parler   4320
Ke trois de ceus anels avoit.
S'il eüst l'un, gari seroit.
Il vint a lui, tant le pria
Ke sur son doi l'un en baillia.

as to dare to touch the cross
or lend a single penny against it.

4285 In London an illness broke out
which afflicted quite a number of people.
They contracted oppressive fevers
and many of them died.
The epidemic lasted for a long time,
4290 for nothing seemed to help.
Nevertheless it turned out well for them:
they remembered Saint Audrey
and, sweetly crying to her for mercy,
they often prayed to her.
4295 One night the virgin appeared
to an ironsmith as he lay in his bed
and told him to go the next day
to his forge, look
on his anvil, and there he would find a penny
4300 with which he was to buy some steel.
He should make small rings out of it
and distribute them to the sick.
Whoever wore a ring
from his forge would get well
4305 and never again suffer from the disease,
otherwise he would die before the third day.
The ironsmith got up in the morning
and did what she commanded.
He found the penny,
4310 bought some steel with it,
made and distributed rings,
and the sick were cured.
When he had no more steel,
he began to forge others
4315 of iron and distribute these
to the sick, and they also recovered.
Brithmar of Haverhill had
such a bad case of this illness that he was dying.
He decided to go pray to Saint Audrey.
4320 Then someone told him about a woman
who had three of these rings.
If he had one of them he would get well.
He went to her and begged so much
that she put one of the rings on his finger.

La nuit, quant il devoit dormir,   4325
Li fu avis k'il vit venir
Un tosard, grant cop le feroit
De un mail de fer k'il tenoit.
A l'autre nuit le referi,
A la tierce tut autresi.   4330
L'angoisse de la maladie
Estoit k'autre cop n'i out mie.
Kant il vint en l'yle d'Ely,
Tut se senti sein et gary.
Tel feim [out] k'il quidoit dever,   4335
Mes il ne trovoit k'achatier
Fors anguillies, tant en manga
Por un petit k'il ne creva.
Un autre en peüt bien morir,
Seinte Audree le fist garir.   4340

En tens un eveske d'Ely,
Hervi out non, ç'avom oÿ,
Apparut seint E[d]mond li ber,
A un home, ç'oÿ conter,   fol 132v col 1
Ke en Exningë out maison,   4345
Si li dist par avision
Ke a l'eveske Hervi alast
Et de sa part le salüast
Et ke pur amur li deïst
Ke une chaucïe[e] feïst   4350
Par mi le mareis atorner
Parunt i peüt bien aler
A seinte Audree en oreison
Pur li requere a sa maison.
Li preudom l'endemain ala   4355
Et fist ce k'il li comanda.
A l'eveske dist le message
Ki out grant joie en son corage.
Ne sout coment il l'enpreïst,
Al covent le mostra et dist.   4360
Un moine de grant honesté,
Johan out non, li a loé
Ke [s]'il l'enprenge, il l'aidera
Et par Deu bien l'achevera.
Li eveske[s] issi l'en prist.   4365
Adesus coranz pontelz mist,

4325   That night, while he lay sleeping,
he thought that he saw coming toward him
a young man who struck him several times
with an iron hammer he was holding.
The next night he struck him again.
4330   The third night was just the same.
The painful illness continued,
but there were no other blows.
When he reached the island of Ely,
he felt cured and well
4335   and was nearly insane from hunger.
But he found nothing to buy
except eels. He ate so many of them
that he almost burst!
Anyone else would have died from it;
4340   Saint Audrey caused him to get well.

In the time of a bishop of Ely
named Hervey, we have heard
that good Saint Edmund
appeared to a man
4345   who made his home in Exning
and told him in a dream
to go to Bishop Hervey,
greet him on his behalf,
and tell him out of love for him [Saint Edmund]
4350   that he should have a road
made through the marsh
by which one could easily go
to Saint Audrey to pray
and make requests of her in her church.
4355   The good man went the next day
and did as Saint Edmund had commanded.
He relayed the message to the bishop
who felt great joy in his heart because of it,
but he did not know how to undertake the task,
4360   so he presented the issue to the monastic community.
A well-respected monk
named John advised him
that should he undertake the project, he would gladly assist him,
and with God's help he would complete it.
4365   Thus the bishop accepted his offer.
He put little bridges over the streams,

Et ros et terre i fist atraire,
E la chauce[e] fist parfaire.
Par seint Edmund ceste chauce[e]
Fu ici faite et comence[e]   4370
De Saham deques en Ely
Ç'ont plusurs veü et oÿ.

Un miracle reconte ci
D'une femme ke pres d'Ely
Manoit, si fu en maladie   4375
Et pleine de paralisie.
Tant fu grevee ke drescer   fol 132v col 2
Ne se pooit ne se seignier.
Mires firent a lui venir,
Ne la purent mie garir.   4380
Tant li dora la maladie
Ke ele fu tote envillie.
A la parfin s'est purpensee:
Porter se fist a seinte Audree
A ouit homes ke la cocherent   4385
Devant la tombe. A Deu prïerent
Et a seinte Audree par non
K'ele li donast garison.
La virge lur prïere oÿ,
Devant sa tombe la gary.   4390
Par ouit homes i fu portee,
Tote seine s'en est alee.

Un miracle volom conter
Ke ne fait mie a oblïer.
A Bradeford out un enfant   4395
Ke ne parloit [ne] tant ne quant.
A seinte Audree fu menez.
Kant en l'eglise fu entrez,
Sa parole lui ad donee
La glorïuse seinte Audree.   4400
A ses amis dist hautement:
« Je sui garri, alom [nus] ent. »

Une femme out en la contree
Ke une fillie out ceue nee.
Par ses amis estoit portee   4405
Dekes al mostier seinte Audree.

had reeds and dirt brought in,
and completed the road.
Thanks to Saint Edmund this road
4370   from Soham to Ely
was started and finished.
Many people have heard of it or seen it themselves.

Another miracle is told
about a woman who lived
4375   near Ely. She was ill
and suffered with paralysis.
She was so afflicted that she could
neither stand upright nor make the sign of the cross.
They had doctors come to her,
4380   but they were unable to cure her.
The illness had lasted so long
that she was a ruin.
At the point of death she made a decision:
she had herself carried to Saint Audrey
4385   by eight men who laid her down
in front of the tomb and prayed to God
and to Saint Audrey by name
asking that she cure her.
The virgin heard their prayer
4390   and there before the tomb healed her.
She had to be carried there by eight men,
but she left completely well.

We wish to recount a miracle
which certainly should not be forgotten.
4395   There was a child in Bradford
who could not utter a single word.
He was taken to Saint Audrey,
and as soon as he entered the church
glorious Saint Audrey
4400   gave speech to him.
Then he said aloud to his friends:
"I am cured; let's go!"

There was a woman in the area
who had a daughter born blind.
4405   She was carried by her friends.
to Saint Audrey's church.

Si tost com ele i fu veneue,
Si a recovré sa veüe
Et vit le ciel encontremont,
Si s'en revint, grant joie en font.   4410   fol 133r col 1

Ci nos reconte d'une chose
D'un home ki out la mein close.
A seinte Audree fu menez,
Iluec fu gariz et sanez.

De Estiefne dist d'Eschaliers   4415
Ke terre tint et fu fermers
De l'eglise seintë Audree,
Cele terre est issi nomee:
Deuz ides et demi devise
Et nief acres et une eglise.   4420
La ferme detint et tolli
Par deuz anz. Les moines d'Ely
S'en sont a l'eveske clamé,
Et li eveske a comandé
K'hom le preïst et amenast   4425
S'il mut tost ne se decrescast.
Quant Estiefnë iceo oÿ
Ou ses amis vint en Ely.
Le jur de la Paske florie
Devant l'eveske merci crie   4430
Et dist ke il estoit chaeis
En poverté et si destreis
K'il ne savoit la ferme ou prendre
N'il ne la pooit mie rendre.
Les moines virent sa poverte.   4435
De la ferme k'il ont sufferte
Li dïent k'il ert pardonee,
Si la terre lur seit mostree
De tote parz la ou el gist,
Et il lur mostrera, ce dist.   4440
Par [le] serment de ses amis
De la mostrance ont un jur pris.
Au jur ke fu entre eus només   fol 133 r col 2
A de ses amis assemblés.
Robert de Conigtone i fu,   4445
Williame k'avom entendu
Le ki pere out a non Rogiers*

As soon as she arrived there
she recovered her sight
and saw the sky above.
4410   So she returned home, and they rejoiced greatly.

We are told a little story
about a man who could not open one of his hands.
He was taken to Saint Audrey;
there he was healed and his hand made well.

4415   The story is told of Stephen of Eschaliers
who held land rented
from the church of Saint Audrey.
That land was thus designated:
two and a half hides allotted
4420   with nine acres and one church.
He had taken the land and kept it
for two years. The monks of Ely
complained to the bishop,
and the bishop ordered them
4425   to seize the man and bring him to him
if he did not pay up very soon.
When Stephen heard this,
he came to Ely with his friends
on Palm Sunday
4430   and cried to the bishop for mercy
saying that he had fallen
into poverty and such distress
that he did not know where to get the rent money,
and there was no way he could pay it.
4435   The monks could see that he was poor,
so they told him that he would be pardoned
for the rent that they had lost
if he would show them
the layout of the land.
4440   He agreed to show it to them
with his friends acting as guarantors under oath,
and a day was selected for the showing.
On the day mutually chosen
he assembled his friends.
4445   Robert of Connington was there,
William, of whom we have heard,
whose father was named Roger,

Si fu Tebaud des Eschalers.
[I]ceus furent mis a serment
K'il ne mentiroient nïent   4450
Pur amur ne pur volunté
K'il ne dïent la verité.
Ricard le prestre et la vilee
Furent tuz a cele juree.
Temoines et entendanz   4455
En fu li eveske et garanz.
Deuz arcediacnes par non,
Williame et Davi eurent non,
Nicholas i estoit un prestre
Et Ricard ke bien i deut estre   4460
Ke de seint Pol estoit nomez;
Plusurs autres i out asez.
Kant la terre fu mesuree
Ou l'eglise il ont plus trovee
Ke cil n'en avoient mostré;   4465
Ateinz furent de fauseté,
Et d'un bon pré ke il celerent
Apertement s'aparjüerent.
Pur iceste ovre seinte Audree
N'a pas sa vengance oblïee: 4470
Estiefne de pez mahaigna,
Ne pot garir, einz mal fina.

Une femme d'Estone nee,
Eldeline fu apellee.
D'ovrer en festes fu engresse   4475
Et en son corage porverse.   fol 133v col 1
Par un jur de feste cosi:
Dedenz la paume li feri
L'anguoillie dont ele cosoit,
Si que sacher ne l'en pooit.   4480
La mein et le braz li enfla,
[Et] dekes au cors li rancla.
Le braz et la mein enmorti,
Tut ariere li acurbi.
As seinz ala pur quere aïe,   4485
Mes el ne fu nïent garie.
Deuz anz, ce dist, cil mal la tint,
Dekes en Hontedone vint.
Une nuit, kant ele dormi,

and also Tibald of Eschaliers.
They were all made to swear
4450   that they would not lie;
neither for love nor money
would they not tell the truth.
Richard the priest and the villagers
were all present for this oath.
4455   The bishop was witness and hearer
as well as protector.
Two archdeacons
named William and David were there.
Nicholas, a priest, was there,
4460   as was Richard who indeed had to be there
for he was appointed from Saint Paul's church,
and there were many others.
When the land including the church
was measured, they found more
4465   than the renter and his friends had claimed.
They were accused of falsehood;
and concerning a good meadow which they had concealed,
they perjured themselves openly.
For this deed Saint Audrey
4470   did not forget to avenge herself.
Stephen suffered with his feet
and could not be cured; thus he came to a bad end.

A woman born in Stonea
was named Eldeline.
4475   She was eager to indulge in pleasures
and was perverse in her heart.
One feast day as she was sewing,
the needle she was using
stuck into her palm
4480   in such a way that she could not pull it out.
Her hand and arm swelled
and the infection spread throughout her body.
The arm and hand became numb
and drew up on her.
4485   She went about seeking help from the saints,
but still she was not cured.
According to the story, this illness beset her for two years
until she came to Huntingdon.
One night, while she slept,

Une dame vint devant li,   4490
Mut belë et mut duz semblant.
A lui parla, se li dist tant:
« Va en Ely a seinte Audree,
Si t'ert iluec santé donee. »
L'endemain s'est cele levee,   4495
D'aler avant s'est atornee.
Plusurs ensemble ou li alerent
Ke de granz mals enfermez erent,
Et un moinë i est alez
Ki de ses pez ert enfermez.   4500
Seinte Audree l'out pris jadis
Hors de prison ou il ert mis.
Tuz ensemble vont en Ely
Iceste gent dont ge vos dy.
La glorïuse seinte Audree   4505
A la femme a santé donee
Et braz et mein out desenflé
Et les autres eurent santé.
Un prestre, ki avoit veü   fol 133v col 2
Les miracles et [le] saleu,   4510
Les seins sona, grant joie fist,
Et par tut le conta et dist.

Qant Estiefne, ce dist, moreut,
Williame la terre receut,
Son fiz ke folement ovra   4515
Vers seinte Audree et meserra.
Ce ke son pere avoit rendeu
Ot delaié et deteneu.
As moines del covent d'Ely
La rente detint et tolly.   4520
Unkes pur roy ne pur asise
Ne lur vout rendre lur servise.
Kant il ne se vout purpenser
Ne vers le covent amender,
Si se pleindrent a seinte Audree,   4525
La roïne bon[e]üree.
Par la vengance Jhesu Crist
Avint se ke Williame fist
Une ovre dont il fu aïz
Del roi empirez et leidiz.   4530
En sa merci li esteut rendre

4490   a beautiful and kind lady
      appeared before her.
      She spoke to her saying:
      "Go to Saint Audrey in Ely.
      There health will be given to you."
4495   The next day she arose
      and prepared to set out.
      With her went several others
      who were sick with terrible illnesses.
      A monk suffering with his feet
4500   also went along.
      Saint Audrey had once taken him
      out of prison where he had been held.
      All these people I have told you about
      went to Ely together.
4505   Glorious Saint Audrey
      gave the woman her health:
      both arm and hand returned to normal,
      and all the others also received healing.
      A priest who had seen
4510   the miraculous healings
      rang the bells with great joy
      and told about the miracles everywhere.

      It is said that when Stephen of Eschaliers died,
      the land went to his son William
4515   who acted foolishly
      and misbehaved toward Saint Audrey.
      He reduced the amount
      his father had been paying,
      thus withholding rent revenue
4520   from the monks at Ely.
      Neither for the king nor for any official order
      would he give them their due.
      Since he would not reconsider
      nor correct his treatment of the monastery,
4525   the monks lamented to Saint Audrey,
      the blessed queen.
      Through the vengeance of Jesus Christ
      it happened that William committed
      an act for which he was hated,
4530   accused and ill-treated by the king.
      He would have to throw himself on the king's mercy

Com[e] de perdre vie ou membre.
Pur dute de cel mautalent
Vers seinte Audree se repent
K'il li out sa rente tollue   4535
Et delaié et detenue.
En oreisons vait en Ely:
A la dame crier merci,
Al covent la terre rendi
Et la rente k'il lur tolli;   4540
Et de ceo ke ariere fu
Cria [merci], li ad rendeu.   fol 134r col 1
Aprés fu au roi acordez
A ki il ert forment mellez.

D'un bon moine reconte ci   4545
Ke estoit del covent d'Ely
Ke leut la vie seinte Audree
En un livre ou il l'out trovee.
En engleis ert la vie escrite
Ou li moine mut se delite.   4550
Un bieu miracle i a trovee
K'il a bonement recontee
De la roïne seinte Audree
Ke primes fu a Tonbert donee,
Un duec ke ert de grant valur   4555
Et mut bien de nostre Seigniur.
Ensemble furent seintement
En bone vie et chastement.
Par un jur la roïne estoit
En sa chambre ou ele entendoit   4560
As puceles ke la servoient
Et as ovres k'eles fesoient.
Le duc ala a li parler
Pur une bosoigne mostrier.
Kant il li out dist et mostré   4565
Et conseil quis et demandé,
Pur ce k'el ne vout otreier
La prist le roi a manacier.
La seinte virge en pes suffri
Si qu'un seul mot ne respondi: 4570
Homblement et en pes se tint.
De l'ewangelie li souvint
Ke dist ke pacïence veint

or risk losing life or limb.
For fear of the king's anger
he repented toward Saint Audrey
4535   for having diluted and retained
rent money due her.
He went to Ely in prayer,
cried for mercy to the lady,
then gave the land back to the monastery
4540   and also the rent money he had withheld,
including any that was past due.
He begged for mercy, and she granted it:
afterwards he was reconciled with the king
with whom he had been on such bad terms.

4545   We are told the story of a good monk
of the monastery of Ely
who read the life of Saint Audrey
which he had found in a book.
The life was written in English,
4550   and that delighted the monk.
He found in it a wonderful miracle
which he then related
about the queen, Saint Audrey,
who was first given to Tonbert,
4555   a duke of great valor
esteemed of our Lord.
Together they lived a good
and holy life in chastity.
One day the queen was
4560   in her chamber supervising
the work that her young servant girls
were doing.
The duke came in to speak with her
about a certain matter.
4565   When he had disclosed it to her
and asked her opinion,
because she did not agree with him,
he began to threaten her.
The saintly virgin suffered this in silence
4570   and did not answer a single word.
She remained humble and quiet,
for she remembered the gospel
which says that patience overcomes

Malice et tres grant ire esteint.
La seinte virge estoit pensant   4575   fol 134r col 2
En son quer, [et] Deu orant.
Ses ganz a de ses meins hostés
Si les a devant li getez.
Seur un rai del soleil avint
Ke amedeuz les ganz sostint: 4580
En pes i ont les ganz geü.
Cel miracle a le duc veü
Et tut [i]cil ke ou li vindrent
Ke a grant miracle le tindrent.
Le duc de ce k'il a leidi   4585
Mut durement se repenti.
Merci li cria bonement
K'ele n'out ver li maltalent,
Et bonement li pardonast
Ke vers li ne se corouçast.   4590
Ducement par humilité
Li ad la virge pardoné.
Icist coruz dont ge vos di
Ne vint pas d'ovre d'enemi,
Mes pur mustrier de Deu la gloire   4595
Et de la virge sa victoire.
Cist moine ke leut en sa vie
Ce miracle ne creoit mie.
La nuit aprés quant il se geut
Seinte Audree li apareut   4600
Et dist li ke il n'out dotance
Del miracle ne mecreance
K'il avoit en livre trové.
Bien le seüt pur verité
Ke c'estoit ele, seinte Audree,   4605
Ke a li estoit demoustree.
L'endemain le moine le dist
Et al covent saveir le fist.   fol 134v col 1
De cele revelation
Mercïerent Deu et son non.   4610

Issi ay ceo livre finé
En romanz dit et translaté
De la vie seintë Audree
Si com en latin l'ay trové,
Et les miracles ay oÿ,   4615

malice and calms great anger.*
4575 As the virgin was reflecting
and praying to God in her heart.
she took the gloves off her hands
and threw them in front of her husband.*
It happened that both gloves
4580 became suspended on a ray of sunlight
and lay there quite still.
The duke witnessed this miracle,
and all those who had come with him
also considered it a great miracle.
4585 The duke bitterly repented,
acknowledging that he had behaved badly.
He duly cried for mercy from her,
asking that she bear him no ill-will,
and that she graciously forgive him
4590 and not become angry with him.
Sweetly and humbly
the virgin forgave him.
This anger I told you about
did not come as the work of the Enemy
4595 but rather in order to show the glory of God
and the victory of the virgin.
However, the monk who read about this miracle
in her life story did not believe it.
The next night, when he lay down,
4600 Saint Audrey appeared to him
and told him not to have any doubt
or disbelief concerning the miracle
that he had found in the book.
He accepted it as truth,
4605 for it was she herself, Saint Audrey,
whom he had seen.
The following morning the monk
told all about it and made it known to the monastery.
For this revelation
4610 they thanked God and His Name.

Now I have finished this book,
told and translated into French
the life of Saint Audrey
just as I found it in Latin,
4615 along with the miracles I have heard.

Ne voil nul mettrë en obli.
Pur ce depri la glorïuse
Seinte Audree la precïeuse
Par sa pité k'a moy entende
Et ce servise a m'ame rende,   4620
Et ceus pur ki ge la depri
K'el lur aït par sa merci.
Mut par est fol ki se oblie.
Ici escris mon non Marie
Pur ce ke soie remembree.*   4625

I do not wish to let anything be forgotten.
Therefore I beseech glorious,
precious Saint Audrey
to hear me out of compassion
4620   and give aid to my soul,
as well as to those for whom I pray:
may she help them through her mercy.
One is indeed foolish who forgets herself:
here I write my name "Marie"
4625   so that I may be remembered.*

Notes on the
Text and Translation

Opening Rubric. "Audree" is the Anglo-Norman Old French form for the Latin name "Etheldreda," founder and patron saint of the church at Ely in Cambridgeshire, England. In Anglo-Saxon the name is "Æthelthryth." She is also called "Ediltrudis" in some contexts, especially in German and Spanish texts. Although she is better known in England as "Etheldreda," we have chosen to use her alternate name, "Audrey," which is closer to the Old French name used in Marie's text.

4. The scribe frequently writes ke (que) for ki (qui) or vice versa. See, for example, lines 61, 135, 142, 182, 263, 630, etc. and 1901, 2241, 3552, 3759, etc. The manuscript also uses si for se and vice versa. See, for example, lines 2457, 3603, 3956, 3958, 4322, etc.

6. "And the Lord God formed the man from the dust of the ground and breathed into his nostrils the breath of life, and the man became a living being" (Genesis 2.7). "...for dust you are and to dust you will return" (Genesis 3.19b [NIV]). Transcending human nature through memory is an Augustinian concept explored in chapter ten of his Confessions. Concerning Augustine on memory, Chadwick writes that memory is "the medium through which the person becomes responsive to grace" (70). See also the chapter on "Memory, Self-Reform and Time" in Stock, Augustine, 207–42.

41. In Old French the term "Engleis" is used to mean both "English" and "Angles."

78. The scribe, apparently unfamiliar with the name Sigilberz consistently writes the more familiar sire gilberz until he gets to line 633,

where the name is preceded by the word roy, thus making it clear that sigilber, as it is spelled here, is a proper name. See also lines 92, 105, 136.

80. After the death of Edwin, the East Angles reverted to their former paganism.

93. A significant number of verses that contain English place names and other proper names are hypometric or hypermetric, which suggests that Marie probably used a different spelling that has been altered by the scribe. We have left these as they are in the manuscript, unless an alternate spelling is attested elsewhere in the manuscript, as is the case in this line. The spelling here is attested in line 606.

99. The spelling of palatal l in this manuscript is typically illi. See also lines 111, 117, 151, etc. The most commonly affected words are fillie, which is a one-syllable word (and should be pronounced like fille), and merveillie (pronounced like merveille). See, for other examples, vieilliesse, line 263; someillioit, line 933; veillie, line 1490; enveillia line 3489; and travaillioit, line 3910; anguillies, line 4337.

123. The word aventure is a favorite word of Marie de France, and she uses it fourteen times in the Vie seinte Audree, compared to nineteen times in the Lais. She also refers to Owein's descent into Purgatory in the Espurgatoire seint Patriz as an aventure. We have often translated it merely as "story" or "tale," but the word carries significant connotations that are impossible to render acceptably with a single word in English. (Howard Bloch has devoted an entire chapter to "The Word aven-

249

ture and the Adventure of Words" in his book, *The Anonymous Marie de France*.) It carries connotations not only of an interesting and unusual story, but also one often tinged with elements of the supernatural or paranormal.

140. In Marie de France's lai *Le Fresne*, Gurun, Le Fresne's paramor, is pressured into marriage by his vassals. See *Le Fresne*, lines 324–28. A similar situation arises in her lai *Equitan*: see lines 203–210, Ewert edition. All subsequent references are to this edition.

168. The biblical parable of the wise and foolish virgins is found in Matthew 25.1–13, as part of Jesus' Olivet discourse in which he speaks to his disciples concerning eschatological matters. Of ten virgins, five had the foresight to take extra lamp oil with them to await the arrival of the bridegroom. The other five had to go out to purchase oil. Since the bridegroom appeared during their absence, only the five well-prepared virgins were able to join the wedding feast. See also lines 1455–56.

169–70. These lines in the manuscript end in *aiznee* and *bontee*, with the *ee* at the end representing not the feminine, but *é*. We have corrected these "false feminines" here and elsewhere (e.g., lines 1887–88, 2259–60, 2831, 2843–44, 3097, 3621–22, 3713, 3777–78. 3994, 4155–56, 4465–66).

175. Hereswith is the name of Audrey's aunt, the widow of Anna's brother Egric and sister of Saint Hilda. She seems to have been confused with Audrey's mother, whose name is uncertain. See "Annotated Index of Proper Names."

183. There may be a lacuna in or around this line. The manuscript text does not make it clear to whose death is referred, although we know it is King Anna's. King Anna's two brothers reigned after his death: Ethelhere for only one year, then Ethelwald for nine years before Anna's son Aldulf became king in 664. Marie explains this in greater detail in lines 702–730. See also "Annotated Index of Proper Names."

188. This is the only metrically regular line in the manuscript that includes the form *abbesse*. Others tend to be hypometric, requiring either an additional syllable added or a *tréma* over a mute *e* preceding another vowel. See note for line 838.

206. The Latin text has "France," not "Britain," which is clearly correct. Either Marie or the scribe has made an error.

214. The monasteries of both Brie and Chelles were located in the old province of Isle de France, north central France, near Paris.

264. A biblical reference to Wisdom 4.7–9 (Roman Catholic canon).

306. Area (375 square miles) in east England, historically a part of Cambridgeshire. In the seventh century Ely was a marshland accessible only by water, hence the term "isle" or "island" of Ely. The extensive fens have long since been drained.

310. *Ales* is the Old French word for *eels*.

350. Marie's interest in spiritual marriage is very much in evidence in the lai *Guildelüec et Guilliadun* (*Eliduc*): the first wife was willing to take the veil, allowing her husband to marry his lady friend, with whom he lived a life of charitable works in "parfite amur" (line 1150). All three ended their days in monasteries.

411. The term *collaciun* (*colation*) used in the Old French refers to religious texts read to monastics while they ate. These texts included writings of the Church Fathers as well as the Bible. According to Janet Fairweather, this particular story comes from the *Collationes Patrum*. She comments: "St Benedict, *Regula 42*, had recommended works of this sort as after-supper reading for monks of his order (*Liber Eliensis*, 19, note 64).

426. This story is suggestive of Abraham's encounter with God's messengers in the Bible. The messengers' feet are washed and they are given food. They inquire after Abraham's wife Sarah. They also discuss intimate matters when they announce that Sarah, though barren and well past her child-bearing years, will have a son. See Genesis 18.

438. Lines 438 and 439 are reversed in the manuscript. However the rhyme requires the order contained in this edition.

453. The wearing of sackcloth is an ancient Judeo-Christian tradition done as a gesture of penitence. The act of lying in sackcloth throughout the night is referred to in Joel 1. 13. King Louis IX established in Paris "l'Ordre du Sac et de la Pénitence de Jésus Christ." See Jacques Seebacher edition of Victor Hugo's *Notre Dame de Paris*, Paris: Gallimard, 1975, note 1 p. 208.

496. March 8.

534. The "sacrifice" in this line could refer to the death of Christ on the cross or to the sacrament of the Eucharist celebrating this sacrificial death.

645. The manuscript is smudged at the end of this line after the letter *a* of *aïe*, but the context and rhyme make clear the word.

702. Ethelhere was killed in the aforementioned battle against Oswy.

755. In Marie's lai *Guigemar* the lady with whom the knight Guigemar falls in love is kept by a jealous husband in an enclosed area accessible only by the sea: "Nuls ne pout eissir ne entrer, / Si ne ceo fust od un batel" (lines 226–27).

784. In Marie's lai *Le Fresne* Le Fresne's lover, the baron Gurun, falls in love with her by dint of the good things he had heard of her: "De la pucele oï parler;/ Si la commença a amer" (lines 247–248).

822. The manuscript indicates that the young people went "a royne"; however, the scribe evidently misread the manuscript he or she was copying, as the Latin source makes it clear that they went to Rome. Gregory saw these Anglo-Saxon slaves on sale at the market in Rome before he was elected pope. The scribe makes the same error in line 1905 and again in line 2902. In each case the context makes it clear that the reference is to Rome.

838. The manuscript contains a significant number of hypometric lines that contain the word *abbesse*, suggesting that the author used the older form of the word, *abbeesse*, the same form that appears in Marie de France's *Le Fresne* in lines 212, 216, 252, 259. Evidently the scribe had "corrected" the word to conform to the Anglo-Norman usage of his or her day. Although in a few cases in *La Vie Seinte Audree*, the irregularity could have been corrected by placing a *tréma* over a mute *e* preceding a vowel, in every single line (with the sole exception of line 188, which is regular without any change), the addition of the [e] corrects the meter. We have chosen this solution consistently throughout the text. See also note for line 188.

843. The text confuses the birth order and kingdoms ruled by the two sons. Marie clearly treated *Egfrid* and *Egelfriz* as alternate spellings of the same name of one of Oswy's sons. Variants of this type occur in other names as well, depending on metrical exigencies (e.g., She refers to King Anna's brother as both *Edelwold*, 184, 710, 724, etc., and *Edwold*, 805). We have followed Marie's lead, using *Egfrid* or *Egelfrid*, as the meter required, though we al-

ways indicate in brackets where the extra syllable has been added. Otherwise we use the name as it appears in the manuscript.

847. Historically, it is King Oswy the father, not his son Ethelfrid, who has grown old and has set Egfrid up to succeed him as king of all Northumbria.

892. Another common spelling of *Ovin* is *Owine*, as is used in the Old French text. In Marie's *Espurgatoire Seint Patriz* the protagonist, the knight Owein, is also desirous of following God, but decides against joining a religious order and remains a knight in the service of God.

907. *Oswy* is a another variant of the name *Owine*. See note for line 892.

913. Saint Chad took Ovin into his monastery at Lastingham in Northern Yorkshire.

918. According to the *Oxford Dictionary of Saints*, Ovin heard heavenly voices shortly before Chad's death.

936. In Marie's lai *Laüstic*, the lady arises nightly from her lord's bed to go to the window to gaze at her lover. The secular love scene is transformed into a spiritual one in the *Vie Seinte Audree*. Like the husband in the lai, Queen Audrey's husband is angered by this habitual nightly behavior and resorts to devious and forceful means. Neither husband is successful in winning his wife's heart.

974. The "Enemy" refers to the devil, Satan.

993. The word *le* in line 993 is in the Picard form.

994. The scribe of this manuscript used *li* and *lui* interchangeably. We have left these for the most part as he or she transcribed it in the manuscript. Only in instances where the object is confusing or where it is required for purposes of rhyme have we corrected it.

1125. Marie de France personified Nature in this text as she does in her other works. A familiar example to readers from her *Lais* occurs in *Guigemar*: "De tant i out mepris nature..." ("But Nature had done him such a grievous wrong" [line 57, Burgess and Busby translation]).

1139. *Relement* is a documented form of *rarement*. See also line 1149.

1211. The line in the manuscript is "Pur priue et veire et aspre et dure." The scribe seems to have read the *te* of *priveté* as an *et* and inserted an ampersand instead. Södergård's rendering is "Pur purpre et veire et aspre et dure," but we believe that our interpretation is more logical, better fits the context, and is closer to the manuscript line.

1213. Marie de France uses this same expression "Donc a primes" in line 6 of the prologue to her *Lais*.

1232. Mary and Martha, sisters of Jesus' friend Lazarus, whom he raised from the dead (John 11.1–44). The biblical reference here is found in Luke 10.38–42. Mary chose to sit at Jesus' feet to hear his words while Martha served him. Jesus commended Mary for having done well in contrast to Martha who busied and troubled herself for him.

1238. Celibacy was not mandatory for monastics in the seventh century, although it was being strongly encouraged by Rome.

1266. A reference to a biblical story set during the Babylonian captivity of the Israelites. Shaddrack, Meshack, and Abednego were thrown into a fiery furnace for refusing to obey King Nebuchadnezzar's orders to worship a golden image. The men were unharmed by the fire, and the king then acknowledged and praised the God of Israel. See Daniel 3.

1274–83. Marie shifts in this passage from past to present tense, which she frequently does to give her text a greater sense of immediacy and excitement. Because the historical present, which is fairly common in French, is not often used in English, we have in the translation continued the narrative, here and elsewhere when it occurs, in the past tense.

1310. Luke 18.14.

1315. Saint Paul.

1318. 2 Timothy 3.12.

1320. Audrey with her two companion nuns had barely left Coldingham when Egfrid came in pursuit of them. Egfrid tried to intercept her en route from Coldingham to Ely. The rock upon which she took refuge is a short distance from Coldingham. The text seems to imply, erroneously, that she was already in Ely when Egfrid arrived.

1334. Not far from the Coldingham monastery. Sneesby describes it as "a spur of rock linked only to the mainland by a narrow neck of sand, presumably sea-covered at high tide (*Etheldreda*, 81).

1394. Saint Ebba's miracle for Audrey reflects a passage from Exodus 17.6. After the exodus from Egypt, the Israelites became thirsty in the desert. As directed by God, Moses struck a rock and fresh water flowed out.

1397. In Anglo-Norman, consonants followed by *l* or *r* were often separated by [ə] rendered in the manuscript as *e*, thus making the line appear hypermetric. For example, in this line *ovri* was rendered by the scribe *overi*, which we have listed in the Rejected Readings.

1456. See note to line 168.

1460. Jacob's daughter Dinah mingled with the people of Canaan, had premarital relations with Shechem who loved her and wanted to marry her. He and all the men of the area were slain by Dinah's brothers Simeon and Levi who believed their sister had been raped. Genesis 34.

1472. Longinus is the name often associated with the Roman centurion who pierced Jesus' side with his lance, causing blood and water to rush forth from the wound (John 19:34). Some critics associate the lance of Longinus with the spear of the Grail procession that occurs in such works as the *Conte du Graal* of Chrétien de Troyes and Wolfram von Eschenbach's *Parzifal*. See Justine E. Griffin, "The Spear of Destiny," *The Holy Grail* (Jefferson, NC: McFarland, 2001), 88–95.

1480. A biblical reference to the saved ones in heaven who wear robes made white by washing them in the blood of Christ. They stand before the throne of God shouting praises. Revelation 7.9–10.

1493. The Latin source uses the term *periclitantibus* (those in danger) at this juncture. It is possible that the scribe has miscopied the line. Since Audrey is praying for *people* at this point, the line as written seems out of place. Although we have not altered the line in the edited text, we do translate it as we think it was probably originally written.

1508. An oblique reference to a biblical passage, Matthew 10.23. In commissioning his disciples to go out and preach the gospel, Jesus tells them that if they are persecuted in one city to flee to another.

1531–32. In the manuscript these two lines end in a Picard feminine *ie*, a characteristic that also occurs, for example, in the *Lais*, ll. 53–54. Some editors have "corrected" it (e.g., Rychner), while others have left the Picard form (e.g. Ewert). Because of the small number of occurrences in this manuscript, we have corrected it to avoid confusion. See also, for example, lines 3091–92 and 4350.

1535. The sprouting of a holy person's pilgrim staff is a common literary topos in hagiography. The flowering staff of Saint Christopher is particularly well known. Concerning a similar motif in the *Pseudo-Turpin*, a work with which Marie may well have been familiar, see McCash, "*Audree*: Fourth Text?" 768.

1537. This line is a near repetition of line 1419.

1541. The name Edeldrestewe (*Edeldrestowe* in translation) is based on the more common English name of Saint Audrey—Etheldreda—which has a variety of spellings.

1593. Södergård noted in his edition that a verb is missing from this line; however, he made no attempt to supply it.

1646. The original church on the island of Ely was founded by Saint Augustine of Canterbury and later destroyed by King Penda.

1672. Aldulf was, in fact, not Audrey's brother, but her first cousin, son of her father Anna's brother Ethelric and his wife Saint Hereswith. Consult "Annotated Index of Proper Names."

1688. John 19.26–27.

1691. A biblical reference to the Parable of the Laborers in the Vineyard: Matthew 20.1–16.

1701. The scribe has written *secante*, which is in all probability a scribal misreading of *setante*, which would be the correct date, 673, as the source text gives. This error is repeated several times in the text. In his edition, Södergård has sometimes corrected it, sometimes not. We have consistently corrected it to *setante*.

1709. According to Södergård, the *English School* referred to here is the *Schola Anglorum* in Rome (199). However, the source text refers only to Bede's *History of the English People* as a source and does not mention an English school. The *Vie seinte Audree* omits at this point a lengthy discussion in the source text of the celibacy of the men and women in the monasteries of Ely and Coldingham.

1714. An obscure passage written in third-person singular transitive verbs ("had founded ... founded") with no subject clearly indicated. The subject of these verbs could possibly be Wilfrid, but certainly not Saint Audrey. Wil-

frid did found churches in Northumbria, but not Coldingham. We have elected to use passive voice.

1744. The Benedictine Rule prescribes baths at Christmas and Easter.

1758. Originally designed as an early morning office, the term "matins" was applied to the night office by the Council of Trent in 567. The Benedictines (including Cistercians) observed matins at 2:00 am. Marie's text refers frequently to the canonical hours, which consist of Matins (2:00 am), Lauds (at dawn), Prime (6:00 am, the "first hour"), Terce (9:00 am, the "third hour"), Sext (noon, the "sixth hour"), None (3:00 pm, the "ninth hour"), Vespers (sunset, evensong) and Compline (before bed, night prayer).

1780. Seaxwulf was succeeded by Wilfrid as Bishop of the See of Mercia.

1797. The manuscript gives "secund Penda," which is either a scribal or an authorial misreading for *Peada* (or *Peda* in the Latin source text). Either the scribe or the author has added the word *secund* in a mistaken effort to make it logical.

1802. After the defeat of Penda by Oswy, the sons of Penda became petty kings under the rule of Oswy of Northumbria.

1822. The Old French text stresses the high rank of those joining Audrey's community, whereas the *Liber Eliensis* points to the inclusive nature of those people "of varying dignity and age" who gathered around Saint Audrey. Throughout Marie's text attention is emphatically directed to the noble status of any of the personae.

1832. Audrey's chaplain was named Huna. See "Annotated Index of Proper Names."

1842. Seaxburga, after the death of her husband, established a convent at Sheppey in Kent on land granted to her by her son, successor to his father as king of Kent. She became the first abbess at Sheppey.

1866. Acts 22.3.

1891. It is interesting to note that Marie uses this word *Elge* to refer to the island of Ely on only two occasions—when she is explaining its derivation (*Elge* meaning "Land of God," lines 1617–20) and here, when Audrey establishes her abbey on holy ground and literally restores it to being the land of God.

1905. See note for line 822.

1928. She uses this same vocabulary in line 343.

1938. This passage concerning the rich and the poor, which does not appear in the source text, may seem irrelevant and out of place in the middle of a description of the protagonist's death. Marie most likely intends it as commentary on the universality of suffering in order to justify the painful death of a servant of God as pure and good as Audrey.

1964. The word as written by the scribe in the manuscript is *enfermeté*, which renders both this line and several other lines that contain this same word hypermetric. However, emending it to the older form of the word, *enferté*, in both cases corrects the meter. Both variants occur in the text.

1982. This expression "s'alme rendi" or a variant of it is used in the epilogue Marie de France's *Fables* (line 22) and again at the end of the *Vie seinte Audree* (line 4615).

1991. In the ancient Roman calendar, "kalends" indicated the section of each month after the full moon. Audrey died on June 23, 679, apparently the ninth day after the full moon.

1995. Audrey was abbess of Ely 673–79.

2020. The scribe evidently omitted a line here, since there is no rhyme for the word *cors* in the previous line. We do not propose that the inserted line is the precise one that Marie may have written; we seek only to provide the missing information contained in the Latin text and to help the reader understand the continuity that was no doubt in the original text.

2035. Södergård suggested the missing word in his edition.

2104. In Marie's text "Fresus" is the name of the man who purchased Yma, whereas Fairweather identifies the purchaser by nationality as a "Friesian" (native of Friesland, a province in the Netherlands, *Liber Eliensis*, 54).

2110. Information contained in the Latin text is missing here from lines 2009–10. It is possible that we have at least two missing lines. The Latin text indicates that when the Friesian (see previous note) realized the situation, he gave Yma permission to go and acquire ransom money to purchase his freedom.

2119. The medieval term *boteillier* or *bouteillier* in Old French, did not have the same meaning or implications of the modern word *butler*. Whereas in modern parlance, a butler is a high-ranking manservant, in the

medieval court he was a nobleman and an important and trusted official in charge of the wines and court provisions.

2138. Södergård inadvertently omitted this line in his edition.

2142. Elger is not mentioned again in the *Life of Saint Audrey*.

2150. We have elected the rarer form *benequist* to correct the meter of this line and to parallel the form used in line 2204.

2154. According to Sneesby, Werburga was the fourth abbess of Ely after her mother, Ermenilda (9, 98). King Ethelfred recalled his niece from Ely and gave her charge of nunneries in the Midlands, including Threckingham and Hanbury. Historically she is not associated with either Wintringham in northern Yorkshire or Winteringham in Lincolnshire.

2186. Reaney has identified Armesworde (*Armsworth*) as Castle End (also called Castle Hill) in the borough of Cambridge (Reaney, *Place-Names of Cambridgeshire*, 36–40).

2190. The scribe has evidently omitted another line following this one, since no rhyme exists for *veüe*.

2208. The scribe has copied this line twice in the manuscript. We have counted it only once in the line count.

2222. The *le* in this line is the Picard feminine.

2257. The biblical story of Moses' encounter with God in the burning bush is found in Exodus 3.1–4.18.

2260. The biblical account of Daniel's deliverance from the lions' den is told in Daniel 6.

2272. A reference to the Christian belief in the second coming of Christ to judge the world, at which time those who died in Christian faith will rise to be with him.

2287. See note to line 1394.

2291. In the legend of Saint Clement, when he was thrown into the sea with an anchor tied around his neck, angels made a tomb for him on the sea bed. The tomb was uncovered once a year by an exceptionally low tide.

2350. Södergård noted that there was a missing word in this line, though he made no attempt to provide it. We are indebted to Rupert Pickens for suggesting that the missing word is *fini*, an echo of line 1981, which suggests a similar idea. The word *finir* means *to die* in a great number of other instances in the text. See, for example, lines 585, 727, 741, 1917, 1981, etc.

2361. The scribe has frequently used the wrong case, which is not surprising since the case system had broken down by the time she or he was copying the text. The insertion of *suer* for *sorur* or *soreur* renders the line (and other lines with similar case problems) hypometic. Correcting the case, as we have done, also corrects the meter. We have corrected for case only when required by the meter.

2400. Werburga actually died in Threckingham but was buried at her request in Hanbury.

2414. The Danes came marauding through East Anglia and destroyed the church at Ely in 870.

2442. See lines 2523–26, 2533–36, and 2817–2820 for reiterations of the same story.

2418. *Bretaignie* should be read as modern French *Bretagne* and should be considered a regular octosyllabic line. Just as *illi* represents the palatal *l* in this manuscript, so the *igni* represents the palatal *n*. See also, for example, lines 3277 and 3292.

2518. The discourse of the cleric in this passage, although he is defending the miraculous power of Saint Audrey, seems pretentiously erudite in its choice of verb tenses. One wonders whether Marie might be parodying clerkly parlance. At the end of the *Fables*, Marie de France expresses her distrust of clerics, when she writes "Pur cel estre que clerc plusur / predereient sur eus mun labur" (Epilogue, lines 5–6).

2533. The Latin *Normanni* refers to "north men," that is, the Nordic people who pillaged the land. Later it became the word regularly used for the Normans, hence the post-conquest confusion over the term. Here the reference should be to a man from the north rather than "de Normandie," since that is the case when the incident is repeated elsewhere in the text. Nevertheless, we have translated it according to the text: "from Normandy."

2690. Genesis 50.4–14.

2708. The translation of the bodies of Audrey, Seaxburga, Ermenilda, and Withburga took place in 1106.

2728. "Epistula Luciani," Migne, *Patrologia Latina*, xli, cols. 807–18. Cited in Fairweather, *Liber Eliensis*, 277, note 748.

2751–52. Without explanation or noting any rejected reading, Södergård gives these lines as "A la mesure, a la leur / De l'autre et tut a la largeur." However, the manuscript is very clear at this point, and the text is as given in the present edition.

2766. According to one account, not only was Withburga's body intact, but her limbs were still flexible, a fact demonstrated to the congregation by a monk from Westminster who waved her arms about. See Jones, *English Saints*, 109.

2788. It is interesting to note that Marie uses the Old French word *translater*, here meaning to translate from one language to another, in a section of the text that immediately follows the important passage describing the *translation* of the bodies of Audrey, Seaxburga, Ermenilda, and Withburga. In all her known works the author engages in such word-play.

2801. Marie's suggestion that Audrey was *parente* [kin] to the angels may be based, in part, on the close homonymic words *angles* [angels] and *engleis* [Angles or English] and suggests the play on words used by St. Gregory of Rome, "Non angli, sed angeli," previously referred to in lines 821–29 of the *Vie seinte Audree*.

2806. Reference to the words of the Apostle Paul who expresses his personal views on the subject of marriage and chastity in 1 Corinthians 7. He encourages virgins to remain so, but also teaches that wives should not deprive their husband of their marital rights. See also 2 Colossians 11.2.

2913. A hide was a measure of land comprising from eighty to one hundred acres.

2932. The story of Leffi and Leflad is similar to the biblical account of Ananias and his wife Sapphira in the early Christian community. Having sold a piece of land, they handed only a portion of the profits over to the apostles. Reproved by Saint Peter of lying to God, both husband and wife fell dead at the apostle's feet. See Acts 5. 1–10.

2941. The manuscript has "fini Wigar," which Södergård has correctly reversed. The change is necessitated by the rhyme.

2951. The manuscript line reads "Pur la vengance ha seinte Audree." However, the *ha* seems to belong in the following line, where we have inserted it. It appears that here, as elsewhere, the scribe has carelessly transposed a word from one line to another.

3010. The biblical story of the rebellion against Moses and Aaron led by Korah, Dathan, and Abiram during the years of wilderness wandering is told in the book of Numbers 16. The ground opened and swallowed the rebel leaders. In this biblical allusion the author of *Vie seinte Audree* refers to the nether world of Greek mythology: Acheron is the river of Hades.

3014. The metathesis of the *re* of the verb *mespernoit* for *mesprenoit* is typical of the scribe when the verb *prendre* has a prefix. See also line 3002 and 3951.

3026. In punishment for his hubris, Nebuchadnezzar went mad, behaving like a beast. He began eating grass with the oxen, his hair grew out into feathers, and his nails became claws. When he lifted his eyes to heaven and began praising the God of Israel, he was restored. See Daniel 4. 33–37.

3127. A "prosa," or "sequence," was a musical addition sung after the *Alleluia* and often related to it. "The sequence repertory is preserved primarily in the medieval *tropers*, manuscripts containing those components of the chant that stood outside the official liturgy. " *New Harvard Dictionary of Music*, s.v "prosa." Today any hymn between the responsorial Psalm and the *Alleluia* can be called a sequence.

3150. Marie writes in the epilogue to her fables that they were written "for the love of Count William, the most valiant of this realm." The Count William of the *Vie Seinte Audree* stands in stark contrast to the one of the fables.

3157. Marie de France frequently speaks in her works of things that are "contre nature."

3165. The destruction of ancient Babylon by fire is prophetically described in the Old Testament books of Isaiah and Jeremiah. See especially Isaiah 47.13–15 and Jeremiah 51. 25, 58.

3173. Lines may be missing just prior to this line, since nothing has thus far been mentioned to motivate Brustan's fear. The subsequent accusations of Robert Malarteis provide at least a partial explanation.

3223. Södergård renders this line as "Matilda ki estoit" in his edition, rejecting the manuscript's "A bone maut ki estoit" and providing instead a hypometric line. Since *Maude* was a common name given to Queen Matilda,

we have given the line as "A bone Maud[e] ki estoit," listing the spelling *Maut* in the Rejected Readings.

3236. This line provides an example of Marie's love of irony, based here on the word *rendre*. To the place where Brustan had come to put himself under heavenly authority, he is instead taken under earthly authority. After his encounter with Saint Audrey, he is able to do as he originally intended. His chains, so miraculously loosened, are brought to the church at Ely, where they will become the agent through which Saint Audrey works still another miracle.

3381–82. The rhyme words in these lines are precisely the same as that used by Marie in the *Espurgatoire Seint Patriz*, lines 277–78. This is but one example of many striking similarities between the two texts. See McCash, "Audree: Fourth Text?" 753–55. The word play on *rendre* is apparent in this line.

3458. Guildford was on the route the monks were following to return to their monastic house in Winchester, from which Simeon had taken them when he placed them in Ely.

3530. The flower placed in the mouth has the power to restore speech, as a flower restored both speech and life in *Guideluëc et Guilliadun (Eliduc)* in Marie de France's *Lais*.

3544. The word *tert* is *cert* in the manuscript, but *tert* (which Södergård also uses) makes more sense, and it is clearly the word in line 3546 [*terst*] within a similar context. The scribe may have confused initial *t* for *c* in the manuscript he or she was copying.

3563. The Södergård edition gives the name of the town as "Gorewelle" and identifies it as a town in Essex. However, it is clearly "Borewelle" in the manuscript, which reflects an older spelling of the village Burwell in Cambridgeshire.

3565. Here Saint Audrey cures a man suffering from the same infirmity that caused her death.

3735. Almost all lines that contain the name *Nel* (see also lines 4016, 4017) have problems. The name in English is *Nigel* and the French equivalent is *Neel*. By the time of the scribe's copying of the text, however, the name had apparently been reduced to one syllable. Often the scribe makes some attempt to compensate, for example, by adding *lui* before the word *ama* in line 4016 but in so doing creates new grammatical problems that apparently did not exist in the original text.

3822. The word *tele* or *itele* occurs ten times in the manuscript; however, in every case but one the line is hypermetric, making it clear that the author's original form was "tel." This is the one instance where the line can be read as metrically regular with *tele*, though the form is still incorrect. To be consistent, we have corrected it to *tel*.

3846. This hypothetical line is based on the Latin original, which contains essentially the same information at this point. The same is the case in line 3866. We do not contend in either case that these are the precise lines Marie would have used, but they are inserted because they contain information that helps to understand the text.

3866. See note for line 3846.

3960. The phrasing of Withburga's revelation of her identify "si sui suer," is reminiscent of the phrasing in the epilogue of the *Fables* when Marie identifies herself in the epilogue of her *Fables*: "si sui de France" (line 4).

3968. See note for line 993.

4055. We have capitalized *Seint* because it refers here and in line 4067 to a place name.

4067. The context makes clear that *Osmon* represents a variant spelling for *Edmund* in this manuscript.

4072. This miracle seems to be unfinished in the text. Additional lines may be missing here.

4081. The form *just* is attested in *Guigemar*, line 544, and is needed here to complete the rhyme, though the manuscript gives *jeut*.

4110. Södergård's note for this line expresses uncertainty concerning the meaning of the verb. The verb *s'aidier de*, according to Frédéric Godefroy's *Lexique de l'ancien français*, has among its meanings "employer ses forces" and "s'empresser." The line seems to mean "He prepared to leave" or "He hastened to leave."

4146. Wulfstan of Worcester lived much later than the others mentioned in this story. Oswald was Bishop of Worcester at this time (c. 969). See Godfrey, "Monastic Revival," *The Church in Anglo-Saxon England*.

4182. Place names almost always present problems in this manuscript. (See note to line Line 98.) Line 228 contains the spelling of

Dereheam. Adding the second *e* corrects the meter in line 4182; however when added to line 4186, it causes the line to be hypermetric. To compensate, we have reduced *amenez* to *menez* in 4186.

4200. A reflection of the biblical story of the Star of Bethlehem that led magi from the east to the infant Jesus. See Matthew 2.1–12.

4242. Although it is evident from the meter that this is the form of the word *boneüree* as Marie usually used it, this is one of the rare times this form is actually attested in this late manuscript. In most cases, the scribe has omitted the *e* in diaeresis and left the line one syllable short.

4249. The manuscript line is "Emfes demein deliveras," which does not work grammatically. We have used the verb *estras* for metrical reasons. The phrase *delivre seras* works in terms of rhyme but not in terms of meter. Another possibility, *te delivreras* (or even *deliveras*), leaves the same metrical problem.

4267. Possibly the cross of St. Osith, wife of King Sighere (664–83). The cross was taken by the Danes in 870 and returned to the church by King Edgar in 970.

4447. In this line *ki* should be read as *cui*.

4574. Although the New Testament gospels and the letters of Saints Peter and Paul commend patience as a virtue, this particular scriptural reference corresponds more closely to the advice given in the Old Testament book of Proverbs. See Proverbs 15.1 and 15.18.

4278. Audrey's gesture may be interpreted as a tacit challenge to her husband, as though throwing down the gauntlet.

4625. Delbert Russell has noted that "the *St. Audree* may ... be missing a final line, since the epilogue which contains the usual prayer ends without a customary 'amen,' and the final line is without a matching rhyme" ("Campsey Collection," 61). While it is indeed possible that a line is missing, the epilogue seems complete as it stands. It is also possible that Marie deliberately left the line without a rhyme in an effort to focus attention on her final word, *remembree*, given the fact that memory is an important motif throughout all her works. On the importance of memory in her works, see especially Whalen, *Marie and the Poetics of Memory*, and Bloch, *Anonymous Marie*, 39–42.

Appendix 1:
Rejected Readings

2 Deveroit 3 deveroit 5 fait e qui 12 v. departi deservi 21 Quil 23 heremite 26 ses f. 27 et viveront 37 lestorie 44 come 52 engendreis 58 la s. 64 del k. 66 a. issi 78 Sire gilberz 80 de e. 87 et e. 92 Sire gilberz 93 bedricheswiorde 94 Qua 95 Et geriz 101 merchenesande 105 Sire gilberz volerent 109 sa a. 111 Et en 116 ke il 124 nos ay ... ci 127 le o. 129 Ceus r. 135 la a. 136 Sire gilberz 143 de honestete 148 poveres 151 e q. 157 a n. 163 ke ceo q. 166 ken 169 Et a. 170 quot g. 172 honestete 181 Sire r. 182 livere 190 v. bien d. 198 al d. 222 M. ele 226 Voit a. 232 livere 235 sa e. 243 sa e. 249 De a. aurier 253 se p. 263 de a. 267 et de s. 283 de a. 292 m. se f. 294 ke ele 306 de e. 310 De a. 313 maries 317 de e. 320 sa m. 324 chastete 335 e. mut s. 336 sa e. 345 chastete 350 Ke a. 352 si come 357 sa e. 360 come 362 espiritelement 364 Ne e. 368 En son 389 chastete 411 come 421 Uncore 436 Tele 442 il ameine 448 Del lantre 461 Ke homme 463 Et t. 481 Werefred 482 home 483 de E. 495 rameseye 515 Et de e. 522 faillie 526 sonestete 541 Ke il 545 Ke il 560 et haucee 563 le r. 578 mortelement 611 est lenglais 622 le o. 636 come 644 Ke une 656 bone be- nuree 658 En kel l. 665 Et ke n. 667 l. ou t. 678 Ke il 681 de a. 696 sa e. 701 come 708 le r. 713 continoit 715 ke il 717 continement 720 ke il 722 Don eveskes oeddes 723 Home 725 Del f. 726 S. ceo c. 729 Fiz le r. 738 b. quele 743 de e. 750 t. en s. 752 habitoit 753 de e.... aubres i ouit 762 Et d. 767 de a. 769 et en b. 772 ke ele 778 come 784 ke il 787 q. il la 789 ke il 795 sens p. 797 desire 800 ke a. 801 de a. 804 uncle sen 815 de u. 822 a royne 825 ke il 845 syriens 852 des a. 860 et si 864 ele p. 876 En m. 885 le h. 891 une h. 894 ke a. 911 Come 917 seinte 920 ke un 922 hant 925 par amur 933 come 934 Et a l. 947 k'ele 948 se ert 950 Ke a 952 K a. 960 ke il 970 de u. 983 honestete 989 sa e. 992 ke il 994 Ne ... ne a t. 995 ke il 999 marie

1000 de o. 1003 charner 1007 la esposee 1017 quele d. 1034 se ert 1040 venceue 1046 Ke il 1049 perpetuele 1056 Et kele 1059 le e. 1066 espiritelement 1071 g. verche 1083 est uochoit 1085 pout 1090 s. et h. 1094 honesteté 1097 De o. 1099 kele 1101 C. deus a. 1104 En le e. 1105 d. deu 1120 de a. 1129 remembrier 1143 Forte 1144 De a. 1145 se je 1146 espiritelement 1156 se ele 1170 delever- ance 1173 de o.... de a. 1176 Qua 1184 quele 1196 Les escriez d. 1198 Saincois 1199 Ou p. 1211 Pur priue et veire et a. 1212 Et e. 1220 ke a 1224 En le d. 1227 saintete 1234 honesteté 1240 de haan 1241 O. ele 1245 de h. 1247 le h. 1260 sa v. 1266 li fens 1271 come 1274 Ke il 1275 de i. 1284 tresques 1295 de e. 1303 et s. 1309 se s. se h. 1311 iceo 1322 ele 1336 Et en m. 1346 ne e. 1347 se o. 1356 Ke u. 1358 Ceo 1362 home 1369 ou ele ne p.1371 grave et 1375 ne ert 1391 Ke un ... de e. 1397 si com overi 1408 Come 1409 ceo a. 1413 come 1427 ne f. 1429 sa a. 1431 ai a 1432 Ke en 1439 Ke a 1442 Quele 1452 p. erent 1469 s. iceo ke e. 1475 ceo ert 1477 estoles 1478 En le s. 1484 le o. 1486 Ele 1494 p. tut a. 1495 Del le c. 1498 Kele 1501 voit 1523 de e. 1526 Quele 1528 de h. 1529 se est 1530 se est 1531 seest 1532 se est 1543 de d et de s. 1545 a. ice 1559 ky a lui a.1562 Ke il n. se e. 1571 price 1573 la cure 1588 deu eus t.1589 le h. 1591 mais l. 1593 apertement 1599 ce a. 1600 de e. 1615 C. edli 1618 est e a. 1620 En la g. 1623 Et e. 1634 g. se les 1644 ke il 1655 ke a. 1664

Quele 1671 Sa e. 1673 aroine a. 1675 Ke e. 1679 Quele 1680 Des 1683 Sembland 1684 j. crist fu 1691 Ke ceus eurent 1692 Et al 1701 secante 1706 A s. 1707 Des h. 1710 Ke a 1720 Et e. 1726 le o. 1727 c. et tut 1734 se est 1736 En le s. 1747 assiduelement 1756 a legeir 1757 tresques au 1759 denfermete 1770 Ke i. 1772 f. en d. 1777 le a. 1778 home 1782 an m. 1783 F. derborc 1785 werboc 1791 sa a. 1793 a. bien t. 1794 Ke il 1797 penda 1800 ke il 1803 Ce t. frere 1806 De e. 1809 ici 1825 soit ice kele 1830 kuns 1833 Le abbesse f. le a. 1838 le a. 1849 En la g. de d. 1857 la amenee 1866 Ki as 1870 se ert 1885 Ke u. pestilencie 1886 descenderoit 1887 moustree 1888 affermee 1895 honestete 1900 le e. 1905 a roine 1908 confermez 1909 Come 1911 par unt i p. 1912 crestienete 1920 Fu done grant e. ke li c. 1923 larguor 1945 creoit 1954 Ke a 1959 ke il 1961 Le h. 1964 enfermete 1970 sa enfermete 1974 Et par la 1975 sa e. 1982 Et en ... sa a.

2001 ke il 2003 Sessante 2004 nees 2007 com je e. 2013 ke en 2014 Ne e. 2016 Sainte 2030 ces f. 2044 il li 2047 ienurent 2050 oscuillierent 2055 Le an 2059 De un 2066 tendeit 2080 se e. 2082 teneu 2083 Cil le 2086 garesit 2088 Si le 2099 Tunuus 2104 li a a. 2115 Sa a. 2126 ne a. 2128 ke il 2132 Des a.... de o. 2136 pieres g. 2137 p. ne f. 2139 de o. 2140 de un 2142 f. mie a 2148 saintete 2150 beneistre et a. 2187 L. versuis 2189 cele p. 2201 le e. 2206 sanoit 2207 e. sui 2222 Ke n. 2224 Testimonie 2230 d. il la 2240 de u. 2241 le u. 2242 Kil lont ... itele 2248 de e. 2249 ke a. 2257 que il 2259 getee 2260 Ky de loinz ... devoree 2262 blesmer 2263 Ore ... honesteté 2265 le u. 2266 le e. 2276 cum au c. 2282 Ne ou ... le o. 2289 le h. 2290 des a. 2294 reine noble b. 2295 sesante 2297 le encarnation 2306 Ke a. 2318 Ele 2322 Ou ele 2327 Ke il 2328 de h. 2337 que il 2340 et par 2349 ceo a. 2356 A lui c. la d. 2359 kil lamoit 2360 Par son s. 2361 suer 2373 suer 2381 Si come 2389 Et q. 2390 sen i ala 2392 le e. 2394 sa a. 2398 de e. et teneu 2408 De e. 2410 le e. 2411 pees 2415 alfedene ... veneu 2418 bretagnie 2424 Ke il ... arme 2425 Le y.... et mai mistrent 2426 Et t. 2428 lavoit ou et e. 2446 Ke e. 2448 De cele 2453 de eus 2455 Cil d. 2457 Si e. 2462 kele 2463 pout 2466 Desques 2468 Eu tutes sunt 2469 Et s'en 2471 De un 2487 De un 2495 ne h. 2503 disimis 2509 ke nos m. 2511 li fist 2525 Ke un 2528 sa t. 2529 clers et 2548 endureroms 2549 Ke e. 2554 ge oy 2556 uncore 2557 que il 2574 Ki al 2577 A li v. 2580 sa a ... l. rava 2584 deskes au 2588 les retrait 2589 A cele f. ceo l. 2590 de home 2599 Ke as 2600 et grant p. 2610 morirent 2614 ala ameison 2615 Ke il 2617 prestres 2625 ke il 2631 n. et li b. 2637 un home 2647 Par ce r. 2648 le y. de e. 2649 le e. 2651 Le e. 2654 Ke il ... le o. 2664 f. atraire 2670 ke il 2671 Mes une 2673 Ki de 2674 overaine ... r. sen a. 2678 quanke il 2680 Et sa e. 2683 covre ki la 2685 Ke il 2691 Le erceveske 2697 Li e.... i fu 2708 icel 2710 o. et la 2713 le o. 2714 le e. 2717 De u. chandelie ... arre 2722 Ceo o. 2724 chandelie 2725 Ky en fu 2728 Si com 2732 pleut 2734 ke ele 2740 ky lur 2744 mervelie 2746 Ke hom 2750 overer 2754 de un 2755 ceo 2764 non ha g. 2765 ke il 2770 li v. 2777 que il 2778 ici 2784 ou beu s. 2792 En le s. 2796 sen est a. 2803 a nos 2808 enteree 2818 De un 2823 de un 2824 de e. 2834 santee 2836 ke a 2840 Reront 2842 restorel de l. de e. 2843 passee 2844 estee 2846 le o. 2874 lur seigniur d. 2881 bonurement 2883 il lentendi 2887 h. sue 2889 granz rentes 2895 le a. 2899 testimonie 2902 Bien a la roine 2904 le h. 2907 De un 2915 aporta 2928 que a. 2930 le o. 2937 ke il 2941 fini wigar 2943 ne ne b. 2945 morirent 2946 le an 2951 v. ha s. 2954 De un 2955 li a. 2956 li ha 2957 le u. 2974 et descoveri 2979 necessaries li ont 2983 la coit v. 2985 Ke a 2987 tele 2992 entreus v. 2993 ne fuissent 2994 Com lur c.

3003 cele d. 3011 costosme 3016 de e. 3018 ke il 3020 de a. 3026 En d. qui 3027 home 3030 li e. 3032 damage 3039 ce e. 3041 Ke il ... se p. 3042 Ne a ... a ceus 3045 Ke l. 3049 ke a. 3055 Ce d. 3065 i sont 3079 de e. 3085 se e. 3090 de e. 3097 espantee 3103 dama 3105 et ou 3107 Jekes 3109 ke e. 3113 se e. 3114 ke ele 3115 Ke il 3118 se e. 3124 ke il 3125 ke o. recoveree 3129 albe de e. 3133 d. jut e. 3134 ke en ... le o. 3144 sa a. 3145 ke il 3146 ke e. 3148 ammone 3177 ke il 3199 Ore le d. 3202 Et il 3208 pareie 3209 Tele 3214 li a 3215 home 3217 dames viues 3219 m. que li d. 3223 Ke a bone maut 3236 se e. 3240 ke e. 3241 home 3242 Deleez ... de e. 3258 avera 3265 cele e. 3267 sa e. 3268 Ke il 3281 sa e. 3294 le o. 3295 De un 3306 sa e. 3308 Ke u. 3312 Ke ele 3313 lui a. 3314 Et lui q. 3319 que a 3326 recovera 3329 de a. 3331 cele m. 3333 Tele ... de e. 3334 li e. 3337 q. si il 3348 que il 3350 ke il 3354 ke il 3355 que il 3359 Tus li c.... ke il 3364 ke ele ... lui a. 3366 Ke un 3367 lo h. 3368 ke il 3371 ke un 3372 a non 3389 Esteez 3392 se apuia 3396 angeles 3400 ke il 3413 De u. 3428 Bristan 3433 home 3435 despeceez 3437 halfedene 3440 de un 3443 Halfedene 3447 de un 3450 temoinies 3451 le or 3455 c. et m. 3457 ke il 3462 quanque il 3464 Ke il 3470 P. si le 3472 de e. 3490 li g. 3494 Ke ele 3496 Ke a 3503 Ke une 3505 ele 3509 deskes a 3510 s. vos de v. 3515 ke ele ... portoit 3517 ele 3519 ke e. 3520 se e. 3526 ke e. 3527 r. arpeler 3531 ke a 3541 tote 3544 li cert 3545 ke e. 3546 desoit 3549 sa o. 3551 ke e. 3557 offrerent 3562 unke 3563 home 3565 enfermeté 3570 ke ele 3576 le h. 3579 home 3581 Jekes e. 3588 home 3589 Jekes 3596 Ke a 3600 jekes 3601 sueffrer 3602 Ke a. 3603 Si en n. 3621 alee 3622 vouee 3624 reporteront 3625 de y. 3630 le y. 3634 Se il 3636 ke il v. tut en a. 3637 De un 3639 neez 3644 sa a. 3645 Le o. 3646 Et en 3650 overast 3653 de e. 3654 et il 3659 Le a. le e. 3664 de e. 3669 ke il 3670 manoier 3671 Encore ... ke il 3679 de e. 3680 le e. 3681 ne out 3682 Ke il 3695 leidei 3709 A les e. 3711 Le e. 3713 nomee 3716 l'en averont 3717 Le e. 3729 sa i. 3731 c. ne o. 3734 de eus 3735 li e. 3736 Ke u. 3738 ne a. 3747 overi 3753 De un ... ke il 3758 Ke il 3765 g. air 3767 le an 3777 menee 3778 alee 3784 te ay 3792 averunt 3793 sa o. 3799 De un 3807 b. genz sont 3809 Ke il 3812 ke il 3813 coveri 3819 ke il 3821 Tele 3822 tele 3823 meimes 3824 Ke en g. maladile 3825 Ke il 3827 ki le 3829 il v. ke il 3831 fist se 3834 geques 3836 ke il 3843 boigsoin 3847 reconosterai 3853 Ke a.... ke en 3860 v. en e. 3861 que a 3864 ke e. 3865 ke il 3867 ce e. 3869 se e. 3871 ke il 3876 li a 3878 ke a. 3879 De un ... ici 3881 tele ke il 3889 Ke al 3898 Come ... li e. 3903 De un 3904 de e. 3905 tele 3909 Ke il 3913 ce li fu 3915 fait 3918 li ad 3925 le eglise 3927 ke il 3929 ke ele 3932 sa aventure 3940 ke en 3943 le e. 3947 ke ele 3949 ke ele 3956 se e. 3958 Si ele li 3964 de sei a. 3968 a lui 3969 se e. 3970 f. cele que ele 3976 ki lui 3977 De a. 3979 De a.... meffait 3983 Le a. 3994 portee 3999 home

4005 les p. 4009 se e. 4010 ke il 4015 se a. 4016 Le e. ne ... lui a. 4021 savereient 4028 foleer 4029 compaignion 4034 veit 4036 apresmer 4037 que il se a. 4038 Ne e. 4039 ke il 4042 li oy 4043 se e. 4044 Et s. companiz 4045 De i.... se a. 4046 Prudome 4047 Sa a. 4050 li out 4051 prud-home 4054 Ke une 4057 ke il 4059 Ke a g. 4061 Messer s. 4062 Ke out 4065 prodome 4076 et estuit e. 4077 ne ert ... sa enfermeté 4083 ke alast 4084 averoit 4085 se est 4086 jekes en 4097 Et p. 4099 li overi 4100 a. de d. 4101 Ke a 4103 que il 4105 Aleez ... si neez 4108 sa a. 4112 Le e. 4115 le h. 4124 aveeuglee 4127 De u. 4129 puissier 4140 Ke o. 4141 sceculers 4143 Ke il 4144 le e. 4145 see 4149 De h. 4151 le o. 4155 ke il e. deposee 4156 genee 4167 le oy 4168 ke i 4172 Ke a 4186 amenez 4188 D. par lui 4189 overi 4190 descoveri 4191 tele la 4199 se a. 4201 clartee 4208 et g. 4209 ke ele 4211 de e. 4212 encontre 4214 Les moines 4222 le e. 4226 le f. 4228 De un ... le e. de e. 4236 se fera 4241 De a. 4245 se aparut 4247 le a. 4249 deliveras 4257 n. dist 4258 De un 4261 le i. 4262 Li e. ke il 4265 Ke en 4273 s. en issi 4274 coveri 4285 enfermetez 4287 Feveres a. se p. 4290 Ke il ne heurent 4295 se a. 4296 fevere 4297 Et li d. 4299 averoit 4303 le a. 4304 fevere 4308 ke ele 4310 Et si 4314 e. des a. 4318 ke il 4320 de une 4322 Si il e. le un 4324 le un 4326 ke il 4327 c. se f. 4328 ke il 4332 ke a. 4333 le y. de e. 4335 ke il 4336 ke a. 4338 ke il 4341 de e. 4342 ce a. 4343 Si a. 4344 ce oy contier 4355 prudom 4356 ke il 4358 Ki en o. 4360 et deist 4361 honestete 4363 il lui a. 4364 le achevira 4366 A deu ... pocelez 4372 Ce ont 4374 De u ... de e. 4383 si e. 4388 Ke e. 4392 sen ieest 4397 meneez 4398 entreez 4408 a reconte s. 4411 de une 4412 De un 4415 de e. 4422 de e. 4425 Ke hom 4426 Si il 4432 poverete 4433 Ke il 4434 Ne il 4436 ke il 4437 ke il 4439 ele 4446 ke a. 4450 Ke il 4452 Ke il 4465 mostree 4466 fause-tee 4467 de un 4468 se a. 4473 de escone 4475 De o. ... engressee 4476 porversee 4486 ele 4494 te e. 4495 se e. 4496 De a.... se e. 4501 prie 4507 desenflee 4508 Et tuz l.... santee 4515 overa 4518 Et d. 4519 de e. 4535 Ke il 4540 ke il 4542 C. si li. 4545 De un 4546 de e. 4552 Ke il 4554 Ke prines 4562 overes ke e. 4567 ke ele 4570 que un 4578 par d. li 4585 ke il 4588 Ke e. ne o. 4594 de o. de e. 4603 Ke il ... trovee 4604 veritee 4605 Et ce e. 4611 livere 4619 ke a 4621 lay d. 4622 Ke ele

Appendix 2*:
Text Analysis and Rubrics
of British Library,
Cotton Domitian A xv (B)

Text Analysis

[I. Vita sancte virginis et regine Etheldrede ("The *Life of the Holy Virgin and Queen Audrey*")]

Audree	MS. *B*	*Acta sanctorum* (AS)	*Liber Eliensis* (LE)
0.[1] 1–16, 1–16, 17–28, 29–36[2]	—	—	—
1. 37–90, 91–124, 125–36	9V[a]–10R[a]	1: §§7–8	1: §1
2. 137–228	10R[a]–10V[a]	1: §§9–11	1: §2
3. 229–64	10V[a–b]	1: §12	1: §3
4. 265–280, 281–320,[3]			
321–94	10V[b]–11V[a]	1: §§13–15	1: §4
5. 395–412, 413–70	11V[a]–12R[a]	1: §§16–17	1: §5
6. 471–500	12R[a–b]	1: §18	1: §6
7. 501–739	12R[b]–13R[b]	1: §§19–22	1: §7
8. 740–918, 919–80	13R[b]–15R[a]	1: §§23–28	1: §8
9. 981–1128	15R[a]–15V[b]	1: §§29–31	1: §9
10. 1129–1268	15V[b]–16V[a]	1: §§32–34	1: §10
11. 1269–1424	16V[a]–17V[a]	1: §§35–38	1: §11
12. 1425–96	17V[a]–18R[a]	1: §§39–40	1: §12
13. 1497–1544	18R[a]–18V[a]	1: §§41–42	1: §13
14. 1545–96	18V[b]–19R[b]	1: §§43–44	1: §14
15. 1597–1714	19R[b]–20R[b]	1: §§45–48	1: §15
16. 1715–1764	20R[b]–20V[b]	1: §§49–50	1: §16
17. 1765–1816[4]	20V[b]–21R[a]	1: §51	1: §17
18. 1817–70	21R[a]–21V[a]	1: §§52–53	1: §18
19. 1871–1918	21V[a]–22R[a]	1: §§54–55	1: §19
20. 1919–50	22R[a–b]	1: §56	1: §20

*Prepared by Rupert T. Pickens and used with permission.

Audree	MS. B	*Acta sanctorum* (AS)	*Liber Eliensis* (LE)
21. 1951–2026	22R^b–23R^a	1: §§57–59	1: §21
22. 2027–54	23R$^{a–b}$	1: §60	1: §22
23. 2055–2142	23R^b–24R^a	1: §§61–62(pt. 1)	1: §23
24. 2143–54	24R^a	1: §62(pt. 2)	1: §24
25. 2155–76	24R$^{a–b}$	1: §63	1: §25
26. 2177–2212	24R^b–24V^b	1: §§64–65	1: §26
27. 2213–62	24V^b–25V^{a5}	1: §§66–68	1: §27
28. 2263–2300	25V^a–26R^b	1: §§69–71(pt. 1)	1: §28
29. 2301–20	26R^b	1: §71(pt. 2)	1: §29
30. 2321–28	26R^b	1: §71(pt. 3)	1: §30
31. 2329–34	26R^b–26V^a	1: §71(pt. 4)	1: §31
32. 2335–46^6	26V^a	1: §72	1: §32^7
33. 2347–80	27V$^{a–b}$	1: §77	1: §35
34. 2381–96	27V^b–28R^a	1: §78	1: §36
35. 2397–2402	28R^a	1: §79(pt. 1)	1: §37
36. 2403–14	28R$^{a–b}$	1: §§79(pt. 2)	1: §38
37. 2415–22^8	28R^b–28V^b	1: §§80–82	1: §39
38. 2423–28^9	28V^b–29R^b	1: §§83–84	1: §40
39. 2429–52	29R^b–29V^b	1: §§85–86	1: §41
40. 2453–60^{10}	30R^a–30V^a	1: §88(pt. 2)–89(pt. 1)	1: §43
41. 2461–70	30V^a	1: §89(pt. 2)	1: §44
42. 2471–78	30V$^{a–b}$	1: §90(pt. 1)	1: §45
43. 2479–82	30V^b	1: §90(pt. 2)	1: §46
44. 2483–86	30V^b	1: §90(pt. 3)	1: §47
45. 2487–2522	30V^b–31R^b	1: §§91–92(pt. 1)	1: §48
46. 2523–2630	31R^b–32R^a	1: §§92(pt. 2)–95(pt. 1)	1: §49
47. 2631–46	32R^a	1: §95(pt. 2)	1: §50

[II. *De secunda translatione Etheldrede virginis* (On the Second Translation of the Virgin Audrey)]^{11}

1. 2647–62	33R^a–33R^a	2: §40 (cf. 2: §§33, 35)	2: §118^{12}
2. 2663–82^{13}	33R^a–34R^b	2: §41(cf. 2: §§36–37)	2: §§140–43
3. 2683–2734^{14}	34R^b–34V^a	2: §§43–44	2: §144
4. 2735–40^{15}	34V$^{a–b}$	2: §46(pt. 1)	2: §145
5. 2741–72	34V^b–35V^a	—^{16}	2: §§146–48 (ll. 1–17)
6. 2773–84^{17}	35V^a–36R^a	2: §46(pt. 3)^{18}	2: §150 (ll. 1–10)

[III. *Miracula Sancte Etheldrede* (Miracles of St. Audrey)]

0a. 2785–2817	36R^a–37V^a	3: §§1–4	—
0b. 2817–22,^{19} cf. 2429–52	38R^b–38V^b, cf. 29R^b–29V^b	3: f. §5 cf. 1: §§85–86	cf. LE 1: §41
1. 2823–40	37V^a–38V^b	3: §§5–7	—
2. 2841–88	38V^b–39V^a	3: f. §7 (=2: §§3–7)^{20}	2: §1
3. 2889–2904^{21}	39V^a–40R^b	3: f. §7 (=2: §§8–10)	2: §5
4. 2905–32	40R^b–40V^b	3: §§8–9	3: §119
5. 2933–52	40V^b–41R^b	3: §§10–11	3: §120
6. 2953–94	41R^b–42R^b	3: §§12–16^{22}	2: §129
7. 2995–3004	42R^b–42V^a	3: §§17–18	2: §130

Audree	MS. B	Acta sanctorum (AS)	Liber Eliensis (LE)
8. 3005–3026	42Vª–43Rª	3: §§19–21	2: §131
9. 3027–76	43Rª–43Vª	3: §§22–24	2: §132
10. 3077–3128	43Vª–45Rª	3: §§25–30	2: §133
11. 3129–50	45Rª⁻ᵇ	3: §31	2: §119
12. 3151–68	45Rᵇ–45Vª	3: §32	3: §28
13. 3169–3240	45Vª–47Vª	3: §§33–41	3: §33
14. 3241–62	47Vª–48Rª	3: §§42–43	3: §34
15. 3263–94	48Rª–49Vᵇ	3: §§44–50	3: §35
16. 3295–3328	49Vᵇ–51Rª	3: §§51–56	3: §36
17. 3329–64	51Rª–51Vᵇ	3: §§57–60	3: §42
18. 3365–3410	51Vᵇ–53Rª	3: §§61–65	3: §43
19. 3411–46	53Rª–53Vª	3: §§66–68	—
20. 3447–72	53Vª–54Rª	3: §§69–71	—
21. 3473–3562	54Rª–57Rª	3: §§72–84	3: §60
22. 3563–78	57Rª⁻ᵇ	3: §85	—
23. 3579–3624	57Rᵇ–57Vª	3: §86	—
24. 3625–36	57Vª	3: §87	—
25. 3637–3734	57Vª–60Rª	3: §§88–98	3: §§47, 51–53[23]
26. 3735–52	60Rª⁻ᵇ	3: §99	3: §57
27. 3753–98	60Rᵇ–60Vᵇ	3: §§100–01	3: §58
28. 3799–3816	60Vᵇ	3: §102	3: §59
29. 3817–78	61Rª–62Rª	3: §§103–07	3: §61
30. 3879–3902	62Rª⁻ᵇ	3: §108	3: §130
31. 3903–3932	62Rᵇ–62Vª	3: §§109–10	3: §131
32. 3933–70	62Vª–63Rᵇ	3: §§111–12	3: §137
33. 3971–98	63Rᵇ–63Vᵇ	3: §§113–15	3: §138
34. 3999–4010	63Vᵇ–64Rª	3: §116	—
35. 4011–50	64Rª–65Rᵇ	3: §§117–21	3: §93
36. 4051–72	65Rᵇ–66Vª	3: §122–23	3: §94
37. 073–4122	65Vª–66Vª	3: §124–28	3: §116
38. 4123–26	66Vª⁻ᵇ	3: §§129–30	3: §117
39. 4127–38	66Vᵇ–67Rᵇ	3: §131–32	3: §118
40. 4139–78	67Rᵇ–67Vᵇ	3: §§133–35	2: §51
41. 4179–4226	67Vᵇ–69Rª	3: f. §135 (cf. 2: §17)[24]	2: §53
42. 4227–56	69Rª–69Vª	3: §§136–37	—
43. 4257–84	69Vª⁻ᵇ	3: §138	—
44. 4285–4340	69Vᵇ–70Rᵇ	3: §§139–40	—
45. 4341–72	70Rᵇ–70Vª	3: §141	3: §32
46. 4373–92	70Vª–71Rª	3: §§142–44	—
47. 4393–4402	71Rª–71Vª	3: §§145–46	—
48. 4403–10	71Vª⁻ᵇ	3: §147	—
49. 4411–14	71Vᵇ	3: §148	—
50. 4415–72	71Vᵇ–72Vª	3: 149–52	3: §115
51. 4473–4512	72Vª–73Rᵇ	3: §§153–55	—
52. 4513–44	73Rᵇ–73Vᵇ	3: §§156–57	—
· 53. 4545–4610	73Vᵇ–75Rª	3: §§158–61	—
0c. 4611–25	—	—	—

1. Major textual divisions are as indicated by rubrics followed by colored initials in **B**.

2. Unless otherwise noted, textual divisions in the *Audree* are as indicated by colored initials in B.L., Add. 70513 ff. 100V–134V. In all but 10 of 99 cases (90%), textual divisions in

B correspond to those in *Audree* or, in 5 instances at the outset, groups of two or more. When the divisions in Add. 70513 do not match those in *B*, Marie's language betrays consciousness of a change. In every case, a new sentence begins at the line in questions, and other linguistic indicators occur twice: "Ici nos dist" (1765) ("Here it says to us") and "Ci conte" (2453) ("Here it tells").

3. The matter from AS 1: §14 ends with 306, after which Marie introduces a digression (307–20) on the island of Ely (see 318–20). In 307–20, Marie selectively draws on material from the introduction to Book 1 (AS 1: §§3–6, LE 1, pp. 2–5) where the island of Ely is described.

4. No textual division before 1765 in Add. 70513.

5. Fol. 25 is erroneously numbered 26.

6. No textual division before 2335 in Add. 70513. Marie substitutes for this prayer a prayer of her own (2335–46) in which "cil qui fist l'escrit" prays God for the strength to finish his task of recounting miracles so that he might earn the thanks of the Blessed Trinity.

7. Marie omits citations of Bede's writings on the saint in AS 1: §§73–76, LE 1: §§33–34.

8. No textual division before 2415 in Add. 70513.

9. No textual division before 2423 in Add. 70513.

10. No textual division before 2453 in Add. 70513. As does *B*, Marie omits AS 1: §§87–88(pt. 1), LE 1: §42: "De victoria Regum Angliæ, & de nativitate Eadgari Regis" ("About the victory of the king of Anglia, and about the birth of King Edgar").

11. The *De secunda translatione*, which circulated as an independent *libellus*, was inserted between St. Audrey's *Life* (AS 1, LE 1) and *Miracles* (AS 3) in the exemplar of *B*.

12. LE 2: §118 (Quod rex Willelmus Godfridum ad Malmesberiam de Ely transtulerit illicque Simeonem pro eo instituit, qui contra morem et loci dignitatem et ipsius regis preceptum nescientibus ecclesie filiis benedictionem percepit ab episcopo Lincolniensi ["That King William transferred Godfrey from Ely to Malmesbury and established there in his place Simeon, who, against the custom and privilege of the place and against the command of the king himself, obtained the blessing of the bishop of Lincoln unbeknownst to the sons of the church"]) pertains to William I's appointment of Simeon and introduces a protracted history of his troubled abbacy that nevertheless contains several miracles (to 2: §139). While the *libellus* begins with a sentence in praise of William as a bringer of peace and prosperity to the church, it attributes Simeon's appointment to King Edgar (AS 2: §40), as does Marie (2659–60) and credits the abbot only with conceiving and undertaking the construction of the new church at Ely, which was unfinished at his death. Marie does not mention William I.

13. No textual division before 2663 in Add. 70513.

14. No textual division before 2683 in Add. 70513.

15. No textual division before 2735 in Add. 70513.

16. AS does not reprint material from the *Life* of St. Withburga, March, II, cols. 606–08.

17. No textual division before 2773 in Add. 70513.

18. After relating Abbot Richard's burial, in AS and *B*, the *De secunda translatione* ends with a poem in praise of St. Audrey not translated by Marie: "Etheldreda ducem rogat hic pia virgo jugalem" ("Here the blessed virgin Audrey begs her husband").

19. This miracle, which is also found in Book 1, appears as an appendix to the Prologue without its own rubric. AS does not reprint the matter from Book 1.

20. AS does not print here the text from Book 2 that constitutes ##2–3 (see 541A, n. b).

21. No textual division before 2889 in Add. 70513.

22. AS does not print in Book 2 (f. §33) six miracles (##6–11) that also occur almost verbatim in the *Miracula* (533Bn.). In Book 2 they appear in the same order as in LE: 11, 6–10 (LE 2: §§119, 129–133), where #11 is separated from the group of five by a series of charters and instances of the Conqueror's interventions in the affairs of the abbey. One other miracle, #40 (cf. LE 2: §51), is found in Book 2, where it is abbreviated, as well as in the *Miracula*.

23. Four chapters in LE correspond to one in the *Miracula*, which Marie's translation follows. One version represents a rearrangement of the other. The openings of AS §88 and LE 3: §52 are alike, but AS 3: §§88–89 continue with the text of LE 3: §47, without the rubric,

while AS §§90–92 correspond to LE 3: §51. AS 3: §93, which reproduces the conclusion of LE 3: §51 in its first lines, then takes up the remainder of LE 3: §52, which concludes in §97. AS §98 corresponds with LE 3: §53.

24. AS does not reproduce the material here, as it also occurs in the Life of St. Withburga, March, II, 606–08.

Rubrics*

[I. Vita sancte virginis et regine Etheldrede ("The Life of the Holy Virgin and Queen Audrey")]

1. Explicit proemium de situ Insule, incipit vita sancte virginis et regine Etheldrede ("Here ends the preface on the location of Ely and begins The Life of St. Audrey, Virgin and Queen") [AS: Est-anglorum Regum series ("The Succession of Kings of the East Anglians"), LE: Incipit textus sequentis libelli in vita sancte Ædeldrede virginis et de quibus carnis originem duxit et quomodo pater eius Anna Estanglorum suscepit re gnum ("Here begins the text of the following booklet on The Life of St. Audrey the Virgin and about those from whom she took the life of the flesh, and how her father, Anna, succeeded to the kingdom of the East Anglians")]

2. Quod pater et mater Sancte Etheldrede sanctam genuere sobolem ("That the father and mother of St. Audrey begat progeny")

3. Quod Sancta Etheldreda in infantia sancte vivere cepit ("That in infancy St. Audrey began to lead a holy life")

4. Quomodo Etheldreda primum data est viro qui parvo tempore vixit ("How Audrey was wed for the first time to a man who lived a short time")

5. Quod Beda exemplum posuit de Beata Etheldreda et sponso ejus Tomberto ("That Bede made an example of the Blessed Audrey and her husband, Tombert")

6. De transitu Felicis Episcopi et ubi sepultus jacuit ("About the death of Bishop Felix and where he lies buried")

7. De interitu Anne regis, et quod fratres sui post eum regnaverunt ("About King Anna's death, and that his brothers reigned after him")

8. Quomodo Etheldreda iterum datur viro, videlicet regi Northanimbrorum, et qui cum illa venerunt, et quam sancte vixit ("How Audrey was wed a second time to a man who was the king of the Northumbrians, and who came with her, and what a holy life she led")

9. Quomodo rex non potuit uti virginis connubio, et per Sanctum Wilfridum ejus animum sibi illicere tentabat; sed ipse monita castitatis regine pretendit ("How the king could not participate in a marriage with a virgin, and he attempted, through St. Wilfrid, to attract her carnal nature to himself; but this man gave advice concerning the queen's chastity")

10. Quomodo Regina Etheldreda, monitis beati presulis edocta, divortium a rege diu postulaverit; sed vix obtinens monasterium subiit, & velamen sanctitatis ab eo suscepit ("How Queen Audrey, instructed by the blessed bishop's advice, for a long time requested divorce from the king, but, obtaining very little, she went into a monastery and received from him the veil of sanctity")

11. Quod Rex Egfridus de monasterio eam eripere laboravit, sed Dei miseratione salvatur ("That King Egfrid worked to steal her away from the monastery, but she is saved by the mercy of God")

12. Insigne testimonium virginitatis ejusdem ("Attested proof of her virginity")

13. Quomodo Etheldreda tetendit ad Ely et quid in itinere ei contigit ("How Audrey went to Ely, and what happened to her on the way")

14. Quod ecclesia Col[l]udi, post illius discessum, igne consumpta est ("That the church at Coldingham was consumed in fire after her departure")

15. Quod Beata Etheldreda in Ely ad possessionem propriam rediit, cetum[que] utriusque sexus sub monachili habitu congregavit, quorum auxiliis illic fun[d]avit ecclesiam ("That the Blessed Audrey returned to Ely, to a possession in her own right, and she brought

*With emendations from LE.

together under monastic rule a community of both sexes with whose help she founded a church there")

16. Quomodo Sancta Etheldreda in Ely a Sancto Wilfredo facta est abbatissa ("How St. Audrey was made abbess of Ely by St. Wilfrid")

17. Quomodo virgo Domini Werburga, habitum religionis in Ely sub Etheldreda suscepit ("How the Lord's virgin Werburga took the habit of religion at Ely under Audrey")

18. De adventu Beate Sexburge in Ely ("About the Blessed Sexburga's arrival at Ely")

19. Quomodo Sancta Etheldreda prophetie spiritum habuit, et quod Wilfridus Roman perrexit; sed rediens, illam obi[i]sse cognovit ("How St. Audrey had the spirit of prophesy, and that Wilfrid traveled to Rome; but returning, he learned that she had died")

20. Quod infirmata palam cunctis penituit ("That the stricken woman suffered in the presence of all")

21. Qualiter majoribus aggravata doloribus, spiritum celo reddidit tertio die ("How, afflicted with greater pain, she rendered her spirit to Heaven on the third day")

22. De Sancto Huna Sacerdote ("About St. Huna the priest")

23. Quod quidam minister beate virginis, per Sacrificium salutare, non potuit vinculis teneri ("That one of the blessed virgin's servants, through the redeeming Mass, could not be bound in chains")

24. Quod virgo Domini Werburga, de Ely assumpta, quibusdam ecclesiis preficitur ("That the Lord's virgin Werburga, brought out of Ely, is appointed to several churches")

25. Post obitum Sancte Etheldrede, soror ejus Sexburga in Ely facta est abbatissa et, divinitus inspirata, levari ossa ejus de sepulcro [jussit] ("After Audrey's death, her sister Sexburga was made abbess, and, divinely inspired, she ordered her remains to be removed from the tomb")

26. Sexburga quosdam de fratribus misit, lapidem querere sepulcralem ("Sexburga sent certain of the brothers to search for stone for a sepulcher")

27. Quod corpus sacratissime virginis Etheldrede incorruptum invenit, et (quod mirabile!) fuit vulnus in carne ejus mortua curatum ("That she found the body of the most holy virgin Audrey to be perfectly preserved, and—how wondrous!—the wound in her dead flesh had been healed")

28. Quod divinitus lapis sepulcralis virginee glebe coaptatur, etsi posito operculo compago non apparet ("That by divine intervention the sepulchral stone for the virginal remains fits perfectly together, and, once the cover is laid down, the join does not show")

29. Quod de vestimentis virginis Etheldrede beneficia prestantur ("That benefits are afforded by the clothing of the virgin Audrey")

30. De locello, in quo sepulta fuit, miracula narrantur ("Miracles are recounted concerning the coffin in which she was entombed")

31. Quod fons oritur i[n] loco sepulture ejus ("That a fountain springs forth where her tomb is")

32. Oratio au[c]toris ad dominam suam beatissimam Etheldredam ("The author's prayer to his lady, the most Blessed Audrey") [Marie substitutes for this prayer a prayer of her own (2335–46) in which "cil qui fist l'escrit" prays God for the strength to finish his task of recounting miracles so that he might earn the thanks of the Blessed Trinity.]

33. De obitu Beate Sexburge abbatisse ("About the death of the blessed abbess Sexburga")

34. Quod Ermenilda postea facta est abbatissa, et Werburgæ filie sue ecclesiam de Scapeia commendavit ("That Ermenilda was afterwards made abbess, and she commended the church at Sheppey to her daughter Werburga")

35. Quod virgo Domini Werburga, post obitum matris sue Ermenilde, monasterium Elge regendum suscepit, et [i]bi sepulturam elegit ("That the Lord's virgin Werburga, after the death of her mother Ermenilda, began governing the monastery of Ely, and she chose to be buried there")

36. Quod apud Ely cultus divini operis sub regimine sanctarum floruit feminarum, donec igne et [flamma] vastabatur a Danis ("That at Ely the cultivation of religion thrived under the rule of the holy women until it was laid waste in fire and flames by the Danes")

37. In quorum temporibus Dani devastaverint Angliam, et de illorum interitu ("In whose times the Danes plundered Anglia, and about their downfall")

38. Quod Dani ad Ely applicantes monasterium combusserunt, et quoscumque invenerunt, neci tradiderunt ("That the Danes, reaching Ely, burned the monastery; and they put to death whomever they came upon")

39. Quod paganus foramen fecerit in sepulcro virginis, sed mox ultione divina percussus est ("That a pagan made a hole in the virgin's sepulcher, but he was immediately struck down by divine vengeance")

40. Exhortatur sacerdos archipresbyt[er]um suum, narratis ei que sequuntur miraculis, cupiens eum amovere de sua temeritate ("A priest exhorts his archpriest after telling him the miracles that follow, wishing to dissuade him from his foolhardiness")

41. De quadam matrona ("About a certain matron")

42. De juvene muto ("About a young mute")

43. De puella ceca ("About a blind girl")

44. De quodam juvene ("About a certain young man")

45. De ancilla Sacerdotis ("About a priest's serving girl")

46. Quod judicum Dei in predicto archipresbytero et consortibus [suis eluxit] ("That God's judgment shone forth in the aforementioned archpriest and his companions")

47. Quomodo Rex Ædgarus regnaverit ("How King Edgar reigned")

Explicit liber primus de historia elyensis insule in vitam beatissi[m]am virginis Etheldrede et quomodo fabricavit illic ecclesiam sive et quibus destructa fuerit ("Here ends the first book of the *History of the Island of Ely* on the most blessed *Life of the Virgin Audrey* and how she built a church there and by whom it was destroyed")

[II. *De secunda translatione Etheldrede virginis (On the Second Translation of the Virgin Audrey)*]

1. De secunda translatione Etheldrede virginis que facta est a Richardo Abbate cum ceteris virginibus ("On the second translation of the virgin Audrey, which was done by Abbot Richard, along with certain other virgins")

2. Quomodo Abbas [Richardus] in suis votis De[i] auxilio sit adjutus ("How Abbot Richard was justified in his undertakings with God's help")

3. Quomodo abbas sanctas inven[er]it, et qualiter eas reliquerit ("How the Abbot discovered the saints and how he disposed of them")

4. Quod ante translationis hujus solemnitatem, propter opus dilatandum, Beatissime sepulcrum Sexburge atque Ermenilde, de loco pristino, ubi eas collocaverat Beatus Ethelwoldus, removit: similiter alme Withburge tumbam dimov[it] dimovens, [quam] casu ministri imprudentes fregerunt ("That before the solemnities of this translation, because the construction project was expanding, he moved the tomb of the most Blessed Sexburga and Ermenilda from the original place where the Blessed Ethelwold had lain them to rest; similarly, he removed St. Withburga's tomb, which careless workmen had accidentally broken to pieces")

5. Quomodo abbas novum mausoleum paravit sed minus aut plus quantitate forme corpus Wythburge ("How the abbot had a new tomb made, but Withburga's body was at times larger and smaller than the structure's space")

6. Quo tempore translate sunt beate virgines, et de obitu Richardi Abbatis ("When the blessed virgins were translated, and about Abbot Richard's death")

[III. *Miracula Sancte Etheldrede (Miracles of St. Audrey)*]

0a. Prologus i[n] Miraculos [sic] Sancte Etheldrede ("Prologue to the *Miracles of St. Audrey*")

1. De Azone nostro monacho ab estu febrium liberato ("About our monk Azo cured of burning fevers") Incipit *Liber miraculorum* sponse Christi sanctissime virginis Etheldrede ("Here begins the *Book of Miracles* of the bride of Christ, the most holy virgin Audrey"

2. Quomodo Rex Ædgarus, divinitus inspiratus, per sanctum pontificem Æthelwoldum, Elyensem restauravit ecclesiam ("How King Edgar, divinely inspired, with the aid of the holy bishop Æthelwold, restored the church at Ely")

3. Priviligium Ædgari Regis gloriosi ("The privilege of glorious King Edgar")

4. Quam districte Deus vindicaverit injurias dilecte sue virginis Etheldrede ("How severely God avenged wrongs against his beloved virgin Audrey")

5. Iterum quomodo Deus vindictam fecerit de hostibus beate virginis Etheldrede ("Again, how God wreaked vengeance against enemies of the blessed virgin Audrey")

6. De quodam fratre, qui mente excesserat, sed meritis sancte Etheldrede sanato ("About a brother who had gone out of his mind, but was healed by St. Audrey")

7. De duobus mutis ("About two mutes")

8. De Picoto Vice-comite, qui multa incommoda huic gessit ecclesie ("About Sheriff Picot, who inflicted much harm on this church")

9. De Gervasio, qui homines sancte Etheldrede valde infestabat et cruciabat ("About Gervais, who greatly mistreated and tormented St. Audrey's men")

10. Quomodo Dominus Deus, precibus sancte virginis Etheldrede placatus, indignationem suam et iram de hoc loco averterit ("How the Lord God, mollified by the holy virgin Etheldredea's prayers, turned his wrath and indignation from this place")

11. Quomodo post mortem Comes Willielmus Warennie sit damnatus in anima ("How after his death Count William of Warenne was damned in his soul")

12. Quod turris ad portam ecclesiæ sancte Etheldrede ab igne fulguris erepta est ("That the tower at the door of St. Audrey's church was saved from a fire caused by lightning")

13. De captiv[o] per beatam Etheldredam soluto ("About a prisoner set free by the Blessed Audrey")

14. Quomodo quidam a dolore dentium curatur ("How a man is cured of a tooth ache")

15. De Magistro Radulpho ab inflammatione gutteris sanato ("About Master Ranulph healed from an inflammation of the throat")

16. Quod quidam, membris omnibus destitutus, pristine redditur sanati ("That a man, debilitated in all parts of his body, is restored to perfect health")

17. Quod apparens sancta Etheldreda infirmanti sanitem promisit ("That St. Audrey, appearing to a sick man, promised him health")

18. Quod sancta Etheldreda a muliere visa est in quadam ecclesia ("That St. Audrey was seen by a woman in a church")

19. Quomodo captivus per sanctam Etheldredam liberatus evasit ("How a prisoner came out a free man thanks to St. Audrey")

20. Que damna extranei loco intulerint ("What losses were incurred in a strange place")

21. De puella, dextro oculo cecata, ad sanctam Etheldredam illuminata ("About a girl, blinded in her right eye, restored to sight by St. Audrey")

22. Quod mulier, invocata sancta Etheldreda, curatur ("That a woman is cured after calling on St. Audrey")

23. Quod quidam languens ad vitam rediit ("That a gravely ill man came back to life")

24. De ydropica curata ("About a woman cured of dropsy")

25. Quomodo nefandorum proditio per sanctam Etheldredam in stuporem omnium detegitur ("How treason by evil doers, to the amazement of all, was brought to light by St. Audrey")

26. De muliere cecata et illuminata ("About a woman blinded and restored to sight")

27. De [quodam] qui [festum] sancte Edeldrede servare noluit ("About a man who refused to observe the feast of St. Audrey")] [The rubric in *B* and *AS* is about a priest who refused to observe the saint's feast. Perhaps a rubricator confused this miracle with another, "De presbitero qui festa sanctarum nostrarum pronunciare noluit" ("About a priest who refused to proclaim the feasts of our saints"), which is found in *LE* (3: §121), but not in *B* and *AS*.]

28. De puero infirmo et sanato ("About a sick boy who was healed")

29. De quodam fratre a morte ere[p]to ("About a certain brother saved from death")

30. De quodam puero monacho per sanctam Etheldredam sanato ("About a certain boy monk healed by St. Audrey")

31. De demoniaco per sanctam Etheldredam liberato ("About a man freed from possession by devils by St. Audrey")

32. Quam severa ostensa est visio de hostibus ecclesie sancte Etheldrede ("How dreadful to behold is the sight of enemies of St. Audrey's church")

33. Quomodo Deus disperdidit hostes sancte sue virginis Etheldrede ("How God brought to ruin the enemies of His holy virgin Audrey")

34. De hom[i]ne erecto ("About a man made to stand upright")

35. Quam benigne virgo Etheldreda, cuidam se diligenti, per visionem apparere dignata est ("How graciously the virgin Audrey deigned to appear in a vision to someone who loved her")

36. De agricolario sancte Etheldrede per visionem ostenso ("About a husbandman of St. Audrey shown in a vision")

37. De quodam ad fontem sancte Etheldrede sanato ("About a man healed at St. Audrey's fountain")

38. Quod mulier ceca ad fontem sancte Etheldrede illuminata est ("That a blind woman was restored to sight at St. Audrey's fountain")

39. Quod virgo quedam, in fontem sancte Etheldrede lapsa, nihil mali passa est ("That a young girl, after falling into St. Audrey's fountain, suffered no harm")

40. Quomodo crux sancta loquelas edidit in protectione monachorum ("How a holy cross spoke words to protect the monks")

41. Quomodo corpus beate Witburge virginis allatum est in Ely ("How the body of Blessed Withburga the virgin was brought to Ely")

42. De hoste juste punito ("About an enemy justly punished")

43. Miraculum de cruce ("The miracle of the cross")

44. Quod per beatam Etheldredam multi sanantur a febre ("That many are cured from fever by Blessed Audrey")

45. [Quod revelatione per paludem fit via ad sanctam Etheldredam ("That because of a revelation a causeway was built through the fens for St. Audrey")] [B and AS have a rubric that does not apply: "Quod quidam exanimis vite reformatur" ("That a dead man is restored to life").]

46. De paralytica curata ("About a paralized woman who was cured")

47. Quod elingui redditur loquela ("That speech is restored to a mute")

48. De ceca illuminata a sancta Etheldreda ("About a blind girl restored to sight by St. Audrey")

49. Qualiter manus arida reformatur ("How a withered hand is restored")

50. Quod inimicus eclesie divina ultione punitur ("That an enemy of the church is punished through divine vengeance")

51. De manu muliercule sanata ("About a girl's hand that is healed")

52. Quod quidam dolosus per sanctam Etheldredam est devictus ("That a certain deceitful man was brought down by St. Audrey")

53. Miraculum beate Etheldrede valde jucundum, quod in vita ejus contigisse legitur ("A very delightful miracle of the Blessed Audrey which occurred, as we read in her life")

0c. Epilogue *Audree* 4611–25

Annotated Index
of Proper Names

Old French names and variants are given first, and the modern English equivalent follows in italics, if different. If the name begins with a different letter in modern English, the name is cross-referenced, with the English equivalent always in italics. Line numbers refer to the Old French text and may sometimes differ slightly in the English translation. Names in bold print within an entry are also identified within this index. References are to line numbers.

Abiron, Abiram. 3021. An Old Testament figure who led a revolt against Moses and Aaron (Numbers 16) at the end of the Israelites' wilderness wanderings. As punishment he was swallowed up by the earth.

Aceo, Acca. 2824. A monk of Ely to whom Saint Audrey appeared. Possibly **Wilfrid's** successor at Hexam to whom **Bede** dedicated several of his biblical works.

Achiron, Acheron. 3022. One of the five rivers of Hades. The name means "river of woe."

Adam. 3977. A constable.

Adam. 4229. A cruel knight.

Adammis. 1553, 1558, 1574. A good monk at Coldingham.

Ailliez, Aelgetus. 4064. A holy man buried at Gretton. Former bailiff of Saint Audrey's lands.

Ailrez, Ailred. 2996, 3001. A mute only partially cured by Saint Audrey because of his insufficient faith.

Aldulf. 153, 169, 183, 185, 1669, 2007. King of East Anglia 664–713. Identified in the *Vie Seinte Audree* and in the *Liber Eliensis* as Audrey's brother, he was in fact the son of Hereswith who was Audrey's aunt, not her mother. Thus Aldulf was Audrey's first cousin, son of her father Anna's brother **Egric** and his wife Saint **Hereswith.**

Alfedene *see* **Halfdene**

Alfelin. 2617. One of several priests who pulled at Saint Audrey's clothing through a hole in her sarcophagus.

Alisandre, Alexander. 3979. A man who wronged Saint Audrey and against whom she took vengeance.

Alfled, Elfleda, Saint. 674. Daughter of King **Oswy.** Sister of King **Egfrid.** Friend of **Cuthbert** and **Wilfrid.** She and her mother Enfleda joined Saint **Hilda's** monastery in Whitby where they became abbesses in turn.

Alvriz, Edfrid. 191. Son of **Edwin.** Grandfather of **Hilda** and **Hereswith.**

Alwine, Aelfwine. 2698. Abbot of **Ramsey** 1043–80.

Alwines, Alfwin. 2069. Brother of **Egfrid.**

Andreu, *Andrew*, Saint. 885. An Apostle of Jesus and patron saint of Scotland, for whom Saint Audrey founded a church at **Augustaldeus** (Hexham).

Angles *see* **Engleis**

Anne, *Anna*. 128, 137, 179, 227, 471, 498, 501, 552, 557, 563, 566, 573, 578, 581, 599, 613, 634, 704, 708, 729, 800, 3365. King of East Anglia 635–54. Father of Saint Audrey and nephew of King **Redwald**. Killed in battle by King **Penda**.

Anseum, *Anselm*, Saint. 2693. Archbishop of Canterbury 1093–1109.

Armesworde, *Armsworth*. 2184. Castle End (also known as Castle Hill) near the ancient walls of Cambridge.

Arondel, *Arundel*. 3329. A town in west Sussex.

Audree, *Audrey*, *Etheldreda*, *Aethelthryth*. 17, 29, 60, 129, etc. *passim*. The saint of whom Marie is writing the *Life*. Patron Saint of Ely, Cambridgeshire, UK.

Augustaldeus. 886. An early name for Hexham in **Northumbria**, where Saint Audrey founded a church at which her friend and counselor, **Wilfrid**, became bishop in 705.

Aüstin, *Augustine* [of Canterbury] Saint. 45. Died c. 604. First archbishop of Canterbury. A Roman Benedictine monk sent by Pope Gregory to evangelize the Anglo-Saxons.

Aüstin. 3961, 3966. Monk of **Ely**.

Averille, *Haverhill*. 4317. A town near Cambridge that dates back to pre–Roman times.

Aÿdan, *Aiden*, Saint. 626. An Irish monk, first bishop and abbot of Lindisfarne (died 626). He was praised by **Bede** for his care of the sick, his love of peace, prayer and study. He lived in poverty and encouraged prayer and meditation among the laity.

Babiloine, *Babylon*. 3163. An ancient city of Mesopotamia ruled by King **Nebuchadnezzar**, the ruins of which are located in modern Iraq. Revelation 18 foretells the destruction by fire of **Babylon**, which there epitomizes man's rebellion against God's sovereignty. This prophecy parallels that of the destruction of Babylon by God in Isaiah 13.

Baseng, *Bagsecq*. 2419. Danish commander, invader of Anglo-Saxon England.

Bede, Saint. 44, 170, 182, 234, 360, 397, 588, 701, 856, 1019, 1421, 1448, 1655, 1704, 1708, 1731, 1904, 1421, 1448, 1655, 1704, 1708, 1731, 1904, 2011, 2061, 2296, 2382, 2900. Lived from about 673 to 735. English historian, Benedictine monk. Also known as "Venerable Bede." Author of *Ecclesiastical History of the English Nation*, one of the principal works on which this life of Audrey/Etheldreda is based.

Bedrichesworde, *Beodricesworth*. 93, 606. Early name of **Bury Saint Edmunds**, a city in Suffolk. Pilgrimage site renowned for its relics, notably those of Saints Edmund and **Jurmin**. *See also* **Saint Edmund**.

Beneït, *Benedict*, Saint. 3187. 3193, 3255, 3428. Lived c. 480–550. Patriarch of western monasticism and author of the *Regula* that came to be recognized as the fundamental monastic code of western Europe in the High Middle Ages.

Berningham, *Barningham*. 3296, 3315. A town in Suffolk.

Bliyeborc, *Blythburgh*. 588. A town in Suffolk where King **Anna** is said to have been buried.

Borc, *Peterborough*. 1775. See **Medeshamstede**.

Borewelle, *Burwell*. 3563. A village in Cambridgeshire.

Botolf, *Botulf*, Saint. 3453. Died in 680. Abbot of Icanho (most likely Iken in Suffolk). An early proponent of Benedictine monasticism in England. His bones were moved to **Thorney**, and his head was given to **Ely**.

Bradeford, *Bradford*. 2472, 4395. Bradford Farm, near **Ely**.

Brandone, *Brandon*. 2936, 2942, 4203. A town in Suffolk.

Bretaine, *Britain*. 42, 205, 50, 2418. The term refers to what is today England.

Briges, *Brie*. 213, 215. A region east of Paris which includes the departments of Marne and Seine-et-Marne. Site of a double monastery at the time of Saint **Audrey**.

Brithmar. 3800, 3810. A monk of **Ely**.

Brithmar de Averille. 4317. A man from Haverhill cured by Saint **Audrey**.

Brustan. 3172, 3255, 3428. A man from **Chatteris** rescued from prison by Saint **Audrey** and Saint **Benedict**.

Burgh Castle see **Cnaresburc**

Bury Saint Edmunds (Saint Edmundsbury) see **Bedrichesworde** and **Saint Edmund**

Calke, Chelles. 213. Located on the eastern perimeter of Paris today, near the Seine River, the monastery was founded by Bathild, an Anglo-Saxon slave who became queen-consort to Clovis II. She herself retired as a nun there in 665 and spent the last part of her life as abbess there (d. 680).

Canterbire, Canterbury. 2691. A cathedral city in **Kent**, spiritual center of the Church of England. The first Archbishop of Canterbury was Saint **Augustine of Canterbury**, who reached the coast of Kent as a missionary sent by Pope **Gregory the Great** in 597. King **Ethelbert** gave him the church at **Canterbury**.

Cantebrige, Cambridgeshire. 2909, 3006. Inland eastern county of England where both **Ely** and Cambridge are located.

Cenwald see **Kenewal**

Cestre, Chester. 2402. A city in Cheshire to which the body of Saint **Werburga** was translated from **Hanbury**.

Chad see **Chede**

Chailons, Chelles. 617. See entry for **Calke**.

Chanaan, Canaan. 2690. Lands that belonged to the descendents of Canaan, the grandson of Noah and son of Ham. They extended through areas that are today part of Lebanon, the Gaza, and the land west of the Jordan River and the Dead Sea, including Jerusalem (see Genesis 10.15–19). This was the land promised by God to the Israelites, the goal of their wilderness wanderings.

Chatriz, Chateriz, Chatteris. 317, 3171. A town in **Cambridgeshire**.

Chede, Chedde, Ceddes, Chad, Saint. 722, 909, 917. Died 672. Bishop of the See of **Northumbria**, then Bishop of **Mercia**. Educated at Lindesfarne by Saint **Aiden** and in Ireland.

Chelles see **Calke**

Ciringcestre, Cirencester. 3473. A town in Gloucestershire.

Clement, Saint. 2290. Died c. 100. Pope and martyr. Fourth bishop of **Rome**.

Cnaresburc, Burgh Castle. 133. A town in Norfolk. Site of a third-century Roman fortress. Said to be the site of Saint **Fursey**'s monastery.

Colecestre, Colchester. 2579. Britain's first Roman city. It was called *Camulodunum*, a Romanisation of its Iron-Age name *Camulos*. Located in Essex.

Coludy, Coludi, Coldingham. 835, 1187, 1194, 1546, 1710. Northumbrian monastery. Saint **Ebba** was abbess there at the time **Audrey** joined the order.

Conigtone, Conington. 4445. A parish in **Cambridgeshire**.

Coteham, Cottenham. 3737. A parish in **Cambridgeshire**.

Coventré, Coventry. 3411. A town in Warwickshire, located in the eastern reaches of the forest of Arden, that grew around a nunnery founded about 700 by Saint Osburga.

Cunit, Cnute. 493. Danish king who ruled **East Anglia** 1016–1035.

Cuthbert, Saint. 1093, 1095. Anglo-Saxon monk and hermit who became bishop of Lindisfarne and patron of **Durham**. Born about 635 and died in 687. Popular saint in northern England. His shrine and relics are in Durham.

Cuthblac, Guthlac, Saint. 737. Lived c. 673–714. Monk at Repton, then hermit in the Fens. A near-contemporary Latin life of Saint Guthlac was written by Saint **Felix**; others were written in Old English prose and verse.

Cynegils see **Kenegis**

Dalehan. Dalham. 2867. A village in Suffolk.

Daniel. 2258. Biblical prophet of the Old Testament, taken as a slave to Babylon. Interpreter of the dreams of **Nabuchadnezzar.**

Danois, Denois, Danes. 399, 2525, 2527, 2652, 2844, 2854. The Danes, also called Vikings and Norsemen, invaded England in several waves from the ninth to the eleventh centuries, pillaging, looting, and burning towns. They were temporarily repelled in the ninth century by Alfred the Great.

Edmund, Osmon, Saint. 3887, 4343. (841–869) King of **East Anglia.** Tortured and beheaded by invading Danes in 870. A *Life* by Abbo of Fleury was written at Ramsey c. 986.

Edrez, Edred. 2446, 2631. King of all England, 946–955.

Edwine, Edwin [*of Deira*], Saint. 71, 73, 177, 192. First Christian king of **Northumbria,** killed in battle in 633 by Cadwallon of Wales and **Penda** of **Mercia.**

Edwines, Edwy. 2631, 2634. King of all England 955–959. Son of Edmund I and brother of **Edgar.**

Edwines, Edwin. 2959. A monk possessed by the devil but delivered by Saint **Audrey.**

Egeriz, Egeris, Egric. 95, 103, 118, 633. King of **East Anglia** 634–635.

Egfrid, Egelfriz. 654, 779, 808, 843, 846, 849, 853, 858, 861, 871, 873, 967, 989, 1011, 1027, 1155, 1273, 1345,1352, 1379, 1412, 1501, 1899, 2063, 2070, 2120. King of **Northumbria** 670–685. Son of King **Oswy.** Second husband of Saint **Audrey.**

Egipte, Egypt. 418, 424.

Eldeline. 4474. A woman born in Stonea helped by Saint **Audrey.**

Elfleda *see* Alfled

Elfrid, Ethelfrid. 643, 842, 845, 847. Son of **Oswy** and brother of **Egfrid, Audrey's** second husband.

Elfriz, Ethelfrid. 813, 814. King of Bernicia 593–616. Father of Saint **Oswald.**

Elge. 1617, 1891. Name that means the "Land of God." Early name of **Ely.**

Elger. 2140. A man (monk?) in the service of Saint **Audrey.**

Elriz, Ethelric. 813. King of Bernicia (northern division of **Northumbria**) 568–72. Father of **Ethelfrid (Elfriz).**

Eltham. 1512. West Halton, a town in Lincolnshire.

Ely. 306, 310, 315, 483, etc. passim. Site of **Audrey's** monastery in her dower land, an island in the marshland. Site of the present cathedral in the city of Ely in Cambridgeshire.

Emborc, Hamborc, Hanbury. 2152, 2400, 2406. A small village overlooking the vale of Dove in Staffordshire. In 680, Saint **Werburga** became abbess of a nunnery founded there by her brother **Ethelred,** King of Mercia.

Emenborc, Ermenburga, Saint. 1806. Wife of King **Merewald.** Her brothers, Ethelred and Ethelbricht, were murdered by **Egfrid's** counselor. In recompense she asked Egfrid for land in **Kent** where she founded a nunnery on the isle of Thanet. She became the first abbess there.

Engleis, Angles. 41, 46, 48, 54, 58, 504, 823, 1630, 2632. One of the two Germanic tribes who settled in England in the late fifth century and formed the foundation for the kingdoms of **East Anglia, Mercia,** and **Northumbria.** *Engleis* also means "English."

Engleterre, England. 572, 986, 1623, 2679, 4178. England takes its name from the **Angles,** one of the Germanic tribes from Angeln that invaded and occupied England beginning in the fifth century, forming the basis of the English language and culture.

Erchenberc, Herchenbert, Herconbert, Erconbert. 180, 199, 693. King of **Kent** 640–664. Husband of **Audrey's** sister **Seaxburga.**

Erkenwald. Eorpwald. 70. Son of **Redwald.** King of **East Anglia** 618–628.

Ermenborc, Ermenburga. 1382. King **Egfrid's** second wife.

Ermenild, Hermenild, Ermenilda. 694, 1639,1782, 1807, 1850, 2377, 2387, 2405, 2736, 2852. Mother of **Saint Ermenburga** and daugher of King **Erconbert.**

Escoz, Scots. 1552.

Estaungle, East Anglia. 57. The region of England from which Saint Audrey comes, located in the middle part of England on the east coast, one of the seven Anglo-Saxon kingdoms.

Estengleis, East Angles. 611, 1629, 1802. Residents of **East Anglia.**

Estefne, Stephen. 4159. King of England 1135–54.

Esteuene, Stephen, Saint. 2728. The first Christian martyr. Allegedly studied with **Gamaliel.** Stoned to death in Jerusalem.

Estiefne d'Eschaliers, Stephen of Eschaliers. 4415, 4471, 4513, 4427. Man who rented land from the church of **Ely.**

Estone, Stonea. 4473. A town in Cambridgeshire.

Estreis, East Anglian Saxons. 53, 56, 712. People of Saxon descent in **East Anglia.**

Ethelwald see **Oderwold**

Eucaliste, Eucalist. 419, 425. An Egyptian shepherd.

Evrewich, Everewic, York. 781, 1372. An early name for York, the county seat of Yorkshire. Ecclesiastical center of northern England. Paulinus, the Roman missionary credited with the conversion of King **Edwin** of **Northumbria,** was the first bishop of York.

Exninge, Exning. 231, 4345. **Audrey's** birthplace and place of baptism by Saint **Felix.** A town in west Suffolk.

Felix, Saint. 81, 86, 472, 485, 494, 565. (Died 647) A Burgundian by birth, he was sent by Honorius, Archbishop of **Canterbury,** to evangelize the **East Angles** when **Edwin** returned from exile to assume rule of **East Anglia.**

Fresus. 2104, 2109, 2118. A man in London who puchased **Yma** as a slave. See note to line 2104.

Fursey see **Phursëus**

Gamaliel. 1866. A Pharisee and celebrated doctor of Jewish law in the time of Saint **Paul.** He advised his fellow members of the Sanhedrin council not to put the apostles to death (Acts 5.34–39); in Paul's defense before the people of Jerusalem, he identifies **Gamaliel** as his mentor at whose feet he sat to learn the Judaic law (Acts 22:3).

Garnier. 2764. Abbot of **Westminster.**

Geforei, Geoffrey. 2702. A treasurer.

Gefroi, Geoffrey. 3564. A man from **Burwell.**

Geldeford, Guildford. 3458. A town in Surrey.

Germaine, Germany. 49. Homeland of the invading Germanic tribes, the Saxons, **Angles,** and **Jutes,** who invaded England in the fifth and sixth centuries.

Gerveis, Gervase. 3045, 3051. A wicked man punished by Saint **Audrey** with death.

Glastingebire, Glastonbury. 3638. A popular site for pilgrimages and, according to legend, the first place of Christian settlement in Britain. The abbey at Glastonbury was a center of learning, where Saint Dunstan was educated. Alleged to be the burial place of Joseph of Arimathea and King Arthur.

Gocelin. 3123. A monk from **Ely.**

Godlondeis, Jutes. 48, 51. Germanic tribe from what is known at Jutland (mainland Denmark and northern Germany) that settled in **Kent,** Hampshire, and the Isle of Wight after the end of the Roman era in the British Isles.

Godriz, Godric. 2964, 3077, 3111. A good monk from **Winchester** who was placed in **Ely.**

Goldeborch, Goldeburch. 1332, 1334. Saint Abbs Head, not far from the **Coldingham** monastery. Sneesby describes it as "a spur of rock linked only to the mainland by a narrow neck of sand, presumably sea-covered at high tide" (81).

Gonter, Gunter. 2700. Abbot of **Thorney.**

Grancestre, Grantchester. 2183. An early name for Cambridge.

Gregoire, Gregory, Saint. 821. Lived ca. 540–604. Known as Gregory the Great. Pope who took the initiative in conversion of the Anglo-Saxons, sending **Augustine** and his monks on a mission to England. His writings enjoyed great popularity, especially his *Pastoral Care* and *Dialogues* (lives of the saints).

Grettone, Gretton. 4051, 4059. A village in Northamptonshire.

Guilliames, William. 3150. Count of Warenne.

Guion, Guyon. 2701. Abbot of **Pershore.**

Guthlac see **Cuthblac**

Halfdene. Alfdene, Halfdan. 2415, 3412, 3437, 3443. Son of the infamous Norse pirate Rognar Lothbrok. Brother of Ingwar. Norse king of York 902–910.

Hanbury see **Emborc**

Hantone, Southampton. 3999. A port city in south-central England on an inlet of the English Channel opposite the Isle of Wight. The Anglo-Saxons called it *Hamtune* or *Suth-Hamtune.*

Milburch, *Milburga*, Saint. 1815. Daughter of King **Merewald** of **Mercia** and his wife **Ermenburga.** Second abbess of the nunnery of Wenlock founded by her father. Known for her healing powers before and after her death.

Mildree, *Mildgyth*, Saint. 1816. Youngest of the three daughters of King **Merewald** and his wife **Ermenburga.** Successor of her sister **Mildred** as abbess at Thanet.

Mildrez, *Mildred*, Saint. 1816. Daughter of King **Merewald** and his wife **Ermenburga.** Educated at **Chelles,** but returned to England to the monastery at Minster-in-Thanet where her mother was first abbess. Known for her generosity to widows and children.

Nabugodonosor, Nabuchadnezzar. 3025. King of **Babylon** whose forces were responsible for the fall of Jerusalem and the destruction of the First Temple of the Israelites in 587 B.C. He took Israelite slaves back to Babylon, among them the prophet **Daniel.** See note for line 3026.

N[e]el, *Nigel*. 3735, 4016, 4017, 4257. Became bishop of **Ely** in 1133. He fell into disfavor with King **Stephen.** He was eventually arrested by the king in 1143 and charged with treason.

Neron, *Nero*. 1483. Emperor of Rome 54–68. During the persecution of the Christians at this time, the apostles Peter and **Paul** were martyred.

Nicholas. 4459. A priest.

Nichole, Lincoln. 2703, 2704. A city in Lincolnshire that was the former capital of Roman Britain.

Nichole *Nicholas*. 3583. A porter.

Norantone, Norhantone, *Northampton*. 4075, 4233. A city in central England (Northamptonshire) located on the Nene River. Northampton has been an important city from Anglo-Saxon times.

Norhomborlond, *Northumbria*. 178. One of the kingdoms of Anglo-Saxon Britain. Located in the northern part of England, north of the Humber River, Northumbria was formed in the seventh century by the union of Bernicia and Deira, Angle kingdoms that had been established about 500 A.D. Much of Northumbria fell to the ninth-century Danish invasions and was annexed in 954 to Wessex.

Norhombreis, *Northumbrians*. 74, 637. People from **Northumbria.**

Normandie, *Normandy*. 2533. An area of France that had been Frankish and Saxon Neustria. After a century of Viking invasions, in 911 Charles the Simple, in the Treaty of Saint-Clair-sur-Epte, gave up the territory to the charge of the Viking Rollo, who in turn accepted Christianity.

Normanz, *Norman*. 3007. The people of Normandy.

Norwiz, *Norwich*. 2697. City in Norfolk.

Oderwold, *Ethelwald*. 659. Nephew of King **Oswy,** king of Deira, 651–655.

Ording. 4056, 4068. Abbot of Bury Saint Edmunds 1148–1156.

Ostrythe see **Hostride**

Oswald, Owald, Oswold, *Oswald*. Saint. 635, 637, 659, 831, 1186. King of **Northumbria** 634–42. Son of **Ethelfrid** and brother of **Oswy.** Fled to Scotland when **Edwin** regained the kingship. Became a Christian at Iona. Killed in battle by King **Penda** who ordered the sacrificial mutilation of his body to the god Woden.

Oswald, **Saint.** 4146. See **Wolstan.**

Oswen. Sewen, *Sewenna*. 1330, 1504. Lady in the retinue of Audrey who, along with **Sewara,** accompanied her on her journey from **Coldingham** to **Ely.**

Oswy. 639, 643, 649, 653, 660, 671, 676, 689, 810, 812, 830, 839, 907, 1186. King of **Northumbria** 642–70. Father of **Egfrid** and brother of Saints **Oswald** (1) and **Ebba.** Killed King **Penda** in battle 655.

Oswy, *Ovin*. 2139. A monk whom Saint **Audrey** had helped.

Owine, Oswy, Ewine, *Ovin*. 891, 907, 1191, 1195. **Audrey'**s faithful steward and governor of the isle of **Ely.**

Pasche, Paske, *Easter*. 1741, 4429. The Christian holiday that celebrates the Resurrection of **Jesus Christ.**

Peada. 1797. Believed to be a son of King **Penda** of **Mercia**. King of Middle Anglia (655–56) during the period of Northumbrian rule of Mercia, his subkingdom likely included **Northampton**, Rutland, **Huntingdon**, and parts of Bedfordshire, Cambridgeshire, Leicestershire, and Lincolnshire.

Penda. 100, 539, 543, 582, 595, 620, 640, 648, 662, 667, 687, 832, 1647, 1765. Pagan King of **Mercia** 632–54. Invaded **East Anglia** and killed **Audrey's** father, King **Anna**, in battle 654. All his children became Christians.

Penthecoste, Pentecost. 1742. The word *Pentecost* means "fiftieth day," for it occurs in the Christian calendar on the fiftieth day after (and beginning with) **Easter** Sunday. It celebrates the apostles' empowerment by the Holy Spirit to proclaim the Gospel throughout the world.

Persore, Pershore. 2701. Town in Worcestershire, site of an abbey founded by Saint **Oswald** in 689.

Peterborough see **Medeshamstede**

Phursëus, Fursey, Saint. 134. An Irish monk who came as a pilgrim to **East Anglia**. On the death of **Sigebert** in the battle against **Penda**, Fursey left for **France** where he died in 650.

Picot. 3007, 3028. A sheriff of **Canterbury**.

Piere, Peter. 3154. Saint Peter's tower in the Church of **Ely**.

Pol, Paul, Saint. 1865, 3982. A well-educated Pharisee, persecutor of the first Christians, who, after a mystic conversion, became the first great Christian missionary to the Gentiles. Author of a number of epistles that form a major portion of the New Testament. Considered an Apostle by the Church.

Rameseie, Rameseye, Ramsey. 313, 495, 2769. Monastery in Huntingdonshire. See **Wolstan**.

Ranulf. 3479. A baron of Wallingford.

Ranulf. 3650, 3655, 3662, 3706, 3714, 3721. A monk at Glastonbury.

Raol, Raoul. 3226. Saint **Audrey's** chaplain.

Raol Bassett, Raoul Bassett. 3180. A judge at Huntingdon.

Raol le Borgondois, Raoul the Burgundian. 3713, 3727. A servant from **Ely** who received **Audrey's** help.

Raos de Dunwich, Ross of Dunwich. 3263. A man cured by Saint **Audrey** of an illness that caused swelling, blindness, and loss of memory.

Rechard, Richard. 3904. A young man from **Ely** cured by Saint **Audrey** of madness.

Redeam, Reedham. 487. A town in Norfolk on the north side of the River Yare. The name is derived from the large quantity of reeds growing in the marshes. It was one of the seats of the Saxon Kings of **East Anglia**.

Redwald. 63, 69. Son of **Tyttla**. King of **East Anglia** 593–617.

Rependone, Repton. 733. Old capital of the Mercian kingdom, a town in South Derbyshire known for Saint Wystan's Church, which was built c. 975. The monastery founded in 653 was destroyed during the Danish raids in 874–75.

Ricard, Richard. 3982, 4460. A deacon of **Saint Paul's** church who was punished by Saint **Audrey**.

Ricard, Richard. 4133. A clerk who prayed to Saint **Audrey** to revive a drowned woman.

Ricard, Richard. 4453. A priest from **Saint Paul's** church who witnessed the measuring of land.

Robert de Conigtone, Robert of Connington. 4445. A witness to the measuring of land.

Robert Malarteis. 3174. A servant of King **Henry** I, accuser of **Brustan**.

Robert de la Rive. 3330. A man from **Arundel**.

Rogiers, Roger. 4447. The father of **William**, who witnessed the measuring of land.

Rome. 39, 822, 1660, 1905, 1909, 2674, 2902. Formerly capital of the Roman empire, Rome became the papal seat of western Christianity.

Saham, Soham. 475, 486, 4371. A town in Cambridgeshire.

Saint Edmund, Bury Saint Edmunds. 608, 3308, 3895, 3989, 4055, 4067, 4369. A city

and is the culmination of the Christmas season that celebrates the coming of the wise men from the East bringing gifts to the Christ child.

Titulus, *Tyttla*. 65. Son of **Wuffa**. King of **East Anglia** 578–593.

Tonbert. 286, 351, 367. 459, 742, 1602, 4554. Saint **Audrey**'s first husband.

Toncestre. *Tonchester, Tunnacester*. 2097. Unknown site. Possibly the Roman Tunnocellum on the River "Tunn" (Tyne) in Northumberland.

Trente, *Trent*. 2068. The river Trent.

Trinité, *Trinity*. 2346. The Holy Trinity of the Christian faith: Father, Son, and Holy Spirit.

Tunnus, *Tunna*. 2099, 2107, 2127. An abbot whose masses always freed his brother **Yma** from captivity.

Ubba *see* **Hubbe**

Ulf, *Wuffa*. 66, 67. King of **East Anglia** 571–578.

Ulf (Eodils) *see* **Hulf**

Ulf. 2996. A mute completely cured by a miracle of Saint **Audrey**.

Ulfer, *Wulfhere*. 687, 690, 692, 696, 700, 1766, 1781, 1785, 1795, 1803. Christian son of King **Penda**. King of Mercia 657–74.

Ulfinges, *Wuffings*. 68. Those of the dynasty of King **Wuffa**.

Walingford, *Wallingford*. 3478. A town in Berkshire built by Alfred, the Saxon king of Wessex. By 1066 it was the most important town in Berkshire.

Werborc, Werburch, *Werburga*, Saint. 698, 1638, 1785, 2145, 2392, 2399, 2405. Daughter of **Audrey**'s niece **Ermenilda** and King **Wulfhere**. Nun and possibly abbess at **Ely**. Buried in **Hanbury** and translated to **Chester**.

Werfred. *Werfrid*. 481. Abbot of Soham.

Westmostier, Westmoster, *Westminster*. 2763, 3233. The abbey at Westminster is built on land that was once known as Thorney Island, a marshy area near London. In the tenth century King **Edgar** donated land for a church there, and under Edward the Confessor in the eleventh century it became an ecclesiastical-royal complex with a palace, a monastery, and an abbey church.

West Sexoine, *Wessex*. 568. One of the Anglo-Saxon kingdoms in England. It had been settled as early as 495 by Saxons reputed to have landed in Hampshire.

Wigar. 2933, 2941. A man from **Brandon**.

Williame, *William*. 3981, 3984. A man from Shelford.

Williame, *William*. 4446. Son of **Roger**.

Williame, *William*. 4458. An archdeacon.

Williame, William. 4514. The son and heir of **King Stephen (Estefne)**.

Williamus. *William*. 3688. A prior of Ely.

Wincestre, Wyncestre, *Winchester*. 2636, 2649, 2659, 2703, 2856, 2877, 2963, 3465, 4145. Ancient capital city of Wessex. King **Cyegils** of **Wessex** brought Christianity to Winchester in 635. It was sacked by Vikings in 860, and in 871 King **Alfred** the Great made Winchester his capital.

Wine, *Winna*. 2939. A friend of **Wigar**.

Wirecestre, *Worcester*. 4146. On the River Seven, Worcester is now the capital city of Worcestershire. In 680 Archbishop **Theodore** of **Canterbury** created the See of Worcester there.

Withburc, Wythburg, Withborc, Withbourc, *Withburga*, Saint. 161, 219, 2741, 2774, 2779, 2959, 4181. Youngest daughter of King **Anna**. Sister of Saint **Audrey**. Reputed to have founded a monastic community at **Dereham**. Her body was stolen from Dereham and moved to **Ely**.

Wolfriz, Wolfrid, *Wilfrid*, Saint. 854, 894, 1012, 1028, 1072, 1092, 1179, 1373, 1433, 1435, 1651, 1656, 1673, 1681, 1715, 1724, 1900, 1909, 1913, 2221. **Audrey**'s spiritual advisor and friend. Educated at **Lindesfarne** and **Rome**, chosen bishop of Ripon then **York**. A builder of churches and patron of the arts.

Wolstan, *Wulfstan*, [*Oswald*], Saint. 4146. Wulfstan is confused with Oswald in the text. Benedictine monk, bishop of Worcester from 961, archbishop of York from 972. Important in the tenth-century monastic revival. Founded several monasteries, including **Ramsey**, the parent house of both Evesham and **Pershore** in Worcestershire. See note for line 4146.

Wuffa *see* **Ulf**

Wulfhere *see* **Ulfer**

Wytringam, *Winteringham.* 1511. A town in Lincolnshire located on the **Humber** River.

Yma, Ysma (Ymma, Imma). 2076, 2123, 2135. A prisoner of King Ethelred, formerly a butler in the service of Audrey's sister **Seaxburga.** The brother of **Tunna.**

Yngulf, *Ingulf.* 2942. An evildoer whom Saint **Audrey** punished with death for himself and his entire family.

York *see* **Evrewich**

Index of
Critical Materials

For names and places within the text, see Annotated Index of Proper Names.